By The Damascus Gate

David Merron

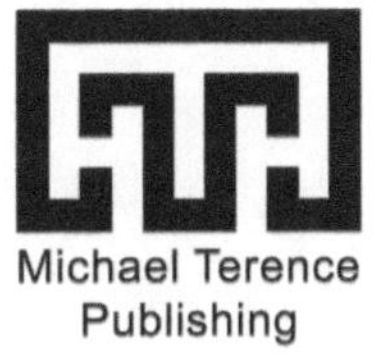

Michael Terence
Publishing

First published in paperback by
Michael Terence Publishing in 2019
www.mtp.agency

ISBN 9781913289270

*A visit to the old City of Jerusalem
inspires a forbidden love between Kate and Amos…*

1

Headlight beams stabbed the darkness and a jeep roared into the deserted bus-station. It braked to a halt, and with the engine ticking over a man swung out of the passenger seat. Tall and well-built with a shock of fair hair, he was dressed only in a blue shirt, shorts and sandals.

Kate stood up and exchanged a brief glance with Jill.

'Wow. What a hunk,' Jill murmured when he strode over to them. 'Just look at those calves.' But the man was looking at Kate, his gaze caught by the smooth, pale face and the reddish tint of her hair in the overhead fluorescent lights.

'Amos,' he smiled when he came up, tanned face and light brown eyes, 'welcome to the Negev, our own desert.' He had a strong accent, but seemed to speak English easily. They all shook hands and Kate felt a light, but firm grip.

It was the late Sixties, and on their boat to Haifa were more than a dozen other young people, some of the thousands from across the globe, all coming to experience at first hand this pioneering, communal society. At the Tel Aviv office, they'd been instructed to take the Beersheba bus to this small country town then phone, and they'd been waiting to be picked up.

'Apologies for the hard seats,' he said, and pointing to the driver added, 'this is Joel.' When the two climbed in the back, he nodded at a young boy sitting there; 'and my son, Ran; loves to come for the ride.'

Amos slid into the passenger seat and picked up an automatic weapon from the foot-well. He laid it across his knees then clicked in the magazine. Kate tensed. He noticed.

'Been pretty quiet, so far.' He shrugged. 'But you never know.'

Kate wondered what he meant by 'pretty quiet'. It was one thing to hear of the tense situation via the BBC news, something else to be suddenly plunged right into it...

The jeep roared through the night. Headlight beams dancing up and down, and side to side along the almost deserted road, through what seemed a treeless countryside. Weary from the day, Kate's mind switched back to how this had all started.

She and Jill were having coffee at Starbucks in Kings Cross late one night. Both had recently finished university and were at a loose end.

'So what made you leave Belfast?' Jill had asked. 'The Troubles'? Alluding to the IRA bombing campaigns.

'You could say that,' said Kate, turning her paper cup round and round on the table. 'But I suppose it was a specific incident that gave me the push, Jill.'

She took a sip of coffee.

'When I finished Queens,' she began, 'I got a part-time social work job through Marina, a college friend.' She paused a moment. 'Anyway, to cut it short, I got friendly with Robert. He was a Protestant youth-worker, and with me being Catholic, it started just by our talking about trying to bring the kids together at the children's centre; everything is so divided there y'know: neighbourhoods, schools, social clubs -- work places too, often.'

'Drink your coffee,' murmured Jill, 'it'll get cold.'

Kate took a few sips.

'Anyway. Rob would give me lifts back to my room. Got stopped more than once by the bastard RUC or the army. Anyway, one night they took our names and recognising mine as

Catholic, despite the drizzle, made us get out of the car while they turned it over.

Well, with my Irish temper, I was about to let them know what I thought, when Robert gripped my wrists and told me to calm down, to avoid more trouble. And that's how it started, Jill. Nothing very deep at first, but then it developed, y'know how these things go.'

Kate paused for a few seconds and took a few more sips.

'Well, we knew it could cause trouble, Jill. My uncle has IRA connections. Dad said it would make it awkward for him. And Robert's cousin was in the RUC, tall, blond fella -- built like a battleship. Threatened to come round and sort me out. It only seemed to strengthen the bond and make us more determined to stand up against the fanaticism and bigotry. But we were naïve; stupid really.'

'Anyway one day his car bonnet was splashed with red paint, and the next morning I found a note in my coat pocket at college that I would get worse. I said we could go to England together. He said his father was disabled and couldn't leave his mother to manage alone; he was an only child.' Kate gripped her mug in both hands; looked down at the Formica table-top. 'So, in the end we split. And it was real painful. So that's why I came to England; to an aunt in Kilburn last year.'

'So, what now?' asked Jill.

'Dunno.' Kate shrugged. 'Something will turn up.'

Jill leaned across the table.

'Listen,' she said. 'Two of my friends have just come back from being volunteer workers on a kibbutz – you know, a communal village in Israel. All found and a bit of spending money.'

Kate thought for a moment.

'But isn't there trouble out there? Nasser closing the Suez Canal or something?'

'Sure.' Jill shrugged, 'but my friends said that's normal for them — and if it heats up, we have out passports and can leave any time.'

'Need to think about it,' said Kate. And they'd drank up and gone out.

The next time they met, with both their funds creeping low, Kate had taken up Jill's suggestion.

'Anyway,' she'd said, 'at least give us time to think what next.'

They booked in at an office in Regents Street, received letters of introduction to the Kibbutz Volunteers' office in Tel Aviv, and the following week they'd taken the overnight train to Marseilles, then a boat to Haifa. And now they were here…

Half-an-hour later, the jeep swung in through a pair of floodlit steel gates set in a barbed wire fence, then pulled up at the rear of a large wooden building.

'Our dining room,' Amos called when he swung out. 'Come. You must both be hungry.'

Kate bundled out of the jeep with Jill and stretched. It had been a bouncy ride in the back and her trim backside had felt it, but at last they were here.

'Married,' murmured Jill, as the burly figure strode ahead and pushed through a set of double doors. 'What a pity.'

'There'll be others,' Kate laughed, but she watched too.

They left their rucksacks in the lobby and followed Amos inside. He motioned them towards an empty table in one of the two rows down the length of the hall.

'Grab a seat,' he said, looking straight into Kate's face. 'Have to take my son back to his schoolhouse. Our secretary will come soon and show you to your room.' And with a smile and a curt *Shalom*, he turned and strode out.

Having been used to college refectories, the pair found eating in the dining hall not a lot different, but rather than having to stand in line at the counters, they enjoyed being waited upon by servers who wheeled trolleys between the tables. Hungry after the journey, they helped themselves from tureens of vegetable soup, and hard-boiled eggs from baskets of brown bread, and took from a salad bowl.

While they ate, Kate looked around. There were tables for six; animated conversations in Hebrew, some laughing at some joke or other, others concentrating on eating, constant sounds and movements. At the far end, loud radio music came though wide doorway, which, Kate guessed, led through to the kitchens.

'People watching?' murmured Jill.

'Harmless enough,' countered Kate and they both laughed.

About half an hour later, the kibbutz secretary came by, and after he took them to book in their details at the *Maskirut* office, they were shown to their billet, a Swedish Hut — one large room with two beds, and a small ante-room with a wardrobe.

Exhausted from the journey, they kicked off their sandals, got undressed and flopped into bed - and before they knew it, had dropped off.

The next morning, they were roused by Jill's tiny, travel alarm-clock.

'Bloody hell,' Jill cursed. 'Half-past-five!'

Kate sat up, her head fuzzy and had to fight the urge to lie back again. She joined Jill at the standing tap by the end of the veranda, where the cold water finally woke her up.

On the way to the dining hall, she looked around. The dusty, yellow-grey ground sloped up to the concrete water tower on a low hill, on which sat a small watchtower. Kate had seen the searchlight sweeping back and forth last night and had a strange sensation in her stomach. She guessed, like the barbed-wire fence and steel gates, the reason it was there.

Other huts like theirs, were arranged in two rows and all facing the same way. In front of them stood a large, corrugated-iron shower hut and further away, the dining hall where they'd eaten yesterday. Beyond, she could see the red-tiled roofs of low houses, where, she supposed, the kibbutzniks lived. And everywhere, small trees in irrigation saucers.

By the dining hall, the two joined about a dozen other volunteers. Then, on a tractor and trailer, all still half-asleep, they were taken out to the fields and set-to hoeing long rows of sugar-beet. By chance, in charge was Amos, whom Kate learned, was head of the irrigated field-crops and also a leading member of the community.

When they broke to sit down for breakfast: hard-boiled eggs, yoghurt, brown bread and huge tomatoes, Kate looked around. Beyond the fields, a grey, parched plain undulated to the horizon. With not another settlement or tree as far as she could see, she was overawed by the isolation.

Back at work, the sun rose higher and sweat soon soaked her shirt. The volunteers only worked till lunchtime, and for Kate that couldn't come soon enough.

'Well, we wanted to experience this pioneering living,' she muttered to Jill as they climbed onto the trailer.

Jill laughed.

'A great life if you don't weaken, they say.'

Before he engaged gear, Amos glanced round to ensure they were all seated and happened to catch Kate's eye, but she was too weary to respond. Yet on the journey back, she found herself drawn to that broad back, the muscles rippling under his sweat-soaked shirt as he gripped the steering wheel or changed gear. He was married, so all she could ever do was look -- but then where was the harm in that?

Back in the hut, as they sat on their beds, exhausted, Jill held out her hands.

'Just look at those palms!' she said, 'they'll be as rough as a navvy's soon!'

Kate grinned.

'Part of the kibbutz experience we wanted, Jill.'

Then, too tired to continue chatting, both lay down on their beds and flaked out again until late afternoon, when they went to shower and then up to supper.

The first days passed swiftly, and while Jill seemed to take everything in her stride, Kate was finding it harder to adjust to this environment: the isolation in the wide plain; the hot, exhausting work; the communal showers -- standing naked amongst women she didn't know; the parents busy with their children after work, then bringing them back to the children's houses to sleep. And from then on, each weekday morning, it was out to the fields in the scorching sun.

'Only the weeds please, not the plants,' Amos called to Jill, who hacked away at the sugar-beet rows with a vengeance, 'we need those!' And suddenly he was alongside Kate.

'Gently. Gently,' he said. Gently took the hoe from her hands and used it. 'Like this or you won't last the day.'

To Kate, it seemed an opening, and when they all sat in the

shade of the trailer at elevenses, drinking black coffee and nibbling crackers, she plucked up courage and turned to him.

'Tell me, Amos, why do the children sleep away from their parents?' Having heard a little about the Collective Education system, she knew it was cheeky, almost as an accusation, but it was the only way she could bring herself to ask.

Amos nibbled a cracker and aware that the others were listening, considered his response. And those grey-green eyes and sharp nose were penetrating.

'Difficult to explain "on one leg", as we say in Hebrew. You see, Kate, we believe that the children are the responsibility not only of their parents but also of our whole society. We also think that our collective living is on a higher level, the future perhaps, and want to bring up our children with those values.'

In the silence that followed, Jill abruptly cut in.

'Amos, does the kibbutz think there really will be a war?' Blunt. Typical Jill.

Kate watched and sipped her coffee. She glanced at Amos and waited for his reaction. Again, he didn't answer at once.

'Well,' he said eventually, 'some do and some don't. Depends --'

'Because Chuck,' Jill cut in and nodded to an American boy sitting nearby, 'Chuck says that when they were loading hay-bales, Motti said he hoped there would be, to give the Nasser a bloody nose for blocking the Straits of Tiran.'

Amos half smiled.

'Bit more complicated than that, Jill.' He shrugged. 'It's not just us and the Egyptians. Starts with the Palestinians. They are used by the Arab rulers to distract from their own problems.' He paused and raised one hand. 'Basically, until we solve the refugee problem and they will have their own state alongside us, there will always be the chance of trouble.' He took another sip of coffee and added sharply, 'war solves nothing!' Then stood up. 'Anyway. Back to work.'

Kate remembered the heated debates at Uni, the New Left students accusing Israel of being a tool of imperialism, of racism etc. Hearing an Israeli speak sympathetically about the Palestinians was new to her. She sensed that it was something about which he felt deeply, and not just on an intellectual level.

They had little chance of continuing the discussions. The days moved quickly towards the end of May and with all outside work dropping to a minimum, the kibbutz began to clear out long disused trenches and dugouts.

'Think we ought to get out of here now, Jill?' ventured Kate, as they listened to yet another news' broadcast. When they had decided to come, Nasser had recently blocked the Straits of Tiran and closed the Suez Canal to Israeli ships and goods, so they'd both known of the tension on the area. Like most though, they hoped it would be sorted out through the United Nations.

'Well, all the other volunteers are staying put,' said Jill, who seemed to be taking it more in her stride. She shrugged. 'Anyway, they say that all civilian flights have been cancelled.'

Although the BBC News on Jill's transistor told of debates at the UN to resolve the situation, along with the rest of the country, the kibbutz seemed to be anticipating the worst. Kate and Jill found themselves helping to clean out the children's shelters and take down tinned food and blankets. Above, children played war games amongst the bushes: 'Pah! Pah! You're dead.' 'No. I shot you first.' 'No you didn't!'

Then, in ones and twos, men began to disappear as they were called up to their various units. Kate hadn't yet got to know many kibbutz individuals, but she felt the gap when Amos went. And when everyone was given emergency tasks, she and Jill were allotted to the children's houses.

By chance Kate was sent to the kindergarten, and found that it was run by Amos's wife, Miriam; medium height and slim, with long black hair tied in a pony-tail and deep brown eyes.

Kate helped her carry plastic bags of towels and nappies down the steep stairs of the babies' shelter. Outside it was hot, but down below the concrete walls were cold and damp, and the air, stuffy. Kate felt claustrophobic but tried not to show it.

'Slip those under the bunks. There, Kate,' said Miriam, pointing with her toe. She spoke English quite well but in the enclosed space, her voice sounded sharp.

Kate dropped the bags on the floor and pushed them into the foot-high space beneath the bottom bunk, while she observed Miriam out of the corner of her eye. She didn't know what she had been expecting from Amos's wife, but she envied the calm way Miriam seemed to be handling the tension -- a mature woman with her own mind; Kate felt quite wispy in comparison.

On the third day, with Amos away, Miriam invited her back to the room for coffee. Kate played chess with her young son, no language required; he beat her each time. She helped the young daughter with her simple embroidery.

Family photographs stood on the bookshelves, the kids and one or two of Miriam and Amos. During work, she'd overheard odd remarks from volunteers who had been here longer, that as well as managing the irrigated crops, he was a leading member of the small community, a great dad, and a reserves' officer. Also that one or two kibbutz women were a bit sweet on him. She could see why, the solid arm around Miriam, handsome, open face, infectious smile and wide-open eyes and strong arms; protective.

On the afternoon before the war began, the BBC reported final efforts at the UN in New York to calm the situation, but the kibbutz seemed to have been informed that hostilities were imminent. The next morning, led by Miriam, the children followed, chattering as they skipped down the steps. At the far end, the toddlers were already gathered around their nurse, Nitza, who was telling them a story.

'Anything else I can do?' Kate asked.

'No. No thanks, Kate.' Again, her voice sharp, firm.

Miriam sat down on the low bunk and started to fold towels. She listened to a portable radio and occasionally translated for Kate -- news of fierce tank battles in Sinai, of kibbutzim shelled from the Golan Heights of Syria, of Jordanian attacks on Jerusalem. And somewhere out there, was Amos. Slowly her movements became more mechanical and sluggish until she sat immobile. Her hands gripped a small white towel; her smooth, olive-skinned face vacant, and her wide, intelligent eyes, dulled.

Kate sat beside her, the edge of the bunk-upstand dug into her thighs and the radio chattered. She turned her head.

'You okay, Miriam?'

Miriam jumped.

'Oh. Yes. Sure. Sure. I'm fine.' She paused. 'Just thinking about this damn war.' Kate thought her eyes were moist. 'You know, Amos and I met in the Sinai war in '56. We said that would be the last. Now, eleven years later, another one.'

'But I heard he's in the reserves. They won't be in the front line, will they?'

'You never know where the front line is.' Miriam half-smiled. 'And Amos takes it all as it comes. "If the bullet's got your name on it…" he says.' Her eyes flashed. 'I hate that fatalism. Wish he wouldn't say it and --.' She stopped. Kate was just a visitor, like all the others, here for a short time then gone. No point in getting too close.

Kate had heard the other volunteers, especially the boys, talking about the impending war, quite scary at times; massive Arab armies with new Soviet weapons -- even possible gas attacks. Now, while the day wore on, she tried hard not to let Miriam notice her anxiety and sought something helpful to say.

'Funny,' she began, 'shouldn't be completely strange to all this, y'know. My father was a regular soldier in the war.' Miriam arched her eyebrows. 'Yes,' continued Kate. 'Hardly ever saw him when I was tiny; Korea, Canal Zone, Malaya. It was all so distant, though.'

'Yes,' Miriam murmured. 'Here it is all too close. Anyway,' she smiled, 'it's our war, Kate. Sorry you have been dropped into it like this.' Suddenly, she sat up. 'Well. This is no way to give the kids confidence is it?'

'On my birthday too,' Kate murmured.

'What. June 6th?' said Miriam.

'Ahah. My twenty-fourth.' Kate grinned. 'Don't think I'll forget this one so easily, that's for sure.'

'Well.' Miriam stood up, 'there'll be something else to celebrate when this is all over.'

Kate admired the way Miriam had snapped out of her forebodings. She was a strong woman and guessed she saw her as just another naïve student.

Over the next few days, a routine settled in; bringing food from the kitchen; sitting with the children as they read or drew pictures, everyone glued to the radio. Miriam or Nitza briefly translated for her from time to time, but with both their husbands out there somewhere, too distracted to explain more than the bare bones of the action.

Kate knew she was scared -- after all they were only twenty-five miles from Gaza and the Egyptian army, and a similar distance from the border with Jordan, and not a lot in between either way. She tried not to show it and wished Jill were down here with her to share it, but carried on as though on automatic pilot.

On the third day, news came of the destruction of the Egyptian air force, then reports of Israeli forces reaching the Suez Canal, the capture of the Old City of Jerusalem, and she managed to relax.

Then, on the sixth day, the radio announced the war had ended in a complete Israeli victory. Everyone in the shelter cheered and the children rushed to the staircase, all wanting to be first ones out into the daylight. Kate felt almost renewed in the sudden, bright sunlight, as though a huge weight had lifted from her, and so pleased to join Jill who had been detailed to another shelter; then to go and shower and later to sleep in her own bed.

The following night, they were woken by loud explosions, not far away.

'Bloody hell, what was that?' said Jill. Kate jumped out of bed, her body shaking and they peered through the shutters. They ran outside and strained to listen while other volunteers came out too. After ten minutes or so, everyone went back inside, but it took her a while to fall asleep again.

At breakfast, they heard that a *Fedayeen* group fleeing from the fighting in Gaza to Jordan, had blown up two tractors left out in the fields.

'The war's over, Kate,' muttered Jill, 'but it doesn't look like peace has broken out.'

A few days later, Kate and Jill were coming back for lunch, and just when Joe brought the trailer to a halt behind the dining hall, an army command-car roared up in a cloud of dust.

'Bloody army drivers!' Joe cursed from the tractor. The car braked and Amos jumped down, sporting a bristly ginger beard and mass of unkempt hair. He pulled his pack from the seat, waved to the driver and hurried away down the path towards the children's houses. Kate turned to watch his burly figure disappearing through the trees, a strange feeling in her stomach.

2

Life in the kibbutz quickly returned to normal. For the volunteers it was back into the fields, where in the meantime, the weeds had taken advantage to grow even thicker. Living in the old huts on the edge of the kibbutz, they also ate early in the evening before the kibbutzniks came in to eat, so Kate didn't have much chance to see Amos, nor continue her friendship with Miriam.

About a week later though, Miriam caught her in the dining hall one lunchtime when she collected the children's lunches.

'Haven't forgotten your birthday party, Kate.' She smiled. 'Waited for Amos to come back. No excuse now not have it,' and leaned forward. 'How about tomorrow, around five?'

'Heck. Had forgotten all about that,' Kate said, laughing. 'But thanks, Miriam. Sure. Thanks --' And, caught on the hop, couldn't say more as Miriam turned and went out, carrying the children's food containers. Like many in the kibbutz, Miriam wanted to make volunteers feel at home, in the hope that the more serious ones might decide to stay. Kate in turn felt that the invitation showed how confident Miriam was in her marriage, to invite her into their room.

The following day, after showering and changing, Kate made her way over to the other side of the kibbutz and knocked on the open door. Miriam was sitting on the bed with her young daughter, Noa. Amos was playing chess on the floor with his son, Ran.

'Ah, Kate. Come in,' Miriam called, getting up. 'A delayed

Happy Birthday, Kate!' and going out to the veranda, came back with a small cake. On top of the icing were a pair, and a group of four tiny candles.

Noa and Ran, as well as Amos, were not slow to join in the celebrations.

'Which birthday?' asked Amos, through a mouthful of cake, not having noticed the arrangement of the candles.

'You don't ask a woman that,' Miriam snapped. 'Peasant!'

'Oh. I don't mind.' Kate grinned. 'Twenty-four.'

'A mere child,' quipped Amos.

Kate had deliberately worn old jeans and a sweater. And now, so close to him in the small room, to keep her equilibrium, she knelt down near the girl and helped embroider a few stitches in a small handkerchief.

With Amos at ease and joking, Miriam was glad she had kept her promise about the birthday party, yet observed that Kate seemed at pains to avoid eye contact with her husband.

'More coffee,' she asked after a while, more abruptly than she'd intended, but enough for Kate to feel a negative vibration. A short while later, having checkmated his father – 'you just weren't concentrating, Dad,' said Ran, he got up and ran out to join his friends. Taking advantage, Kate thanked Miriam, said *shalom*, and went out.

A fortnight later, the kibbutz organised a trip to the Old City of Jerusalem. Kate and Jill, and half a dozen other volunteers, came up with a truck-load of kibbutzniks to see the ancient city. Until the war, it had been across the Jordanian border, completely inaccessible.

Everyone jumped down from the back of the Dodge truck,

and when it drove away to find a parking spot, they all clustered on the dusty, sun-baked area, gazing at the massive, ancient ramparts and the slim, round Tower of David rising over the arched entrance to the Jaffa Gate.

Cars, buses and lorries were disgorging their human loads and crowds of Israelis and foreign tourists were streaming through the gateway into the Holy City.

'Just a month or so previously,' said Joe, 'this was a no-man's land, choked with barbed wire and mines.' He pointed at the wall. 'And Jordanian snipers peering through those crenellations.'

Kate was so glad that she had come, to take a breather from the kibbutz and also get away from the stupid girlish crush she was getting on Amos -- and from his sharp-eyed wife. While the kibbutzniks and most of volunteers made their way to the Wailing Wall, she and Jill decided to take off at a tangent.

'Can't stand crowds,' Jill called to the others. 'Going to the Mount of Olives.'

'Want to look down on the Old City from "the other side" as it used to be,' added Kate, and they pushed through the gateway and joined the crush down the narrow, shaded Street of the Chain.

Soon both were seduced by the twisting alleyways of the Souk with its myriad shops and stalls under long, arched passageways, all bright with dresses and silver jewelry, copper pots, intricate marquetry chess and backgammon boards, and blue Hebron glassware. And everywhere the smell of spices and exotic fruits, and the aroma of cardamom flavoured Turkish coffee from cafes in the cul-de-sacs.

By the time they'd reached St Stephen's Gate on the East side of the city, the afternoon was scorching, and their intended climb up sun-baked slope of the Mount of Olives to the modern colonnades of the Inter-Continental Hotel in the midday heat, seemed daunting.

'Best try it another time,' said Jill. 'It'll still be here in a month, Kate.'

Kate wrinkled her nose but nodded. Her sandaled feet had begun to feel the pounding from the cobbled streets. They turned to stroll back up the Via Dolorosa towards the Jaffa Gate but just then, an old man darted out from a row of shops in the wall to their left. He was dressed in traditional long, beige *abaya* with a neat brown jacket over it and pointed black shoes.

'Lovely silver, ladies. Best in Jerusalem.' He smiled under a thin grey moustache. 'Come, ladies. You look. You my guests.'

Kate glanced around. Jill had been remarking how few tourists there were in this area; they were almost alone. The man held aside a hanger of dresses revealing a dark doorway in the wall beyond.

'Please. Come inside,' the man beckoned. 'I bring coffee.'

'Seen one. Seen them all,' Kate muttered, nodding to the dresses.

'And end up in some harem,' murmured Jill.

The shopkeeper sensed their hesitation.

'Please. Many Americans come to me… I make these myself.' He spoke clearly but with a pronounced accent as he held up another hanger dripping with silver chains and earrings. Turning to a small boy who was sitting on a stone step opposite, he called: 'Araf. *T'laateh. Udrup!* Wide-eyed, the boy sprang up and hurried into an alleyway to bring coffee.

Kate and Jill looked at each other then Jill laughed.

'To hell with it! As long as it has central heating.' Then, to Kate's questioning eyebrows, added, 'the harem, I mean!'

Kate was more circumspect. The old man had soft eyes and

wasn't as pushy as most of the shopkeepers in the Souk, and recalling Amos's positive sentiments about the Palestinians, suddenly felt an urge to be friendly. In addition, with Jill she felt safe, as if both of them couldn't be mistaken and turned to enter the low, arched doorway.

The man, who'd introduced himself as Yusuf, motioned them to sit on the floor cushions. A single bulb in a table lamp cast an uneven light around the arched, rough masonry walls that rose to a pointed vault in the centre. When they were settled, he showed them a letter lying on the table.

It was typewritten, from an American woman, thanking him for a Sufi ring. Kate was wondering what was particularly special about the Sufi ring, when the boy returned with three tiny cups of Turkish coffee and three glasses of water. She was always careful about water and didn't drink it; Jill gulped hers in one go.

The boy, whom Kate found out later was the silversmith's nephew Araf, sat cross-legged on the ground next to her. He had smooth black hair and large, dark, wondering eyes, smiling and shrugging whenever she returned his gaze. The old man took down some strings of necklaces and chains and handed them to Jill, draping one of the chains around her neck, his eyes discreetly averted from her deep cleavage.

'You won't see like these in the Souk!' he said.

Jill chose a silver necklace, and orange and brown wool weave to hang on her wall. Kate was looking at some silver-set, green malachite earrings; Miriam had worn similar. She had already bought a braided silver bangle, but decided to buy a pair of these as well.

They chatted, and when the man asked where they were staying, Kate started to explain about the kibbutz — the farm, tractors, cowshed, orchards, all way out in the desert. When Yusuf translated for Araf, the boy stared eagerly into her face, wide eyed and enquiring as though the whole description was of another world. And from that moment, she felt a strong empathy with the boy, whose childhood was probably confined within these high stone-walls of the ancient city.

In the short time she had been here, Kate had already gathered differences of opinion in the kibbutz about the Arabs. While they had been in the shelters, Miriam mentioned Amos's struggles against the few extremists in the kibbutz, and how they tried to counter the children's constant exposure to war news, and to see Palestinians only as enemies.

'Y'know,' Kate said quietly to Jill, 'wouldn't it be great for this lad to see the kibbutz — and for the kids to meet him?'

'Great idea,' Jill smiled, then muttered, 'still, need to test out the waters in the kibbutz first.' Kate recalled how they tried to get the Protestant and Catholic children together in Belfast, and had already made up her mind. She was sure Amos would approve too.

They were telling Yusuf more about the kibbutz when the doorway suddenly darkened and a young man came in. He was dressed in a light blue, open-necked shirt and black trousers. Surprised, he stepped back and made as if to go out, but before anyone moved, the old man stretched out his arm and called over to him.

'*Esteneh e'shwieyeh!*' adding quickly in English, 'Wait. These are my guests.' He turned to Kate and Jill. 'Ah. Ladies. This my nephew, Shafik, Araf's brother.'

The man came forward and Yusuf turned to the boy.

'Araf. Coffee for Shafik.'

Kate was sure he had spoken in English to reassure them.

The man nodded a greeting to each of them, then eased himself down onto a low stool in the corner, hands clasped, elbows on his knees. He had a smooth, clean-shaven face with wavy black hair and a sharp, angular nose. In the dim lighting, a gold ring glinted on one finger. When he had settled, the man turned to Jill and Kate.

'You are from England? America?' he asked.

'I'm from England,' said Jill, 'but Kate's from Northern Ireland.' Kate bit her lip; Jill opening mouth before engaging brain. To her dismay, the man's expression showed that he had picked it up.

'You are a Catholic or a Protestant?' he asked, in a strongly accented but otherwise correct English.

'My family are Catholic,' said Kate, having long distanced herself from the sectarian divide.

'Ah. A friend of my cousin studied there. Belfast. Electronics,' he replied, then immediately continued, 'and how do you find Israel?'

'In what way?' asked Kate.

'Well… ' He paused, as though searching for words. 'We too have had our land taken over by colonists. Have become second-class citizens.'

For a moment, the room was silent. Outside, a donkey brayed and a child shouted in the street. Yusuf rubbed his hands together, eyes half closed. Kate's mind flipped back to her year at the LSE. The heated debates; the New Left allying itself with African and Arab students and calling Zionism white colonialism, like South Africa, while others equated Jewish settlement with the Protestant takeover in Ulster. But for this stranger to spring it on her like that? The blood rose in her face while she hesitated and sought the right comeback.

Jill sensed her embarrassment and raised her hand.

'Look, mate. We're not responsible for the world's problems.' She tossed back her mop of fair hair. 'We've just come to say hello to Yusuf and Araf. Okay?'

Shafik took the rebuke with a faint smile.

'Please. Don't be offended. You both seem too intelligent to be just tourists. So I really would like to know what you think about... ' He waved hand to one side, then back again, 'about what you have seen in the city.'

The short exchange allowed Kate to recover her composure and the sudden annoyance subsided.

'Well. It's a different situation, y'know. Have you ever been to Ireland?' she asked, looking straight into his eyes; deep, almost black, brown eyes. He shook his head.

'I don't need to,' he sighed. 'For us, this war was just another stage of Israeli colonial expansion. And...'

'Wait a minute. Just wait a minute,' snapped Jill. 'Who started it? Who blockaded the Straits of Tiran? Your friend Nasser! And who started shelling the Jewish city in Jerusalem? Your King Hussein!'

Again, Shafik took it coolly.

'He's not *our* king. He too was just an occupier and his soldiers were no friends either.' He would have continued. So would Jill. Her blood was up and she relished nothing more than a good argument, but just then the boy returned with Shafik's coffee. Yusuf seized the opportunity and stood up.

'Yes. Yes. All very well.' He spread his hands and looked around the room. 'But Shafik, these are my guests. Enough politics for one day,' he said, adding a few sharp words in Arabic.

Shafik sat back against the wall, took the small cup and sipped as they all sat silent for a moment. Then, setting down his cup and looking at Yusuf, he said softly, 'Well, perhaps I could show them the Mosque of Omar?'

'Oh. Yes. We'd like that,' Kate said quickly.

'Yes. Why not.' Yusuf nodded and smiled. 'You will like it, I'm sure.' But as they all stood up and went out, Kate had the feeling that the old man was uneasy -- that perhaps his nephew's radical views had offended them.

They walked up Al Mujhadeen Street and Shafik pointed to a tall, many arched stone building on their left.

'The Omariyya School,' he said, 'one of the oldest in the city,' and added pointedly, 'long before the British came.'

'Your old school?' asked Jill.

'No. It's very traditionally Muslim,' he replied. 'Mine was in the new part, past Sheik Jarrah. Mixed, Muslims and Christians.' He paused and pointed to his chest where black curly hair showed from his half-unbuttoned shirt. 'Made us all first and foremost Palestinians. That's what makes my generation different from Yusuf's.'

They started walking again along the Via Dolorosa but when they reached where it joined Al Wad road, Jill glanced at her watch and suddenly stopped.

'Heck, Kate. Just realised. I have to buy some presents to send home to the family. Won't have time.' She shrugged. 'Look, I'll see it next time -- it won't have gone anywhere! You go on. See you back at the truck.' She laughed. 'Don't be late.' And strode off, turning once to wave.

For a moment, Kate hesitated. She would be alone with a strange man in a strange city. Then supposing that Yusuf wouldn't have let her go off with him if there were any qualms -- and her own intuition, relaxed.

As they walked on, Shafik, looked at her.

'Tell me, Kate?' he began. 'You are not Jewish, but you came to Israel?'

Kate stopped and turned to him.

'Actually, Shafik, most of the volunteers are not Jewish. Jill neither. It's the idea of kibbutz that attracted us.' She paused, then added, 'and Israel, a new country, I suppose.'

Shafik nodded and seemed to relax as they walked on, Kate feeling easier now in the open air, wanting to know more about him, not just his politics, and from time to time finding herself unconsciously comparing him to Amos. Apart from the jet-black hair, he was slightly taller but leaner and less muscled.

'Tell me,' she began, 'what do you do, Shafik. Y'know, I mean, work. Study? Or shouldn't I ask?'

He didn't react at once then, looking straight ahead, began: 'Well, I finished studying Economics, in Ramallah. Then I had another year in Amman.' He looked at her. 'And for the past few years, not much.'

'Nothing?' Kate's eyes opened wide. 'You mean really nothing. I mean, I thought there was a shortage of educated people. Of teachers. Of that kind of thing.'

Shafik smiled. She felt it almost patronising.

'We may be in what you call Third World, Kate, but the one thing Jordan did have was a good education system. That and the various church schools gave we Palestinians the highest literacy and education in the Arab world.' He waved his arm as if pointing over the horizon. 'It's our main export: education and talent, to the whole Arab world -- Kuwait, the Gulf, Egypt, Iraq, Saudi Arabia.'

'And you?' pressed Kate.

'Unless,' he continued, as though she hadn't interrupted, 'you were "known". Blacklisted.' He paused. 'I was active in the student organisation. I won't bore you with the details, Kate, but it was enough for King Hussein's puppets to prevent me getting any government position.' He looked past her again. 'I could have gone to Kuwait. Or the Gulf.'

'So, what will you do now, Shafik?'

'To be truthful, Kate, I don't know.' He looked away. 'The occupation has upset everything on the West Bank and we are all in a kind of limbo. But when things settle down again, I shall have to decide.'

They turned left again into the narrow, shaded, Al 'Uddin Road, at the end of which was a low archway through which she could see a flight of stone steps.

'The *Haram*,' said Shafik. 'The holy area around the main mosques.' He looked at her, half-smiling. 'Until the Israelis came, only Muslims were allowed up here.'

'And only men, I heard!' added Kate, wanting to be devilish.

'Yes,' he said sharply, 'but if things need changing, modernising, we'd rather do it ourselves.'

Up on the raised piazza, Kate was stunned by the beauty of the 7th Century Mosque: the dazzling, gold dome, the façade of blue and green mosaic tiles, slender white marble pillars, all with proportions and geometry so different to anything she had experienced in her travels through Europe.

Around the mosque, the wide expanse of worn, stone paving was dotted here and there with small, arched colonnades, clumps of cypress trees and purple bougainvillaea. At the southern end, a tall minaret rose from another building into the clear blue sky.

'The Al Aksa mosque,' said Shafik, 'from where Muslims believe The Prophet took off for Heaven.'

In awe of the place and of the stillness, Kate hardly spoke as they wandered past the great dome and across the sun-baked pavings, out to the ramparts overlooking the Valley of Kidron. Below them, were the dark green trees of Garden of Gethsemane and the gilded onion domes of the Russian Church. And beyond, rising sharply, the bare, Jewish grave-studded slopes of the Mount of Olives.

'My God. What a view,' Kate said softly, as though raising her voice would be sacrilegious. 'Just fabulous.' Turning to face him, she added, 'no wonder everyone is fighting over it.'

Shafik stared up to the summit, his eyes glazed. He remained silent for a moment then turned to her.

'You know,' he said suddenly and more firmly, 'when the Zionists wanted to colonise this country at the end of the last century, they sent out one of their famous poets from Russia. When he came back, they asked him what he found. 'The bride,' he said, 'is beautiful. But she is married!' He looked straight into Kate's eyes.

With the sad tone, she sensed his bitterness. She was on the point of telling him that back in the kibbutz, people like Amos did understand -- or at least tried to, but didn't want to talk politics just now.

They sat on one of the huge stone blocks that topped the ramparts, the wall falling away to a sheer drop beneath them. Kate looked down to the dark green of the garden around the Church, all in such stark contrast to the sun-baked rocks close by.

'So, Kate.' Shafik's voice, confident again, broke into her reverie. 'You are glad you came?'

'Oh. More than glad.'

'Well I am glad that I brought you here, Kate. That you agreed to come.' He paused. 'Pleased that you trusted me, I suppose.' With the sun was beating down on the stone pavings, the reflected heat had become unbearable. 'Come,' he said. 'Let's find some shade and a cool drink, Kate.' And they went down into the alleyways of the Old City again.

On her way back to the bus station, Kate mulled over the visit to the *Haram* — it was almost like another world. Shafik explaining its significance had been great, but although she found him attractive, the complications: Muslim, Palestinian, family, had also sparked her instinctive wariness. She had wanted to ask him about the ring he wore -- after all, as a Moslem, if he was married he wouldn't want to be seen walking alone with another woman. Next time, she vowed, she would ask him outright.

Either way, she was glad they'd had the chance to chat, to see things from 'the other side' and hoped they would meet again. It would also help to stop herself being sucked into the attraction to Amos. But she had to take care. Events had a habit of overtaking her.

3

The young boy with his wide eyes and eager face wouldn't leave Kate's mind. So a few weeks later, on her next visit to Jerusalem, alone, following some friendly small talk with Yusuf, she suggested that perhaps Araf might like to visit the kibbutz. She could pick him up later, after shopping.

As Yusuf had translated, the boy jumped up, clapping his hands and grinning, repeating, 'Thank you, Miss. Thank you!' the few English words he knew. And when Kate stood up to go, Yusuf took both her hands and shook them energetically, thanking her too, again and again. She could have sworn his eyes were moist as he sent the boy to their house nearby to collect a few things for the journey.

On her way through the Souk, Kate wondered how the idea of taking the young boy to the kibbutz had occurred to her, even in their very first meeting. Was it from admiring Mairead's efforts with her joint Protesant/Catholic nursery in Belfast -- something about children being able to bridge the divide and promising a better future, that a seed had been planted? Did she hope that Araf meeting with the kibbutz kids could start something similar? Or was it that she was seeking Amos's approval -- that they had to take advantage of the occupation to speak directly to the Palestinians? Either way, after buying a few toiletries for Jill and herself, Kate had a warm feeling about her decision.

Araf was waiting when she returned. Following a short, animated exchange with Yusuf and much handshaking, she took the boy's bag and led him up to take the local bus to the inter-city bus station.

It was late afternoon when they jumped off the bus, and after taking a spare mattress for Araf from one of the other huts, Kate took him up to the dining hall.

As in many newer kibbutzim, this was still a wooden structure but sturdily built, with a terrazzo-tiled floor, at the rear of which were modern kitchens. Holding the boy's hand, Kate pushed through the double doors into the entrance lobby then went over to check where she was working on the next day's work roster. Next to the roster were various colourful notices of committee meetings, cultural activities and other social events. With most people having been in their separate workplaces during the day, the lobby served also as a social venue especially around the evening meal — 'the village pump,' Jill joked.

Kate went through into the hall. Servers wheeled aluminum trolleys between the two rows of tables, some to give out main items of the meal, others with bowls of soup for each table. A third came round with a bucket and cloth to clean up after each table had finished. With not enough tables for the growing population, the main meals were served in two shifts.

She scanned the room to see if she anyone she knew, then noticing that there were two places at Miriam and Amos's table, Kate went over and asked if she could join them.

'Sure. Why not,' said Amos, with a broad smile.

'Who's the lad?' asked Miriam, nodding at the boy as they sat down. Her English had a slight American accent, 'from my schoolteacher,' she'd once laughed.

'He's called Araf.' Kate grinned, then gushed, 'you see, I met this silversmith in the Old City and this is his nephew, he's about ten or eleven. Well, I was telling them about the kibbutz, and when his uncle translated, the lad was totally spellbound. Sounded like a fairytale I suppose. So,' she continued almost in the same breath, 'I thought, sure, wouldn't it great for the lad to see a kibbutz?' She laughed and raised both hands in the air, 'do my bit for international peace and friendship!'

'Good idea,' said Amos, laughing too. 'Why not!'

The boy was short and thin, with smooth, jet-black hair and dark eyes; and dressed in a light khaki shirt, navy short trousers and open sandals. Embarrassed at being the focus of attention, he ate head down while Kate told how his father had been killed in a work accident about two years before and now his uncle, Yusuf, looked after him.

'And they let you take him,' asked Miriam. 'Just like that?'

'Well, I've visited them a few times and we chat a lot. And they trust me, I suppose. He has an older brother too and we've talked a lot about Israel and about the kibbutz,' Kate gushed, the words spilling out without a pause, 'and the boy was so keen, y'know.' She laughed again, the freckles dancing on her cheeks. 'But he doesn't understand much English. We manage mainly with sign language!'

'Sure, a nice idea,' said Miriam, 'but I'm wondering whether perhaps you should have cleared it with the kibbutz first.'

Kate coloured, then glanced at Amos and was about to say something, when Motti came in through the swing doors with his wife, Orna. Looking around, he stared at Amos's table stopped short.

'Is that an Arab kid?' he snapped, pointing at the boy. 'What the hell is an Arab doing here?'

Motti, tall lean with smooth black hair and sharp face, was head of the cereal crops, deeply suntanned from long hours out in the open fields. He too had recently returned from the war, having served with the Paras.

'Seeing everything we've got,' he continued, 'the fences, the night guards. He'll go straight back and tell them all about the kibbutz layout!'

The boy looked up, then turned to look at Kate, his eyes wide and puzzled.

'Oh, stuff it,' said Uri, the farm manager, who was eating at the next table. 'He's only a kid.'

'Kid or no. He's a security risk. Who the hell gave permission to bring an Arab here?'

'Oh. Come on,' said Amos. 'The damn war's over and no one needs permission. Can't you trust anyone?'

'Not Arabs,' snapped Motti. 'No!' And as Orna turned her husband away, he muttered loudly, 'Amos trying to impress the bloody volunteers!' And they went to eat on the far side of the dining hall.

Kate couldn't help noticing the bigoted slant of his mouth as he sneered the word '*Aravim!*' Just like the Prods in Belfast when they spat 'fucking *Taigs!*'

Amos winked at Uri.

'Colonel Motti!' And they both shrugged and smiled.

For a few moments there was a tense silence in the dining hall, then as the hum of conversation resumed, Kate looked across the table. 'Is there a problem, Amos?' she asked.

'Look, Kate,' said Amos. 'Take no notice. Motti's our local hardliner. Sees a *Fedayeen* terrorist in every Arab.'

He shot her a warm smile, at which Miriam narrowed her eyes. But although resenting Amos's promptness to side with Kate, Miriam couldn't stand Motti's bigotry either. She reached a hand across the table.

'No one else cares about the boy, Kate. Really. It'll blow over.'

As she was talking, Amos stood up.

'Anyway, got to turn on the sprinklers in the cotton. Have to excuse me.' He shrugged and nodded to Kate. 'Don't worry. It'll blow over.'

After leaving the dining hall, Amos drove out to turn on the sprinklers. They always irrigated at night; by day, the wind and burning sun would evaporate half the water before it even reached the soil.

Just after nine, he came up from the tractor shed in his muddy boots and carrying a twelve-inch Stilsons wrench, but as he clomped into the lobby of the dining hall to check the next day's work roster, he walked straight into a furious argument.

Kate, who'd been standing in the corner, ran over to him.

'Amos. Please. What's happening, Amos?' she pleaded, looking as though she was about to burst into tears. 'Why are they arguing about the boy? Sure, he's just a harmless kid.'

Amos didn't need to enter the heated discussion to find out.

'I want him out of here,' Motti was shouting, his wiry body shaking, his face thrust forward. 'This is no place for an Arab, however young he is. Remember that little bastard with the hand grenade? It's bad enough having Bedouin living over the road.'

'Come on, Motti. That one was at least sixteen. And that was three years ago,' said Yaacov, the kibbutz secretary. 'I've no objection, that's for sure. And it won't hurt our kids to get to know each other.'

Joe, and others standing beside him, nodded agreement, but Motti came back.

'I don't need to know any more about Arabs,' he snapped.

Rami, Motti's workmate, joined in, siding with him, but although Joe and most of the others standing by backed Yaacov, Motti wasn't backing down.

Amos turned to Kate and spread his hands.

'Look, Kate. For twenty years, everyone saw them as the enemy. People will take a while to get accustomed to the new situation and some,' he nodded towards Motti, 'some never will.' He glanced at the secretary then back to her. 'Anyway, don't worry. Yaacov will sort this out.'

Amos listened to the argument for a few seconds more, then asked, 'Where's the boy now?'

'In our room,' she whispered. After supper Kate had taken took the boy back to the room, and with Jill, brewed coffee and broke out a packet of '*Osem*' biscuits.

'Good. Best he stays there.' Amos smiled. 'It'll blow over, Kate. Don't worry,' he said, his smile wavering this time.

As he turned to go, Kate glanced down and caught her breath. His boots were muddied and his trousers soaked to the knees from the sprinklers.

'Holy God. You're soaking! I shouldn't have kept you here. I'm sorry, Amos. But thanks a lot. Thanks so much.'

'No problem.' Amos smiled and turned to go out, then stopped and swung back.

'Look, Kate. If there's still trouble — any trouble at all, just come over to our room and call me. Any time. Okay?

When he reached his veranda, Amos's head was still burning. Why the hell did they have to put up with someone like Motti? Fuming, he threw the wrench into the work clothes cupboard. So Motti was a good worker. So what? Was that all kibbutz was about? A few years ago, someone with his chauvinist ideas would have had to shut up, or been kicked out. He unlaced his boots and kicked them off. What the hell was the kibbutz coming to?

After a shower and a change of clothes, Amos had calmed down and went to look in on Noa and Ran in the children's houses. He knew they'd be asleep but having been away throughout the war, he liked to do that most evenings now.

Back in his room, he sat in the easy chair, leafing through Yigal Yadin's book on the Bar Kokhba discoveries in the Dead Sea caves. Miriam was out at an education committee meeting.

The next thing he knew, there was a light tapping on the door.

'Yes,' he croaked, sitting up and trying to clear his head. 'Who's there?' He must have dozed off with the light still on. A soft, wary voice came through the door.

'It's me. Kate. I'm really sorry to bother you, Amos. But I saw the light on. Thought Miriam would be here. Have you a moment?'

Amos swung off the bed, and glanced at his watch. It was gone ten! Miriam's meeting must be fraught — they were deciding on a new *metapelet,* a nurse for the next toddlers' group. Stepping across the room, he opened the door. Kate stood on the veranda in jeans and a thin, black sweater, her hair loose and her face pale.

'What's up, Kate?'

'The boy. They say he's got to go. And now!' she blurted out, her eyes red. 'Security reasons, they say. Can't stay here overnight, even.' Her knuckles were white where she gripped the doorjamb. 'They want to take him back to Jerusalem in the jeep. Now!' She clenched her hands together. 'Oh God, Amos. How can I take the lad back at night? His family will be asleep.' Tears started to form in her eyes. 'How will I explain it?'

Amos rubbed the back of his neck.

'*Le'at. Le'at.* Take it easy, Kate.' He was only beginning to fully wake up. 'Is the boy still in your room?'

'Yes. He's fast asleep.'

'Well. As long as he stays there, what's the harm?'

'That's what I said. Oh, I don't know. Please. Amos, can you speak to them?'

Amos pulled Miriam's work jacket from the cupboard.

'Here,' he said, 'you're shivering. Come inside and wait. I'll go and knock some sense into Yaacov.' He buckled on his sandals. 'Wait here. I'll be back soon.'

As soon as he had gone, Kate went in and sat in the easy chair, wondering where Miriam was. Probably still in some meeting or other. They often seemed to go on so late into the night that she wondered how anyone ever got up for work at six the next morning. Those who were active in the kibbutz seemed to live such a hectic life -- and all for nothing extra, Jill joked…

Although she had been to the room before for coffee, Miriam and the children were here. Sitting alone, it felt different. She glanced around. The walls were a matt cream colour, the floor of terrazzo tiles with a folk-weave rug in the centre. A settee stood against one wall, a bookcase and shelves along the opposite wall and a table and chair under the window. Two nylon-webbing, easy chairs were the only other furniture. A narrow doorway led through to a sleeping area not much larger than the double bed and built-in wardrobe. Outside the front door, leading off the small veranda was a small shower and toilet.

Kate glanced at the bookshelves. Nearly all the books were in Hebrew, but a few in English, mostly educational ones like Susan Isaacs' *Early Years*, Bruno Bettleheim's *Children of the Dream* — which made Miriam boil whenever a visitor mentioned it, the renowned educationalist 'condemning our kibbutz education system after just a three-week visit and not knowing the language,' she'd snapped.

Others were on archaeology -- Amos's she guessed, Kathleen Kenyon on Jericho; a British Museum booklet on flint tools and a stack of pamphlets of the old Palestine Exploration Society. From the dust jackets, many of the Hebrew books seemed to be on archaeological subjects as well.

One section, at the far end, held art books: Reubens, Michelangelo, Mogdiliani and others. Kate took out a Phaidon edition of the Pre-Raphaelites and slowly leafed through, but so preoccupied was she with what might happen with Araf, her eyes saw little.

By the time Amos came back she had idly leafed through three other art books, and hearing footsteps on the veranda, hurriedly replaced the last one as Amos came in.

'Sorry.' Kate blushed. 'I meant to put them back earlier.' It was getting late and she felt guilty; he had to get up early for work tomorrow.

'Not to worry. You're welcome. I didn't think it would take so long.' Amos rubbed his ear, standing awkwardly.

'Look, Kate,' he began, spreading his hands, 'the boy will have to go back tomorrow. I'm really sorry. Best I could do and I feel terrible about it.' He sank onto the bed, slapping one fist into the other hand. 'People are so damn stupid. Bigoted. I'm so ashamed, I can tell you.' He paused and took out a cigarette then offered her one. She declined and he lit his with a small plastic lighter.

'Problem is, Kate, Motti has telephoned the local army headquarters. Got them involved. Said there would be an official complaint.' Amos cursed. 'Bloody idiots!' He paused and looked into her face. 'If we had a chance to bring it to our secretariat, Motti and his crew would be voted down for certain. But it's late and we couldn't argue all night.'

Kate stood up.

'No. Please. I'm grateful for what you've done, Amos. And I'll take him back tomorrow. On the early morning bus.'

'No. No. No need. Take your time. As long as he isn't here by tomorrow evening, Kate. Motti is making a lot of his seeing our night-time security arrangements and all that.' He looked around the room, then back to Kate. She looked so tense and miserable.

'Please. Sit down, Kate. Have some coffee.' And without waiting, he went out to the veranda and plugged in the electric kettle. Kate followed him out. It was late, and despite his easygoing manner with his wife not there it didn't feel right.

'Thanks. But Miriam must be back shortly. You'll both want to get some sleep,' she said. 'I've imposed enough.'

Amos pulled out the plug and turned to face her, hands hanging at his sides.

'Look, Kate. People like Motti just cannot forget old scores. They make a lot of noise, but they are a tiny minority in the kibbutz. Believe me.'

Kate watched his face as he spoke, his intense, light brown eyes looking straight at her, tired and pained, as though he were suffering as much as she.

'No. It's my fault, Amos. This isn't my home and I shouldn't have brought the boy here without asking first. Just that he was so enthusiastic, and I thought it would be a good idea.'

The corners of her mouth drooped as she spoke. Thin, red lips in a pale, lightly freckled face, with that mass of reddish hair hanging loose down to her shoulders, her small breasts outlined under the thin sweater. At that moment, perhaps because he was so tired -- or so incensed by Motti and his bigotry, Amos felt something more than just wanting to help her, of seeing her not just as an attractive volunteer, but as a warm and caring woman.

They stood motionless for a moment. Around them the kibbutz was silent. Through the stillness of the desert night, the footsteps of the night guard sounded along the path behind the house. The war had ended but no one was taking any chances yet.

'Anyway,' she said, turning to go, 'I must get back to the boy. He might wake up and not find me there, you know.' She held out her hand. 'Thanks. Thanks so much, Amos,' Amos took it and gripped it firmly for a few seconds. She had a strong, warm handshake too.

'No problem,' he said. 'Sorry I couldn't do more, Kate.' Then something made him add, 'look, I'll see you across to the huts.'

'No, no! I'll manage,' she protested.

'Let's go,' he said sharply. 'And you'll need a jacket.'

In the clear, still night, the light of the three-quarter moon reflected from the asphalt paths and tiled roofs. Beyond the fence lights, the grey desert glowed dimly. Kate felt drained and in the cool air she hugged the thin summer jacket about her body -- his wife's jacket.

'Here!' Amos threw his own jacket around her, 'you're shivering,' his hands momentarily resting on her shoulders.

Outside her door, Amos waited as she went in. The boy had fallen asleep on her bed she said, as she came out to say goodnight and hand him back the jackets.

'Where will you sleep?'

'I've got his mattress on the floor. I'll be okay.'

'And blankets?' She nodded. 'Okay. Goodnight then. And safe journey tomorrow.'

"Night, Amos,' she said, and unconsciously reaching out, her fingers touched his bare arm. 'And again. Many, many thanks.'

That soft touch stayed with him on the way back, but as he turned down the path to his room, Amos had to tell himself to stop thinking like a stupid teenager -- and to keep his equilibrium when telling Miriam what had happened, when she came in.

The next morning, when Amos woke, the events of the previous evening welled up into his head.

'I'm so angry with that bastard Motti -- involving local army headquarters,' he said to Miriam as they dressed for work. 'And throwing that boy out because he is an Arab is against everything we believe in. I'm not letting him get away with it.'

'I agree. But what can you do now?' said Miriam. She was annoyed too, but wondering whether Amos was so wound up about the boy -- or the girl.

'Something, that's for sure.' And it bugged him all day at work.

That evening, after they had taken the children back, Amos grabbed the kibbutz secretary in the dining hall.

'Listen, Yaacov. Why the hell did you let Motti make that stupid fuss and send the boy back home like that?'

'I agree with you, but once the army was involved, not a lot we could do at that time of night.'

'Well, I want it brought to the next general meeting. Urgently. This Saturday.'

'Okay. Since I agree with you, sure, why not. Meanwhile, I'll go to the local HQ and chat with them.' He smiled. 'I know the commander from old times.'

During the week, from time to time the image of Kate's anxious face outside his room flashed across his mind, and with it, the touch of her fingers his bare arm. And on Friday, he was pleased to see it was the first item on the agenda of the general meeting the next day.

That Shabbat evening, the dining hall was packed, Motti and his colleagues from the cereal crops sitting at one table in the corner. As usual, some of the women had brought their knitting – 'doing something productive in all this hot air,' Sarah laughed.

Yaacov opened the proceedings, outlining the motion that Amos and Eli would propose, condemning what had occurred.

'Not allowing an Arab to stay in the kibbutz negates all our bi-national principles of equality and friendship between the two peoples,' Amos ended his brief introduction, 'a basic tenet of our principles.' Yaacov added that the areal commander wasn't told that it was just a young boy, and that had he known, he wouldn't have been bothered.

The discussion didn't last long; a show of hands supporting the motion and condemning what happened. No one spoke against. Motti said nothing, just scowled and muttered to his friends from time to time.

The meeting also voted to accept Eli's proposal that the kibbutz send someone with the volunteer woman to make *shalom* with the boy's family. Yaacov suggested Amos, as he had been involved. Amos shrugged, as if he didn't care one way or another, but Miriam noticed a little smile playing around his mouth as it was agreed.

The meeting passed on to other items on the agenda, and Motti and two of his friends rose and walked out, scowling and muttering.

Out on the path, Motti turned to Rami.

'As if we can live off stupid bloody principles.' He swore. 'Amos and his lousy Arab friends.' Being publically humiliated like that made him determined to get back at Amos. It was no longer just about that Arab boy. Now it was personal.

4

The *Egged* bus was crowded and stifling. It seemed as though the whole country was going to Jerusalem – celebrating victory and deliverance of the Six Day War. Up the winding asphalt road through the pine forest of the steep, rock-strewn valley of Shaar Ha Gai, an endless pilgrimage of trucks and buses, cars and vans, up to the Eternal City.

Amos was going up too, on his own pilgrimage -- to make excuses to the Arab silversmith on behalf of the kibbutz. The confrontation with Motti and the other extremists had been a long time coming but he was glad it had -- and given the kibbutz a chance to re-affirm its basic principles.

He was also pleased also that it had demonstrated all that to the new influx of volunteers, and that he had been the one to initiate it. However long Kate and her friend – what was her name again? and all the others stayed, it was important to let them know that the kibbutz was not a breeding ground for sectarian hatreds.

During the week, he had struggled to control his anticipation, deliberately avoiding mentioning it -- until Miriam did the evening before.

'You'll be back in time for the kids?' she'd asked. But it wasn't really a question.

'I'll try to -- buses and all that.' And they didn't mention it again…

The bus continued on and up, past the old, stone-built pump-house captured by *Palmach* shock troops twenty years and two wars before, their crude black graffiti still visible: '*Barukh Jamili was here*'. On past the burned-out chassis of convoy trucks that had saved the eternal city in that spring of '48, now painted red-oxide and set on concrete plinths, each carrying a small marble plaque showing the date of its demise.

Air-brakes hissed. The slow bus made its last stop at Beth Shemesh, before continuing direct, non-stop to Jerusalem.

'*Yerushalayim! Yerushalayim!*' the driver's voice called above the babble of voices as yet more people mounted the steps, packing into the already crushed centre aisle, while from the bus radio blared the silver-sweet voice of Shuli Natan:

'*Jerusalem of Gold, of copper and of light; to all your songs, I am the lyre…*' the kitsch lyrics suddenly transfigured through the war into a battle hymn, a thanksgiving for salvation — a dirge for loved ones who would never return.

On up the highway and out of the forest into the scrub-covered, terraced mountains, each hilltop stained with blood of the young from one war or another: '48, '56 and now, '67. And as the bus changed gear for the steep grind uphill past Mount Castel, the bitterly contested redoubt, Amos thought of his cousin, Naomi, making her visits each spring to lay red anemones on the rose-flushed limestone. Never missing a year; crying at the melancholy refrain of '*Bab el Wad*'. Never marrying. Who could replace Yuval?

Amos stared up at the tiny cluster of deserted, white stone houses. Now that the border had gone, would Abdul Kader's widow come here too, he wondered?

At the Jerusalem terminus, he changed to the local number 12 bus. It rattled down the narrow Jaffa Road between the old stone houses and past Zion Square to the stop opposite the main post office. Jostled and pushed through the exit door with everyone impatient to see the Holy City, he made his way down from the New City.

'I'll come from the Eastern quarter,' Kate had said when they were discussing arrangements the previous week. 'I could meet you just inside the walls.'

'Sure,' he'd nodded. 'By the Damascus Gate.' Although he had never been here before, from army maps, as well as his archeological interests, Amos was quite familiar with the general layout of the Old City.

In front of the Jaffa Gate, Amos stood and looked up at the round tower of King David's Citadel. His stomach was bubbling and his chest tinged with the anticipation of meeting Kate, relishing the opportunity to talk alone to an intelligent outsider, someone new and from a different world. But was it just that?

It was still early; they'd agreed midday to allow for any bus hold-ups. So to kill time, he joined the thousands of booted and sandaled feet that trod the ancient stones day after day. Unlike the crowds around him though, he was neither in a hurry, nor in mood to see the sights; the loss of Ya'ir, his best friend still so painful, his blood still fresh up there on the rocks of Ammunition Hill…

On and down the dark, narrow steps of the shaded Bazaar and along the Street of The Chain towards the Temple Mount, joining the horde of Israelis and tourists heading for the Wailing Wall, the hallowed, surviving remnant of the Holy Temple.

In the small courtyard, shaded by the high walls, Amos stood for a moment, looking around. Just being here in this previously hidden and forbidden place was incredible, the hushed awe broken only by the sound of feet scraping on the cobbles.

Some were still in khaki, rifles or Uzis slung carelessly over their shoulders; others wore white shirts or summer dresses. Beside him, old men wept and prayed silently. For over a thousand years, Jews had risked their lives here to pray -- pray for the Messiah; to rebuild the Temple and gather in the Exiles.

People were touching and caressing King Herod's massive, hewn stones of the temple's remaining west wall that towered course above course up into the sunlight, stones that through the ages had seen so many tears and so much bloodshed, before being moved along by the persistent pressure of new arrivals.

The stones reminded Amos of that discussion with Kate as they'd loaded empty onion boxes onto the trailer one afternoon.

'Look. Jerusalem is not just about religion,' he'd explained, 'it's more of a national symbol. Part of our history.' Like many Israelis, Amos wasn't religious; detested the religiosity of the black-coated ultra-orthodox with their bigotry and hypocrisy. Kate, though, had some difficulty with the concept of a non-religious Jew.

'Look,' she had cut in, 'there were some Jewish students at Queen's and the only thing that set me apart from them sure, was their religion.' Amos had rested his elbow on the wing of the tractor. It was going to be another of those intense discussions, her grey-green eyes sharp and piercing, her head jerking to emphasise this point or that.

They'd been hoeing the sugar beet, and because she had shown a real interest in the workings of the kibbutz, he had bothered to answer her questions -- or as far as was possible in the snatched conversations as they moved from row to row. She spoke in a tight, clipped way with strange vowels and sharp consonants, her voice often rising with a 'you know,' at the end of a sentence. It was quite distinct from that of the other English volunteers, or the American members of the kibbutz.

'You have a strange English accent, Kate,' he'd remarked one day.

'Yours isn't so hot either,' she had snapped.

'Okay. But I'm a "bloody foreigner",' Amos countered, grinning.

'Touché,' Kate had laughed and continued weeding then looked up, 'and we're not English either!'

Amos smiled to himself. He recalled that discussion and others that had followed. She was nothing if not determined, but although Jerusalem was to him principally an historic, national symbol, even he felt moved as he shuffled through the narrow space by the Wailing Wall. Yet Amos knew that this was also a city holy to the Palestinians who had always lived here – and despite being on the losing side, they would never forget that either.

Soon, he felt he had seen enough and glancing at his watch, he hurried towards the narrow exit. Squeezing through with the crowd, he turned left and walked away between the high, rough-stone walls of the Via Dolorosa thinking about the meeting.

Ostensibly, he had come to meet the Arab boy's family, to absolve the collective conscience of the kibbutz over the boy's abruptly truncated visit. 'Why you?' Miriam had said on their way back to the room after the kibbutz vote. He'd shrugged, surprised at her reaction, just as he'd dismissed Eli's teasing the day before: 'behave yourself in the Holy City, mate.'

Now, as he headed towards El Wad Street and the city's northern ramparts, Amos began to consider; would he have come so readily, had it not involved Kate? He was sure he would have. One of the reasons he was on this particular kibbutz was precisely because of their bi-national ideals. Nevertheless, as he thought of being on time to meet Kate, he quickened his pace.

In the hostel, Kate sat up and glanced through the east-facing window to the Mount of Olives. She had come up to Jerusalem the day before. The ancient tombstones glared white in the early sun; the sky was a cloudless blue. Soon it would be baking hot outside. Turning back, she swung her feet onto the tiled floor and straightened out the single bed then grabbed her wash bag and padded barefoot along the tiled, whitewashed corridor to the bathroom.

Back in the room she picked up her hairbrush and sat down by the small table, flicking the bristles and aimlessly staring at her toes. Amos's bus wouldn't arrive much before midday -— and it was only a few minutes' walk down to the Damascus Gate.

Across the room, a long dress hung on the wardrobe door. She'd bought on a whim in the Souk the day before. It was the colour -- blue with a touch of iridescent green like that of the hand-blown, Hebron glassware. It fitted neatly round her waist and had a loose flared skirt, and was really cheap too. With so many tourists and Israelis flooding the Arab Old City, prices would soon rise. Buying on impulse though, was so unlike her. Was it because she was meeting Amos? Jill was sure to tease when she got back.

Kate brushed and brushed her long hair. It caught a stray sunbeam and reflected a soft, ruddy glow onto the wall alongside. She hunched forward and gripped the brush in her lap, and her mind wandered back to that traumatic evening; to how Amos had been so sympathetic, and how she had felt so grateful -- and more, afterwards.

She laid the brush back on the small table, then glanced around the room again, once a nun's cell; plain and whitewashed. The room was nice and cool now but must be freezing in the Jerusalem winter. The Sisters presently occupied only one wing of this old stone building in the Arab quarter, the rest now a women backpackers' hostel.

A nun, sure. Her older sister, Eileen, had entered cloisters three years ago. Wouldn't that have saved Kate all that trouble in Belfast? She had run away to the LSE in London. But that didn't seem far enough. And when this Middle East crisis blew up, and fellow students like Jill wanted to set off for kibbutz in Israel, she'd joined them. And now she'd begun to get herself involved with the two sides out here.

An open letter from her mother lay on the table -- Mam probably telling the women at the Holy Cross how Kathleen is in Jerusalem; near the Holy Sepulchre and all that.

Poor Mam. She was a Dubliner and most of her family still lived there. Kate had deliberated many months before going to London, knowing she was leaving her to deal with her father's drinking, his brawls, his coming home late at times almost legless and having to help drag him up to bed. 'He'll have a terrible accident one day, if he doesn't stop,' she'd said more than once. But Mam had urged her to go. 'He's not a bad man, Kathleen, I'll manage. And there's always Eileen or father Eamon to help me, sure. Go. You have to live your own life, Kathleen.' The day she'd left, they'd hugged for a long time in the passage before she shouldered her rucksack and went out.

Kate stared absently out of the window again, up to the spire of the brown-stone walls of the Augusta Victoria Hospital on the adjacent hill, then glanced again at her watch. Amos said he would catch the early bus from the Beersheba. That usually arrived about eleven -- then at least another half hour for him to get to the Old City.

Yet again she told herself that he wasn't coming to see her;

that she was just the go-between to Yusuf and the boy. After taking him to meet the old silversmith, he would probably need to catch the bus back to the kibbutz in time to see his kids. End of story. Yet perhaps he would stay awhile and they could chat over a coffee, like they did while working out in the fields.

The tingling in her chest tough told her she was hoping for that -- and more. But what? Something like the closeness of that traumatic evening? She had told herself not to act like a moony schoolgirl. Amos was happily married; two kids and a lovely wife. She had to start thinking before she acted. And wasn't it so like her to bring the boy without first asking permission?

Kate checked her watch yet again. It was nearly eleven. She must stop treating this like some assignation; wear some sort of shapeless shirt with jeans? Pulling off her nightshirt, she threw it on the bed. Then, taking her underwear from the back of the chair she began to dress. For a moment she hesitated, then mouthing 'to hell', stepped across the room and opened the cupboard door, took the blue dress from the wire hanger, and slipped into it.

She looked at herself in the long mirror and spun one way, then the other. The soft, thin fabric flared and swirled, the low neckline revealing just a hint of cleavage. To hell with what Jill would say! Strapping on her sandals then tying back her hair with a thin, blue ribbon, she took her shoulder bag, stepped into the corridor and locked her door. She skipped down the stairs, evaded the curious glance of the sister -- and her own soul-searchings, and went out.

In the street, the brilliant, late-morning sunlight reflected off the rose-flushed, Jerusalem limestone walls of Sheikh Jarrah. Kate stood for a moment and screwed up her eyes. She ought to go and fetch her sunglasses, but didn't want to go back, and anyway, once inside the shade of the Old City it wouldn't matter.

Jerusalem was built on several small hills that nestled in a hollow some three thousand feet up, and all the roads sloped up or down. Ahead, she could see the crenellated ramparts; people streaming in and out of the massive, 15th century arched gateway of Suleiman the Magnificent. She hitched up her shoulder bag and strolled down the gentle incline towards the North Walls. Inside, she hoped Amos would be waiting.

Amos glanced at his watch and quickened his pace. In this part of the city there were far fewer tourists. Instead young, dark-faced men with bristling moustaches and women in embroidered, long black dresses flowed in from the Eastern bus station and Wadi Joz, to do what they had done here for centuries: buying and selling in the old covered markets and the narrow alleyways, but now, apprehensive at the horde of strange people thronging their city after twenty years of fear and enmity.

Standing on the high step set into ramparts by the public toilets, Amos scanned the crowds streaming in and out through the massive arched gateway. It was just after twelve and the midday sun cast deep shadows under the arch. And suddenly it was Kate. She strode out of the shade in a long, blue dress. Her hair was tied back and glowed in the bright sunlight.

Amos stepped forward. Kate saw him and waved.

'Hi. What a crowd!' She grinned as they met and shook hands. 'Thought you'd never see me.'

Amos laughed. 'With that red hair? Couldn't miss you.'

They stood for a moment, the excitement tempered by apprehension, Amos wary of being recognised. Israel was a small country and so many people were tripping up to see the sights. True, Kate was taking him to see the Arab family on behalf of the kibbutz, but already his conscience made him feel vulnerable.

Kate broke the silence.

'Amos.' She grinned. 'I could murder a cup of coffee, y'know.' Whenever she grew emotional or excited, unconsciously Kate slipped back into her mother's Dublin vernacular.

'Me too,' he nodded.

After the noise and crush of the Damascus Gate, their footsteps echoed in the empty, side-street. Narrow windows looked out from the high, stone walls either side and although he had relaxed as they left the crowds behind, instinctively Amos kept glancing right and left, aware that the locals must resent the Israeli occupation -- and that he was obviously an ex-soldier.

Kate led him to the small Arab cafe beyond El Hamra Street that she'd found with Jill. They sat at a pink and green plastic covered table and ordered cardamom spiced Turkish coffee and glasses of water, Arab style.

Butterflies flitted in Amos's stomach and wondered how to begin, and what to say. He was here to meet that Arab boy's uncle, to apologise for what had happened. But he was also meeting Kate alone, away from the kibbutz. And although everyone knew the purpose of the joint visit, sitting in this small out-of-the-way café just the two of them still made him wary.

Wary of what, though? After all, they were doing nothing wrong.

He looked across the table and smiled. Kate smiled back.

'Glad you made it,' she said. 'Have much trouble getting out?' It could have been referring to work. Or the buses. Or to… He rubbed his ear with the back of his finger; she'd noticed he did that whenever he felt awkward.

'*Mistadrim,* we manage.' He smiled again. 'And I'm glad you could make it, too.'

The barman was looking at them sideways. Amos felt his gaze, part hostile, part curious, probably trying to figure out why these two '*faranji*' had chosen his cafe in this obscure back street. He what the man was really thinking, and suddenly remembered Abu Gosh, the village in the hills on the way up.

The highway to Jerusalem wound through the centre of this, the only village in the area where the Arabs had stayed put in 1948 when all others had fled. Through the bus window, Amos had noticed the old men sitting in cafes by the roadside under fluttering blue and white Israeli flags. They twirled strings of worry beads and watched the hordes going up to Jerusalem. Women with baskets of produce on their heads, walked past at a slow measured pace, as they had done for hundreds of years in this, their land too.

What did they really think, he'd wondered? How did they feel during those six days, when they saw their brother Arabs in Jordan, Syria and Egypt humiliated and defeated and watched on television the new wave of refugees fleeing the West Bank across the Jordan River? Their land. His land. Two peoples, pulling at the same child, but no one with the Wisdom of Solomon to resolve it…

'A *grush* for your thoughts,' said Kate, and looked straight into his restless, light brown eyes. Together with his outward brashness, she sensed an edge of mystery -- suffering, perhaps? Whatever, it was something that made her want to draw closer; to get to know him.

'Worth at least a *lira!* Amos smiled and cast a glance towards the bar. 'Tell you later.' It was paradoxical that this girl from Northern Ireland, was more familiar with the Old City than he, who had been born in this land. But then she, a *faranji* and a Christian, would always be more accepted by the Palestinians than any Israeli would ever be.

Kate was from that far country about which he knew very little, apart from that it was riddled with religious divide and probably her reason for leaving. 'Sure,' she had smiled, when Amos questioned her about coming to Israel with its own ethnic conflicts, 'there are similarities. But here it's different. Not mine!'

They sat silent again for a moment, and the picture of her striding through the Damascus Gate flashed into his mind.

'Nice dress,' Amos said. 'Suits you.' The tight waistline, the silky cloth clinging to the small, rounded breasts and her angular hips moving as she walked.

'Got it in the old Souk,' she smiled. 'Yesterday. Dirt cheap. Thought I'd get in before the tourists hike up the prices.'

Kate sipped her coffee. She'd acquired quite a taste for the strong, cardamom-spiced beverage. Israeli men had appealed to her ever since she had arrived with Jill. Sure, they seemed just as macho as the lads back home, but they had something else. Intellect? That wasn't it. The boys at college were no idiots. Mediterranean passion? No. She had had enough of that in Italy. Perhaps it was the combination: pioneer country, Jewish intensity, melting-pot, siege mentality.

Amos, tall and broad shouldered, with his unbounded energy and boyish face, had intrigued her since she had arrived, and she felt good to be here alone with him. Kate took another sip of coffee and mused that had it not been for his confrontation with Motti over the Arab boy, perhaps she would never have managed to get closer to him at all.

From that evening, and even more since the kibbutz delegated him to go with her to see Yusuf, she had thought a lot about him. Yet having been down in the shelters together with Miriam, she had come to like and to admire her and felt some guilt at being alone with her husband like this.

She would, of course, never do anything to take it further; was experienced enough to rein in a schoolgirl crush. Sure, it was so good to be alone with him, but this was as far as it had to go. And she would make sure of that.

Amos, set down his cup with a click and made her start.

'Do you stay with the boy's family when you come here?' he asked.

'Oh no. No. At a women's hostel. Simple and bare but quiet and clean y'know. Run by the nuns.'

'Keep you out of mischief,' Amos grinned. Kate ignored the quip.

'It's odd,' she said, 'I feel good in the kibbutz. But I feel somehow more at ease here, amongst the Arabs in the Old City — as if there is less tension. Less stress.' She laughed. 'Though really, there should be more. And strangely,' she continued, 'as a woman, despite their attitudes, I feel much more at ease here than in say, Tel Aviv.'

'Careful,' Amos grinned across the table. 'You're becoming a real kibbutznik. We all hate Tel Aviv!'

Amos hated it too, the rush, the bustle, the dust, the crowded bus station. Some, like Shmuel, their treasurer, loved driving to town, having early breakfasts in the small cafe near Tel Aviv vegetable market, while exchanging news with functionaries from other kibbutzim. Then sitting in endless committees and meeting Jewish Agency and Bank officials.

He'd done his share, been both farm manager and general secretary at one time or another, pounding the corridors of the ministries for drought compensation and cotton quotas. But he was happiest just managing the irrigated crops: cotton, maize, potatoes and sugar beet, and feeling the nut-brown soil trickle through his fingers. That, and taking time off for his real passion, archaeology, tramping the hills and deserts, taking part in digs and joining the meetings of the Israel Exploration Society.

A regular clip-clop came from the narrow street outside; a loaded donkey trotted past the doorway. Even though he had never been inside the Old City until now, Amos knew the layout quite well. He recalled the archaeological discussions with Abbé Pirie from the French Seminary in Mamilla Street, who came over to the New City from time to time. Now, being here provoked an urge to renew the contact. When things settled down.

Amos sipped some water.

'So, how is Araf?'

'Oh. The boy is fine.' He watched her small, white teeth as she laughed. 'Tries out his English on me, but back at school now.'

He glanced at his watch. He had to see the Arab boy and his family. Kate nodded and drank up.

'Come,' she said, 'Yusuf will be waiting.'

She stepped across to the counter, put down some coins and smiled to the barman. Amos jumped up and started towards her, but she tossed her head. 'Yours next time,' she grinned. 'Ah, sure, aren't we all socialists!'

The sun had passed its zenith and the street was half in the shade when they stepped out onto the warm stones and turned to walk towards St Stephens Street. Amos had a rough idea of where they were going and what he would say to the boy's family when they met. But now, he enjoyed so much to be with her, he had begun to think of afterwards. Make sure they left time for coffee perhaps, before he had to take the bus back.

5

Kate led the way through the narrow streets, she and Amos chatting casually about Jerusalem and the boy's family. But by the Chapel of the Flagellation, as they turned left into Al Mujahadeen Street, Amos suddenly stopped dead. Kate had carried on a few paces before noticing, then turned, puzzled.

'It's quite safe, you know.'

Amos ran a hand through his hair. 'I know,' he murmured, a tightness had gripped his chest. 'It's not that. It's… It's just something that happened.' He nodded towards the distant gateway. 'Down there,' adding softly, 'only I was coming the other way.'

Ahead, at the far end of street and set into in the old ramparts, was St Stephens gate --the 'Lions' Gate', the Israelis called it from the motifs carved in the lintel stones.

Kate looked into his eyes as she walked back to him. They were dull.

'Bad memories?' she asked.

He shrugged. 'Uhuh.'

'Like?'

'A friend. My best friend.' He looked away. 'I'll tell you some time.'

In his mind was that day at dawn, waiting in his armoured column that were about to break through into the Old City. Ya'ir, his best friend and a paramedic, had been seconded to the parachutists. Ever since the Sinai campaign they had been together in the Reserves, survived more than one ambush. But as the Paras stormed the Jordanian Legion on Ammunition Hill that night, Ya'ir had caught a bullet. Amos heard of the assault over the unit radio, but all night long as his column waited he was sure his friend would survive this one too.

From first light, there'd been little time to think as his unit had sped down from the Mount of Olives, the first tank crashing through those iron gates, the column following through the archway into the deserted streets. It was only after the surrender, as they sat and rested against the cold, stone-walls of the Omariyyeh School, that the terrible news reached him; Ya'ir had gone, his tears coursing down his cheeks and falling onto the old, worn cobblestones.

Now, as he looked down this same street again, Amos saw that the steel gates had since been repaired and painted blue. He glanced back up the Via Dolorosa, remembering, and clenched his fists. Nothing. None of this was worth Ya'ir's life. None of it. Ya'ir and his poems, his stories, his flute playing something out of this world. Gone. For a heap of stones. His head burned. *Le'azazel:* To hell with it! They could have the whole damn lot. If only it would bring him back.

Kate waited, silent, the muscles of his face twitched and his neck tendons knotted. Perhaps she shouldn't have brought him. But then he hadn't mentioned it when they discussed the visit. How was she to know? Though they never talked about it, she guessed many men in the kibbutz probably had bitter memories -- one battle or another; friends dead or wounded.

For a brief moment, Kate thought of suggesting that they turn back. Instead she grasped his forearm gently, and for a moment, they stood there and looked into each other's eyes. There was something in his gaze; it seemed to penetrate deep into her soul.

'Come.' Amos shrugged; he tried to smile. 'Nothing we can do about the past, Kate. Let's have a go at the future.'

They walked on until just before the gateway, Kate abruptly turned and dived into a low doorway to her right. Amos would hardly have noticed it, hidden as it was by the tourist paraphernalia hanging on the wall outside: rows of copper pots and trays, brown and white sheepskins, and wire coat-hangers dripping with silver chains and ornaments. Alongside, hung full-length, Arab peasant-women's dresses in black and purple, richly embroidered in red and orange across the chest.

Turning to follow Kate, instinctively he paused just inside the opening for a few seconds to become accustomed to the dim light. By a rickety table, an old man sat on a low chair. Around him, embroidered cushions were scattered on the floor and wool weaves and embroidered tapestries hung on the arched walls that met in a point high in the ceiling. Silver chains and ornaments, necklaces and earrings dangled on boards and from cords, and glinted in the dull, bluish light that reflected from the whitewashed walls.

The old man rose, hands outstretched.

'Ah. Kate. Welcome. Welcome,' he said in a thick accent and a broad smile crossed his dark, lined face. He was quite short and very thin, a brown jacket over his cream-coloured *abayya*, and shiny black shoes. He clasped Kate's hand in his two hands, then while he still held it, looked past her and caught Amos's eye.

'Hello to you too. Welcome. Welcome.' He waved towards a cushion. 'A friend of Kate is always welcome.'

'This is Yusuf. Araf's uncle,' Kate explained, and gently withdrew her hand.

'*Ahalan wesahalan,*' Amos greeted him in Arabic.

He stepped forward and they shook hands. For Amos it

revived childhood memories of Haifa during the British Mandate, in the late forties when Arabs and Jews lived together in the town. He recalled his father to meeting Arab trade unionists in Wadi Salib. Seemed in a different century now.

They sat on cushions and Kate wrapped her dress around her ankles, then the old man called towards the doorway. The boy, Araf, ran in, a wide grin across his face as he shook Kate's hand. He listened to his uncle, then hurried out and for a moment there was an awkward silence. Kate picked up the open letter that was lying on the table and handed it to Amos.

'Yusuf makes great things in silver. See this.' He saw it was a signed, typed letter from a woman in California, thanking Yusuf for the wonderful Sufi ring he had made for her. Amos knew that the Sufi were a sect of Muslim mystics, but little else. He wondered what was special about a Sufi ring.

'Ah. She was so grateful. A lovely woman,' he said, and took back the letter and placed it carefully on the table.

The single lightbulb cast a ruddy glow to Kate's hair as she told Yusuf about Amos, how he was the manager of the cotton and maize crops, had been farm manager and spoke English, all the while carefully avoiding any reference to the war.

Amos stared to where the arched-ceiling ribs sprang from the walls, like the vault of some ancient castle. Old Jerusalem was like so many medieval cities, building upon building, that rested on foundations and cellars of even older structures. He thought of how just two months ago, to sit in the Old City would have seemed like a dream. Now, in the space of six days, everything had been turned upside down. But if it hadn't been for Kate, he doubted whether he would be here at all. She seemed to have such high expectations of him; he didn't want to let her down.

Araf, coming through the doorway, broke his reverie. Amos

sat up and took a tall glass of tea from the silvered tray. Kate smiled at him across the room almost conspiratorially as they all sipped the hot, sweet *chai*.

Yusuf was bemoaning that trade had fallen through.

'Before,' he said, 'all the tourists came from Jordan, up by Jericho and in through the St. Stephens gate. Now,' he added wearily, 'the tourists come from the New City and in through the Jaffa gate. My shop is one of the last to be seen -- if they come this far!'

'I'm sure that tourism from Jordan will soon be renewed,' Amos said, 'it's in our interests too.'

'*Insh'Allah*,' said the old man.

Amos apologised for the boy having to come back so soon, the huts were needed for a school harvest-camp, he explained. Kate had gone along with this story from the start. The old man thanked him profusely for having let the lad see the kibbutz.

'Hasn't stopped talking about the cows and the tractors ever since,' he added.

Amos looked across at Kate again. In the dim blue light that matched the colour of her dress, with the pale complexion and the loose hair down to her shoulders, she looked as one of the Impressionist paintings he'd seen in Miriam's art books. It took him again to that night after the argument with Motti -- her pale face, the touch of her fingers on his arm. And again, he tried to fathom out why that had affected him so and why he'd wanted so much to go to Jerusalem with her.

Amos was glad he had come and had managed to talk to the old man, but now he wanted much more to be out and alone with Kate. And as the man offered them more tea, Kate was surprised that before she could respond, Amos cut in to decline, and said that he had to catch his bus.

It was mid afternoon when they left Yusuf's shop. The cobbled street was in deep shade, but a soft yellow light reflected from high up on the old, stone-walls. They strolled up the crooked street of the Via Dolorosa, Kate explaining the Stations of the Cross.

'Okay,' said Amos, longing to reach out and hold her hand, 'but why "stations"?'

'Stations – from the Latin *Statis*: Stops,' Kate smiled. She recalled her childhood and the nuns who related the story. 'It's where Jesus stopped to rest the heavy cross. Twelve of them,' she said.

'Twelve. The old magic number. Twelve moons, twelve tribes, twelve apostles, every faith taking over the ancient lunar magic.' Amos paused and tried to stay calm while his body was tingled as they crossed the small square. 'Well, we suppose that Jesus -- if he really existed, Kate, would have been just one of many turbulent preachers before the 1st Century Jewish revolt against the Romans, which led to the destruction of the Temple.'

Although he had studied the history and archaeology of the Old City, Amos was bewildered at the multitude of churches, monasteries and seminaries, and all the different Christian sects. Kate, despite her Catholic upbringing, was also baffled by the multiplicity of holy places, but she so enjoyed their walking and chatting together. Despite the tourists, both felt as though they were alone as they wandered on through the Church of the Condemnation and then the Armenian Church, and Kate wished he would take her arm -- and perhaps hold her closer.

By the Ecce Homo basilica, Kate suddenly stopped.

'Heck. Enough religion for one day I think, Amos.'

'Uhuh. Come.' He smiled. 'Come. Let's have coffee.'

'Holy God,' said Kate as they sat and drank, 'reminds me of

what Arthur Koestler wrote in his *Street of the Prophets*. "So much religiosity, so little religion".'

'So much wealth,' added Amos, 'so many sects, and each one thinks that only they have the correct way.' He grinned. 'A bit like left-wing politics!'

'Don't have to convince me,' said Kate. 'Had enough of religion as a kid with the nuns. Luckily, when I was fourteen my grandmother died and my mother didn't feel that obliged, so I went to an ordinary school. Of my friends who stayed, only three became devout Catholics. Most lapsed, or rebelled and went the other way completely.' He loved the way her whole face lit up as she laughed, adding, 'and two were pregnant at sixteen!'

'But you're a rebel too, Kate,' Amos said, turning to her. 'Otherwise why would you have come out here?'

'Well. Yes. A bit of one sure, but not extreme. Now my friend Mairead, she's into the Civil Rights and all that.' Amos had already noticed her strange way of pronouncing the 'u' sound, her lips pursed and tight. Now, with her face upturned and slightly toward him, her tiny front teeth white in the sunlight, he had to control a sudden crazy urge to lean forward and kiss her, but if he misread the signals it would foul up a lovely day. To distract himself, he turned away for a moment and looked at a dragon-headed gargoyle opposite. Then swung back.

'So. What about you. Kate?'

Kate looked directly into his eyes and smiled, and his chest tingled from the warmth of that smile, and the way her intense face suddenly seemed to soften, as though he'd touched a chord.

'That's another story,' she said. 'Needs more time, Amos.'

'I'd like to hear it, Kate.'

When they came out of the Jaffa Gate, Amos's heart still pounded from the intimacy of their conversation and the near-miss kiss. To distract himself, he pointed over the broad expanse of newly graded, waste ground.

'Impossible to believe, Kate' he began, 'just a few months ago, all this was a no-man's-land; massive, concrete anti-shrapnel walls, mines and barbed-wire entanglements. For twenty years we used to stand at those old houses over there, Yemin Moshe, and stare at these walls and David's Tower. Couldn't even see the Jaffa Gate itself.' He paused and turned back to her. 'Still seems unreal.'

Trucks and cars were parked on the stony brown soil, many of them army vehicles being 'borrowed' for day trips while still on active service. Amos recognised some of the units. The intoxication of victory was already producing its hangovers. It would soon have to end.

They crossed the open space and walked up the Mamilla Road, then stood at the bus stop and waited for the local No 12. The moment the silver and blue bus approached, the crush began to move forward and when the door opened, they had to join a mad scramble up the metal steps to get on at all. When it bumped its way up the Jaffa Road, they were thrust together in the aisle of the crowded bus. But neither moved away.

The main bus station was seething too. Originally built for a provincial city at the end of a cul-de-sac of territory, it was now struggling to cope with its new status as a main crossroads. Standing with him in the queue for the Beersheba bus, Kate was jostled and crushed as those behind tried to push forward.

'Y'know,' she winced, 'waiting patiently doesn't seem part of the Israeli character.'

'No,' Amos grinned. 'After getting kicked around for two thousand years, allowing someone else to stand in front of you doesn't come easy.'

They talked more about Jerusalem. About what she was going to do for the next couple of days until she came back to the kibbutz, and while they talked, Amos realised that they had only a short time before they would have to part. He even hoped that the next bus would be cancelled, as sometimes happened, and they would have to wait for the one after -- as long as he got back before the kids were asleep.

And in these last few minutes, Amos began to sense Kate's reluctance too, that they were their about to part -- and that like him she wanted the clock to stand still. His body grew hot and the blood rushed through his head, and he regretted more and more that he had no excuse to stay longer in Jerusalem.

Kate glanced at her watch when the scheduled time for the bus approached and a tightness gripped her chest. She too wished he could stay and regretted not having planned to go back with him; to sit close on the long journey back.

The parting was sudden and violent. The *Egged* intercity bus arrived and nosed into the bay, the door opened with a hiss of air, and in the mad rush to get in that followed, Amos saw that it wouldn't be a matter just to grab a seat, but to get on at all.

'I'd better go,' he gasped, their handshake rudely torn apart as Kate was squashed between a large woman and a bearded man with a huge bag, while Amos had to muscle his way up the steps and into the bus.

Kate scanned the windows and her heart thumped. She had to see him to say goodbye -- had to! Then, when the driver started the engine, Amos managed to lean down from the centre gangway.

'*Shalom*, Kate,' he called through a half-raised window. His hand poked out and she reached up. '*Lehitra'ot!*' Their fingers touched, then clasped. 'See you soon,' he shouted.

"Bye, Amos. Bye,' she gasped. 'Safe journey,' and squashed back against the barrier, managed only to catch one last glimpse as he waved again from inside the bus, before it reversed into the roadway, turned and accelerated away. And it was gone -- he was gone.

Kate stood by the kerb, her stomach clenched tight -- and felt empty.

Amos stared through the side window. The journey up to Jerusalem had been so full with anticipation. Now, all the way down the winding road to Bab el Wad, there was only a void that grew with every kilometre. But then, after they passed Masmiyya junction, and the nearer he came to the kibbutz, he began to think of Miriam.

Eleven years. A large chunk of his adult life. So why was now being so stupid?

In the past, when bumping into an old girlfriend in Tel Aviv or joking with the boys in the garage over innuendos about this one or that, he had sometimes felt the odd frisson, but it went no further. The kibbutz was a small village, everything seen and known -- the most conservative revolutionary society in the world, Joe would quip. So an affair with Kate would be nigh impossible.

Perhaps, he pondered, he allowed himself to consider it because she was only here for a while -- no long-term threat of a serious involvement. But it mustn't happen, not least because Miriam would inevitably find out, and the last thing he wanted to do was hurt her or make her do something drastic which, being Miriam, she certainly would. And the kids! A sudden dryness in his throat almost choked him. He closed his eyes for a moment. There was no choice; it must all be forgotten. The next time he saw Kate he must treat her just like any other volunteer.

The bus left Kastina junction and sped down the road to Beersheba. Amos stared through the side window; stubble fields stretched away either side, and in the East, the distant, blue-tinted, the rounded hills of the *Shefelah* thrust like breasts against the darkening sky.

After they passed the ruined mud huts of Faluja, the sky turned deep red, then purple, and the sun set towards the sea in the west. In half an hour it would be dark and he would be home; go to say goodnight to Ran and Noa, then supper with Miriam, and to tell her about Jerusalem. He usually told her everything. But now? The bus dipped as it crossed the dry wadi. He rose and pulled on the bell cord.

Amos paused by the roadside. The bus drew away, headlight beams swinging and searching, and negotiated the narrow, undulating road before disappearing, Soon, the roar of the engine faded too and he was alone in the silence of the night — and the fence lights of the kibbutz.

On the far side of the road, about a kilometre to the east, pin-points of orange firelight flickered from the Bedouin tents. To the south glimmered the distant fence lights of the neighbouring kibbutz. Three isolated communities under a vast, star-studded, indigo vault in the desert night.

He turned and began to walk the few hundred yards down the side road. Ahead, the fence lights of the kibbutz had already come on. Time to see the kids. Already, Jerusalem seemed a long, long way away. Kate even further. And the closer he approached the gate and into the full glare of the fence lights, the more Kate, Jerusalem and everything around it seemed to come into question.

By the time he'd passed the dining hall and strode down the path to the children's houses, his mind had turned to more pressing matters. Making sure he had the new Fordson diesel tractor to finish cultivating the cotton, and checking that the school harvest-camp was coming from town next Sunday to pick potatoes. But first, to see the kids before they went to sleep.

<h1 style="text-align:center">6</h1>

It was nearly eight o'clock when he called in at the toddlers' house. Noa was in the small bedroom she shared with three others, sitting on her bed in pyjamas and taking two red bows out of her straight, fair hair.

'*Abba! Shalom!*' she shrilled, surprised, adding the inevitable: 'what have you brought me?'

For the children, the three hours at home from four to seven were sacrosanct. Mum or Dad -- usually Dad, not being there, was the next thing to a heinous sin. In compensation for not being there, Amos never failed to bring back some small present whenever he went to town: sweets or a small trinket. 'Something from town' had become obligatory.

'Like blackmail,' Amos had protested once. 'We should be able to show our love and care without material gifts each time.'

'No it isn't,' Miriam had responded. 'It shows that they are still in your mind even though you are not here. Children can't think in abstracts.' Amos didn't argue. She knew more about kids than he ever would. Or was it just the way women loved presents, giving as well as receiving? Like most of his friends, Amos never could never quite get to the bottom of it.

So there was always the mad rush to the sweet shop just before catching the bus home, or searching out some rubbishy stall near the bus station for unusual beads, or a dinky toy. This time -- for the first time ever, with the excitement of meeting Kate and the emotional parting at the bus station, he had forgotten. And all the way home on the bus, he'd agonised with making an excuse. And had to lie.

'I'm so sorry *khamudi*. I bought Pezim sweets in a Goofy head, but left them on the bus.'

Noa put out her lower lip and looked down. Amos crouched down and hugged her.

'But I'll bring two next time. I promise.'

'Promise?' she said, and reached up and touched his cheek.

'Promise. Promise,' said Amos, giving her another hug.

He sat by her on the bed, while she drew him a picture — a house with a red, pitched roof – even though many of the kibbutz houses had flat concrete roofs. Something about security; a protective cover, Miriam explained. Educational psychology wasn't his strong point, either.

'Now then. Say goodnight, children.' Nitza, the *metapelet*, the children's nurse was making made the rounds of the two bedrooms that led off from the dining room. She smiled as she saw him with Noa.

'Shalom, Amos. *Nu?* How was *Al Kuds?*' using the Arabic name for the Old City as the *sabras* would. Amos nodded and smiled back.

'Still there. Just.'

They'd known each other since they were kids together in Haifa. Their fumbling, teenage romance had swiftly faded but had left them still quite close. Trusting. The barely warm, yet comforting embers of a long dead fire.

Miriam sensed -- and at times seemed to resent it. Despite three kids, with her mass of curly brown hair and wide mouth, Nitza was still vivacious and attractive. He wondered whether she could sense anything now. She would be the first to notice; could read him even more clearly than Miriam. 'You'd never make a good liar, Amos,' she'd once told him.

He just hoped Noa had believed him. He returned his daughter's hugs, and by planting two more kisses on her forehead eventually managed to disengage, then backed and waved from the doorway, blowing still more. 'Bloody Oedipus,' Joe, who had a daughter in the same group, would joke, 'I blame him for it all,' and by chance he was outside as Amos turned to go down to the schoolhouse.

'Hey. Amos. How long do you need the Fordson?' Joe, short, earnest and balding had come with a dozen others from New York some five years ago. He insisted on using his Hebrew name, Yosef, but everyone except his wife Aviva still called him Joe. A fan of Noam Chomsky and Marcuse, he travelled to Tel Aviv every fortnight to take part in *Seeakh*, a New Left group. Amos stopped and thought for a moment.

'About four days, Joe. I need the big three-point linkage for the new cultivator.'

'Just my luck,' Joe laughed. 'I wanted the new cultivator for the orchards, before we start irrigating again.'

Amos didn't want to get into complicated negotiations right then. Ran would soon be going to sleep. He stepped to one side.

'Look. I'll make sure you have it as soon as we're finished. But see Uri to make sure no one else has bagged it.'

'Okay,' said Joe. 'Thanks.' And ambled away, his arms swinging like windmill sails.

It was always like that. Each working in their own branch, often miles from each other, meant that evenings were the only times that managers could meet to co-ordinate schedules of irrigation and machinery. Otherwise, it would be during the hours with the kids. Some, like Uri or Yossi would often do that, knocking at the door, interrupting a game or a story. Not Joe. Crazy about his new daughter. Amos acknowledged that he himself might even have done that more often, if it wasn't for Miriam.

Ran was seated with Gadi and Yoram around a classroom table, and played Chinese Chequers.

'You can't do that.' Gadi was indignant. 'Only two jumps. Not three.' Ran tried to calm him down.

'Okay. Okay. Let Yoram take two, then it's your turn. Okay.' Suddenly he spotted Amos coming through the door. 'Hi Dad. When did you get back?'

'Just now. How's things?'

'Fine,' said Ran then jumped up, wide eyed. 'Saw an African Black Eagle today circling over the wadi. Ephraim said it must have come up with the hot winds from Sinai!' Amos ruffled his son's hair. It was like barbed wire, sticking out everywhere and defying the strongest comb. Ran had inherited his love of the countryside, and of archaeology. They often spent hours together in the room, pouring over encyclopedias from the school, or in sorting out the artefacts that Amos brought back from his field trips.

In less than half a minute, the boy seemed to have forgotten that Amos had been away, just held onto his hand for a while and went back to playing with his friends. In three years, thought Amos, Ran will be going away to the kibbutz high-school, boarding and coming home only at weekends. Yet it seemed only yesterday that they had called out the army to escort Miriam to Beersheba hospital at two in the morning. Even Noa was five.

It was pitch dark when he came out, the narrow paths weaving between the young acacia and pine trees, barely lit by the lampposts. He had also forgotten to get something for Ran, and was glad the boy had been too engrossed in the game to notice, but he didn't feel good about that. He mustn't do it again.

In the kindergarten, Miriam was sat on the floor in a circle of twelve children, and read from *The Jungle Book* before putting them to bed. Two of the boys sucked thumbs, while one girl twisted strands of hair through her fingers and each lived every tense moment of Akela and the wolf cubs.

Amos poked his head around the fly screen door. She looked up and smoothed back her hair, while her dark eyes smiled a welcome. 'Eight thirty', she mouthed, then turned back to continue reading, before the spell was broken. Amos nodded and smiled, then ducked out and walked swiftly up towards the brightly lit dining hall. Why the hell he had even briefly harboured fantasies about getting involved anyone else?

In the lobby of the dining hall, he checked the work rosters to make sure the two volunteers he'd requested had been arranged for the potato picker machine. Then he sauntered outside and sat on one of the concrete benches in the paved area around the entrance, and greeted friends coming up to eat. Like every evening: arrangements for the tractor or irrigation water; arguments with the treasurer or the work organiser, and he still had to see Uri about the old huts for the harvest camp. He glanced at his watch. Miriam would still be a quarter of an hour, and after supper she had a meeting with the area education officer.

Crickets chirped in the nearby bushes. Moths fluttered against the street lamps and bats flitted out of the darkness before they vanished again in split seconds. And while he sat and waited in the darkness, for the first time since getting off the bus, Kate suddenly entered his head. It was as though in this first quiet moment he had to himself, a huge wave held back by a wall of the evening's activities, had burst through to flood his brain.

Amos closed his eyes and visualised her coming through the Damascus gate, his crotch growing hot as he saw again the soft, thin fabric of the blue dress that flowed over her hips and thighs, and imagined pulling her against him, to run his hands up her back and --.

'Hey, sleepy.' Amos jumped and opened his eyes. 'How about supper?' It was Miriam. He sprang up, reached out and pulled her against him. Miriam, surprised by the sudden passion, tensed.

'What's got into you?' she said.

'You,' he said emphatically.

They kissed, holding together for a few seconds in the darkness.

'Come,' she said, and leaned back, 'I'm hungry.' And, arm around her waist, they went in to eat.

Kate had walked away slowly from the bus station. Her fingers still prickled from their brief finger-clasp through the side window and her stomach turned. At the last moment, she'd felt a crazy urge to jump on the bus, to try to buy a ticket from the driver and join him on the journey back. Just as well the bus was packed full, and anyway her rucksack was still back at the hostel.

Head down, she crossed the square towards the No. 12 bus stop. She'd planned to stay in Jerusalem for another day to enjoy the calm and undemanding atmosphere of the Old City, away from the hectic life of the kibbutz -- and to see Araf again.

Kate had grown fonder of the young boy ever since she had taken him down to the kibbutz. She recalled his joy at the liberation from the confines of the walled city and his traditional Muslim family; the open countryside, the modern farm and the free and easy world of the kibbutz children.

She pictured how he had run about in the cowshed, snatching

handfuls of hay from the bales, darting from one cow to the next and giggling as the huge wet lips slurped against his wrists, then clambering up the tracks of the huge D6 caterpillar in the tractor-shed, pulling at the clutch levers, and making engine noises, 'Brrm. Brrm.' Just like any other kid.

She had wanted so much for him to meet the kibbutz kids -- and for them to see him; that he was just like any other child, wanting to play, to learn, to make friends. She recalled Brigid trying to arrange joint games with kids from Protestant schools. Here, like there, the adults on both sides already had their preconceptions and suspicions. But the children, the curiosity of the young, the openness, they were the future, could break down the mutual suspicion and bring hope. Unlike his dogmatic older brother, Shafik, young Araf still possessed that innocence.

The local bus drove through Zion Square and climbed Koresh Street towards the Old City. Along the pavements, black-and-white chequered *keffieh* headscarves mingled with the summer dresses of the New City, Arabs and Israelis mixing freely, as though the last twenty years had never been. The honeymoon period, Shafik called it. Wouldn't last, he said. 'They will only want a united Jerusalem on their terms, Kate. Under their control,' his dark eyes narrow and hard. 'Golda Meir, their prime minister, doesn't even recognise the Palestinians as a separate people. To her, we are all just Arabs!'

She got off near the still boarded-up Barclays bank, a remnant of the old British Mandate. It had once been cocooned by the no-man's-land of barbed wire and mines. Now, from the roadside, roughly graded waste ground ran up to the corner of the Old City wall, the city council having lost no time in trying to make the two cities into one.

Kate headed for the hostel, walking swiftly along Sultan Suleiman Road and past the crenulated ramparts of the Damascus

Gate, the gate that would now always hold such a special meaning. But despite the feeling that lingered in her chest, when she turned left away from the city walls and into the modern part of Arab East Jerusalem, the picture of the birthday party swam into her head, Miriam inviting into her room, the cake, the happy family. What right had she to threaten all that?

Kate crossed the road, and the more she walked on with sharp, quick steps, the more she acknowledged that she had to give up on her stupid fantasies. For his sake in the kibbutz, for Miriam, and for his family, if she wanted to stay here, she had to nip it in the bud and let Amos him know it, and now.

Instead of staying on here, tomorrow she would catch the midday bus to Beersheba and back to the kibbutz. Quite suddenly, the evening seemed colder and her stomach empty as she walked on, past the new stone-built villas and young trees planted in small, square plots in the neat paving. Two men in light coloured suits came towards her, one spinning a string of amber worry-beads. They stepped off the narrow pavement, glancing sideways at her as they went, then carried on. A donkey staggered past with an enormous, white-*keffieh'd* man astride it; how on earth did those spindly legs carry such a weight?

In the hostel, as she entered the cool, half-lit corridor, Kate remembered that she had agreed to meet Shafik again the following morning. While acknowledging that her interest in Shafik, a 'view from the other side' was a chance to get to know another world, it had also been a counterweight to her growing interest in Amos. Right now though, going back to the kibbutz was the priority and she had to cancel their planned meeting. It wouldn't be fair to Shafik, but when she opened the door and stared at the small bed, Kate knew that she had to.

The sun cast its last hazy beams across the roofs of the New City and onto the crenulations of the ancient walls, when she hurried through the Damascus Gate. Inside the Old City, tourists still thronged the narrow alleyways of the Souk, lit with bare electric lamps strung on wires between the stalls. But in the dimly lit St. Stephens street, it was quiet, the dresses and jewellery already stowed away behind closed shutters, and Yusuf's shop was shut too.

Rummaging in her shoulder-bag, Kate tore a sheet from a small notebook and began to write a note for Shafik. Suddenly, door swung open and he stepped out, his black wavy hair neatly combed and wearing a white shirt and faded blue jeans. Kate jumped back, her mouth open.

'Oh. Shafik. I --,' She was thinking fast, 'glad I caught you.' The words cascaded out. 'Really sorry, but I have to go back tomorrow. Jill left a telephone message at the hostel.'

At that moment, Yusuf came out backwards. He was about to lock the door when he saw her and swung round.

'Ah. Miss Kate. A surprise.' He smiled broadly. 'Indeed a surprise.'

'I just came to tell Shafik I can't come tomorrow. I hoped someone would be here.'

Shafik remained sullen, and made no attempt to hide his disappointment.

'I'll see you to the Damascus gate then,' he said curtly,

'Oh. Sure. Thanks,' said Kate, 'and goodbye Yusuf.'

'Goodbye Miss Kate. Come and see us. Whenever you like. Goodbye.'

Kate smiled and waved, and he hurried away. Shafik didn't.

'Dear old Yusuf, Miss this, my lady, Mrs that,' he muttered as they reached the top of the street. 'Twenty years since the British left and still he lives in that sham world of colonial politeness.'

Kate sensed his annoyance — and knew it wasn't with his uncle.

In her bid to distract herself from Amos, had she led him on? Heck. Why was she getting so mixed up with men? Hadn't she come here to experience kibbutz, to see a new society and country, and perhaps contribute to it somehow. Instead, she'd been getting all giddy, like some stupid schoolgirl.

They walked along the Via Dolorosa and Kate tried to relax, but from time to time, Shafik glanced at her out of the corner of his eye. They'd met again since that first occasion, and wandered through a different part of East Jerusalem, while he told her more about himself and his people, their resentments, doubts and hopes.

Each time when she returned to the kibbutz, she would play devil's advocate and confront Amos and Miriam, or argue with Jill and other volunteers, then would bring their views back to argue with Shafik, trying to make sense of it all. Often to end up more bewildered than before.

'You're trying too hard, Kate,' Amos had said one day, while they sorted seed-potatoes. 'It's difficult enough for us living here to understand, let alone anyone from outside.' But she did want to understand. Both sides.

She had tried to do that in Belfast, had bridged that divide for herself, as had many of her student friends. Much good it had done her. It was the majority, 'working-class bigotry on both sides,' Robert had said. And out here it seemed to be the same if she had understood Amos correctly, the educated, European-origin Israelis inclined to understand the Palestinians, while the poorer, mainly oriental immigrants regarded them as the permanent enemy.

They walked on in a strained silence, and her mind switched back to the tiny cafe in the alleyway off the Souk, where Shafik had taken her on their first meeting.

Music from Radio Ramallah was coming through the grille of a battered transistor on the counter; two old men were playing *Shesh-Besh*, one pulling smoke through a *Nargila* water flask. And as usual, over coffee, they'd talked politics, Kate trying to show him 'the other side'; convince him of 'The Good Israeli'.

'Look, Kate,' Shafik sighed, picking up the argument where they'd left off, 'I don't dispute what you say. But those Is-ra-el-is' -- pronouncing the word in four syllables, 'they are not the ones who make policy.' Leaning conspiratorially towards her, he added, 'do you know, they are passing new laws to expropriate the neighbourhood around their Wailing Wall and hand it over to religious Jews? And that's right under the walls of the Haram with its the great mosques.' He moved back. 'And there's nothing we can do. Nothing.' And looking straight into her face and added, 'maybe that Israeli man you meet in the kibbutz doesn't give that impression, Kate, but that is how it is for us.'

Kate tensed. Why had he mentioned Amos? Was it getting personal for him? She had to be wary.

'Tell me, Shafik,' she said quickly, 'why does Yusuf appear anxious about us being together? Does it compromise you with the family?'

Shafik half smiled.

'You noticed the ring.'

'Actually, Jill did. Joked about it. Said you might be married. But then I wondered, would you be here, alone with me, if you were? Anyway. Apologies, if it's rude of me to ask.'

'No. No,' Shafik began, looking away. 'Well, I am not married.

But yes, I am betrothed to a girl from Yusuf's family. My father and Yusuf were brothers and it would bind the families together and keep our property in one piece. We have some land near Jenin.' He paused. 'Old customs here die hard. And for independently minded people, it is difficult – especially for women. They often end up in terrible marriages.' He looked up at her. 'We have a young Palestinian writer: Leila Balbeki. She describes it well.'

Kate sensed his embarrassment and looked away past the Mount of Olives, to where the barren, white hills of the Judean desert peeped between the nearby hills.

'You see,' Shafik continued, 'Jamilla is a lovely girl, but still very traditional. It would not work. We both know that. But,' his face grew taut and dark, 'but when my father was killed in a quarry accident I became head of our family, and all the relatives insisted that we marry. Yusuf too.' Kate realised now why the old man always seemed uncomfortable as they left the shop together.

'So what will you do, Shafik?'

'To be truthful, Kate, I don't know. That is why I didn't leave to find work in the Gulf. This had to be settled first.' He looked away. 'Now the occupation has upset everything on the West Bank. We are all in a kind of limbo. But when things settle down again, it will have to be resolved.'

'Just that?'

'Just that,' he said softly.

So that was it. She wasn't just 'that woman who was Yusuf's friend', to whom he was being pleasant and polite. Shafik was 'a free agent', as Jill would say. Sure, at first as well as being interested in his views 'from the other side', she had taken advantage of their meeting to divert her feelings away from Amos. Now Kate realised that in thinking his betrothal was a 'safety net', she had sent out the wrong signals, and as they walked along his sullen face told her he was really hurt.

They carried on through El Wad road towards the Damascus Gate, both silent, and by the time they came out through and crossed the stone causeway over the dry moat, the short twilight had gone and it was dark.

'Can I see you to the hostel?' said Shafik suddenly. 'It's getting late.' His voice had softened. Protective. Had he sensed that she was hiding something?

'Sure. If it's no trouble,' said Kate as they walked past the East Bus Station. 'And look. I'm really sorry about tomorrow, so I am.'

'Oh. It's okay.' Shafik shrugged, 'Just that I arranged my cousin's car. Still, he won't mind.' His resignation added to her guilt, as though she was kicking someone who was down, already feeling defeated and occupied.

At the doorway to the hostel, Kate stopped and held out her hand.

'We can do it another time Shafik. I'm sure.'

'*Ma'alesh.*' He smiled, gently shaking her hand. 'So be it, Kate. Good night.'

'Good night, Shafik. And thanks a lot for seeing me back.'

Kate breathed deeply as she climbed the stone stairs to the front door, her sandals slapping on the treads, and up in her room, quickly undressed and slipped into bed, but couldn't fall asleep. She saw Amos sitting opposite her in the cafe, his light brown eyes wide and looking straight at her, his unruly fair hair and broad, trusting face, and then that desperate fingers-clasp as the bus pulled away. But then she saw Miriam's anxious face as they sat in the shelters that day, remembered her birthday party, their room. No. It had to end before… before. Yes tomorrow, she would go back and let him know.

Exhausted by her soul-searching, Kate turned on her side. It took her a while to fall asleep.

7

The next day, after a cool Jerusalem morning, by midday it was hot. It was even hotter in the crowded bus, and no one would give up a seat to a young, healthy woman. Kate gripped the overhead rail, swung from side to side as the *Egged* driver took the bends down the mountain road *Le Mans* style. Buffeted by other passengers, she held her small rucksac tight between her feet; nothing was safe in such a packed bus.

At Kastina junction, the bus made its usual fifteen-minute stop. A new, tarmac-surfaced bus park had replaced the ruined mud houses of the abandoned Arab village. On the far side of the main road, the white modern blocks of Kfar Akhim, the new immigrant township, stood beyond the last remaining single-storey shells.

From this junction, one road followed the coast southwards to the border just beyond Ashkelon, and once, on to Gaza and Egypt. The other road, originally a British military track, branched off to wind inland across the dry loëss plain of the northern Negev, past Amos's kibbutz and on down to Beersheba.

The driver announced a fifteen-minute break for drinks at the bus-station cafe. Most of the passengers would carry on to Beersheba, but Kate watched for those with bundles getting off. Scrambling to the rear, she thumped down in a vacated seat; sweat-soaked hair clung to her cheeks.

While they waited, Kate's thoughts turned to her future – certainly no future for her in Belfast the way it was going. She had enjoyed her year in London, but didn't feel that was permanent either. In her more pessimistic moods, she felt an empathy with the Flying Dutchman, doomed to wander the world and search. To search for what? Purpose? Happiness? Love?

The driver jumped up the steps, started the engine and broke her train of thought. With a hoot and the hiss of doors closing, the bus swung out onto the roadway and sped south. Mentally exhausted by her soulsearching, Kate dozed and almost missed her stop, luckily alerted as the bus dipped through the dry, concrete watersplash of the *wadi*.

She jumped off and strode up the side road. Ahead, the kibbutz rose like some green island from the gently undulating landscape, baked grey and yellow by the relentless desert sun. Hot air rippled from the black tarmac, and the gateposts of the perimeter fence shimmered like a mirage.

She glanced at her watch. Three-thirty. Keeping a wary eye for snakes in the straggly grass, she took a shortcut through the young eucalyptus trees that hung grey and listless in the afternoon heat. She'd had to come back to sort it. Now, if she hurried, she might make the showers before the field-workers came in.

The volunteers were housed in the old huts where the kibbutzniks had first lived. Some, like hers, were red-tile-roofed, Swedish timber houses, quite spacious with a small ante-room. Kate shared with Jill, who apart from her irritating untidiness, was easy going and considerate. 'I know. I'm a slut,' she'd laughed, 'and proud of it,' her rebellion against her all-too-prim family in Solihull.

Jill was drying her hair in front of the hut with a large blue towel. She had been on dining-hall rota until midday, and had another two hours serving duty in the evening. 'Hello, wanderer,' she smiled as Kate came up. 'You're back early. How was the

Holy City this time – and how was your man?'

Kate just grabbed her wash-bag and change of clothes.

'Tell you in a bit. Want to get to the showers before the masses.' She grabbed her wash kit and towel, and hurried away.

Just as she reached the courtyard, a tractor pulled in with a trailer full of field workers. They quickly scrambled off and everyone made a bee-line for the showers. Kate quickened her step; she must get in before them -- then abruptly stopped dead and her heart thumped. Amos was on the blue Fordson -- here, just fifty yards from her.

She was about to raise her arm and call out, to let him know that she had come back. Then, remembering her decision, stopped and just stood there while the first workers, tired and sticky and sweating from picking grapes, reached the doorway to the showers. In a moment, they would all be inside and she would have to wait ages to get under the sprays. But still she hovered, her stomach clenched, hoping he would see that she had come back.

'Hi. Didn't think you were coming back 'till tomorrow,' said Harriet, a tall, psychology student from Boston. 'Boy, are you glad you missed the grape-picking.' She plucked at her black stained shirt and waved her sticky hands. 'Just look at me.'

Ellen, a pale, virginal blonde that no amount of sun seemed able to tan, pulled off her head-scarf and leaned closer.

'We're having a party tonight. Graham brought some wine back from Rishon. And,' she grinned conspiratorially, 'we've invited over a few of the soldiers from the patrols.'

Kate smiled back, feigned interest and waited for them to go in. She continued to stare across the courtyard. Amos was bent down. He had to look round. Now. He must! But, he pulled out the pin from the drawbar, then climbed back up into the seat, and without a second glance round, flicked up the throttle and sped away down to the garage in a cloud of blue diesel smoke. Kate bit her lip, then turned and went in.

The showers were now crowded and she barely found room along the benches to put her clothes. Women in assorted stages of undress waited their turn to get under the shower-heads. Others hurried back, hair wet and clinging, bodies dripping, all laughing and joking over the day's events. Amidst the smell of dampness and scented soap, a mixture of English and Hebrew echoed from the tiled walls.

Some were more open and moved freely, others, mainly the newer volunteers were still self-conscious about their nakedness in front of so many strange women. Kate remembered how quickly she herself had grown used to it. She sank onto the bench and slowly took off her shoes and socks, and waited for *kafkafim*, a pair of shower sandals: slabs of bare wood held on by strips of old inner tube. '*Kafkaf* is also what we call someone as thick as two short planks,' Amos had laughed.

Slowly, Kate undressed. No hurry. After the showers, she could spend her evening as she liked, with all the time in the world. Amos was married, kids to play with for the next three hours, then supper with his wife and after that responsibilities: arrangements for tomorrow's work or some committee meeting or other. Sure, they might live in the same village, but the rhythm of their lives was totally different.

Leaning forward, Kate rested her head in her hands.

'Here, daydreamer. Try these for size,' Harriet's voice cut in as she slid a pair of *kafkafim* across the wet tiles. Kate looked up.

'Oh. Thanks, Harriet.' She nodded and slipped them on. Then she picked herself up off the bench and clattered along to the showers.

Amos hadn't lingered in the courtyard. Miriam was on afternoon shift in the kindergarten and he wanted to home at least by the time the children came. He'd managed to extract the Fordson back from Joe every afternoon by agreeing to pick up the grape pickers, but it made him finish later than he would have liked.

As he had driven in through the gate, the Jerusalem bus had stopped out on the main road, but he hadn't bothered to look. Kate had said she would only come back tomorrow. And again he resolved to find a way to let her know that Jerusalem had been a pleasant time, and that was all; the most important thing was his family.

He backing the tractor into the corrugated steel shed, took out the key and tucked it under the seat. Pulling out the oil dipstick, he wiped it on the corner of his navy work shirt, and dipped it into the fuel tank to note the level. At that moment, Joe puttered into the garage on the red Ferguson. He had already showered and changed.

'Need to fill up fuel,' Amos called over. 'Almost dry, Joe.' He had filled the Ferguson and he wasn't going to do both. But if it ran dry, the garage wouldn't be pleased at all when they had to bleed it through again.

'Yes. My fault,' Joe smiled. 'But I don't want to get all messed up now. I'll do it in the morning. Thanks.'

Amos hurried up through the grove of young pine trees they'd planted at *Tu B'Shvat*, the New Year of the Trees, last January. Already they were waist high. Soon, it would be *Succot*, Tabernacles. Nearly a year gone. And a war.

Noa came hurtling round the corner with her friend, Inbal, when he hurried across the lawn towards his room,

'*Phooyah, Aba*', you're dirty, she called out. 'Go and shower! Inbal wants to play Chinese Chequers.' And he did as he was told.

Miriam came home shortly after.

'Had time to make a small apple pie whilst the kids were still resting,' she called through the fly netting on the porch door. Noa jumped up and opened it.

'A big bit. Like that,' she said, running her tiny finger across the crust. Miriam lightly tapped the back of her hand with the flat of the knife.

'Don't be greedy. Save some for Ran. He'll be home soon from volley-ball. And Inbal wants some too, don't you?' The girl continued to suck her thumb and nodded.

'And I suppose I don't count,' called Amos.

'Crumbs for Daddy,' Miriam chirped.

'Yes. Crumbs for daddy.' Noa jumped and clapped her hands, laughing, 'Only Crumbs for daddy.'

Amos scrambled up from the floor where they had been playing, grabbed his daughter and whirled her through the air, round and round -- as though to dissipate the tension that now built up within, from time to time.

At seven thirty, Miriam and Amos took the younger one back to her children's house one hand each, and swung her up and down all the way along the path. Noa ran in through the door, hurled herself at Nitza, and threw her arms around her neck, and they both left.

Half-way along the path back to their room, Aviva, the work organise caught up with them. Short and round, with long black hair coiled up on her head, like him Joe's wife spoke Hebrew with a strong Brooklyn twang.

'Hi, Amos,' she said. 'So how was Jerusalem?'

'Still there,' he said jokingly, as the city's name prompted a flash of memory; Kate's consoling touch on his arm as he'd looked towards the Lion's Gate.

'Listen, Amos, I've been looking for you,' she puffed as she walked alongside them. 'You last did guard duty two months ago.'

'So?'

'Well. Yochanan is down for next week. But his wife has just given birth. And you're next in line.'

'No way.' Amos shook his head. 'We start cotton picking in ten days. I can't.' In the short silence that followed, Miriam knew the argument would take time and tapped his elbow.

'See you back in the room,' she said. She wanted to spend some time with Ran before he went back. Amos wouldn't give in easily but Aviva wouldn't have asked him at this season, if she hadn't been desperate. He would have a job getting out of it.

Back at the room, Miriam stepped onto the porch and kicked off her sandals. Who would be a work organiser? A hundred and fifty holes to fill each day — and only a hundred and twenty pegs with which to fill them.

Aviva was indeed desperate.

'Look, Amos. I know about the cotton. But there's just no one else.'

As she paused and looked at her notepad, Amos thought about the cotton. He couldn't neglect that. True, most of the machines were ready. But there were the trailers to check out and rotas to confirm with the cotton gin, though perhaps he could do that when he got up in the afternoons.

He was about the protest again, when a thought struck him: Guard duty, the kibbutz asleep and a chance to speak to Kate! Let her know that Jerusalem had been a one-off and that was that. Yes, why hadn't he thought of that before?

'Look, Aviva, I might agree to half a week, but no more. And I must speak to Yossi first. I'll let you know at supper.'

'Three days. Start Friday night.'

'Tomorrow?'

'Yes. Friday night. Like always for guard duty.'

She turned and hurried away and Amos continued along the path to his room.

'Poor Aviva,' he said to Miriam as he came in. 'She was so desperate.'

'So why not do a few days?' said Miriam. 'It'll be a rest before your crazy season.'

'Maybe.' Amos waved his hand in the air. 'Luckily all the machines are ready.' He shrugged, 'but I'll only agree to three days.'

When they took Ran back to the schoolhouse, Amos glanced up at the sky. A thin crescent moon has just risen and myriad stars sparkled in the clear desert night. Yes it would be a chance to knock it on the head, before it started. Then his thoughts turned to the next day. He was going with Shmuel to a Ministry meeting in Tel Aviv about cotton quotas, and would take advantage to see Azriel, an old friend at the Agriculture Faculty in Rehovot to discuss a recent crop failure. He could also use the meeting to have a heart to heart chat.

The next morning in Tel Aviv, Amos arranged to meet Shmuel at the Ministry later then headed for the road beyond the vegetable stalls. When he crossed in front of the bus station, he glanced up at a shining new Leyland bus. The Jerusalem line always got the smart ones first, immediately reminding him of Kate.

The express bus stopped just once at Rishon before leaving the urban sprawl of outer Tel Aviv. On either side of the road, deep-green orange groves were criss-crossed by darker, tall cypress windbreaks. Ahead, beyond packing sheds along the railway lines and by the white buildings of the Weitzman Institute, was the Faculty where Azriel lectured.

Azriel had taken a bullet in the calf during the Sinai campaign, which had left him with a slight limp. When he came out of military hospital, he'd wanted to stay near the land and decided to study and qualify in plant genetics. 'Absolve my conscience in deserting the kibbutz,' he'd quipped. He was now head of department.

'So,' Amos smiled after they met and hugged, 'what are you wasting your time on now?'

Azriel ran his hand through his short, black hair, now showing a few grey ones.

'Something dead sexy! Show you later.'

They went into a tiled, lab annex and sat at a small table, swapping information on mutual friends and acquaintances -- the *sabra's* bush telegraph. Starting in the army and continuing through time and space, it covered the whole country, forever enriched by intermittent meetings such as this.

After a short while, as if exhausted from the conversation and reminiscences, they both sat in silence for a moment before Azriel sprang up and plugged in an electric kettle.

'The melons won't run away. Time for coffee.' He grinned. 'Only "instant" I'm afraid. Grab a seat.' And as he set the two cups on the table, he looked across to Amos.

'You seem a bit down, my friend. Still thinking about Ya'ir?'

Amos nodded. 'Uhuh. What a loss. And what for, Azriel? Still no peace. Nothing's changed. Except that now the religious nuts and Begin's extremists are calling the shots, wanting to hang on to the "Historic Territories". Which means there will be another round sooner or later. Bloody depressing.'

'True, too true. That's why I'm going to this Peace demo in Tel Aviv next week.' He grinned. 'Coming?'

'Not really.' Amos shrugged. 'Too much on my mind.'

The melons' crop failure?'

'Uhuh. But not just that, Azriel.' Although he had made his decision finish with Kate -- before it started, he still felt the need of friend's advice. 'Look,' he began again. 'Just between us -- and definitely not for Gila or anyone else -,' he looked straight across the table, 'I'm trying not to get involved with a woman. But it's proving tougher than I imagined.'

'*Elohim*! Serious?'

'No. Or — maybe yes. A bit.' He looked down at the table-top. 'Could justify it with Ya'ir going, the political stalemate, the battle to keep our kibbutz principles. But there it is.'

'So. Who with? One of the members?'

'No. No. From outside. One of the volunteers.'

Azriel leaned back.

'Oh, come on! With all these hippie American students here, I can tell you it would be all too easy.' He paused and half-smiled. 'Look, mate. We grew up in a puritan, pioneering society, but now the wide world is bursting in.' He shrugged. 'But you and Miriam? That was always rock solid.'

Amos sat back.

'Well it is, but . . ,' and he went on to tell about the Arab boy, about the day in Jerusalem. 'Just that I feel life slipping by, Azriel. And when I'm with her, Azriel, I feel so much more alive. Really alive, you know.'

Azriel looked straight into Amos's eyes.

'Look mate. Things like this have a way of getting out of

control. Just think of the pain, the chaos it would cause.' He didn't have to mention the kids.

'Sure. I know. I know.' Amos half smiled. 'Actually, I've already decided to end it. I'm just waiting for the right moment to tell her.'

'Good,' said Azriel. 'That's good. Miriam's a wonderful woman. Nip it in the bud, my friend, while still you can.'

Amos hadn't expected his usually easy-going friend to be so critical and couldn't help feeling a little resentful. What did Azriel know of Kate? Of his feelings for her? But then what had he expected?

After a short silence, Amos nodded, finished up his coffee and looked across the table. 'So, about my damn watermelons?'

That spring, a whole crop of early watermelons had gone bad; they had lost the lot, an expensive failure. And all the agronomists at the Ministry were as puzzled as he.

'Well,' Azriel began, 'from my studies here, I think it's almost certainly some interference during the fertilisation process -- unseasonal bad weather or something like that.'

'So it could happen again,' Amos muttered.

'Possible. But quite unusual.' Azriel sighed. 'Just bad luck, mate.'

For moment, both were silent. Then Azriel stood up, adjusted his glasses and grinned. 'Come. I've something to show you. Something real pornographic.'

Azriel led him through to the experimental greenhouses, the plots covered by thin mesh stretched on wires. Leaves and tendrils of cucumber and courgette sprawled across the red soil. At the back, were huge marrows and pumpkins.

'There it is.' Azriel waved his hand over the gauze-covered

frames. 'My thesis: Pollination and fertilisation in Cucurbita.' He laughed. In other words, 'The Sex life of the Cucumber!''

'Riveting,' Amos smiled. 'Lots of kicks, eh. Does Gila mind?'

'Dead jealous,' said Azriel. 'And you should come more often, Amos. Gila would love to see you.' Yes, she would, thought Amos, remembering that late night clinch when Azriel was in hospital, which was why he didn't. And he took the bus back to meet Shmuel and go to the Ministry meeting. And no wiser about Kate.

8

On the journey home Amos knew he had to see Kate soon, tell her that Jerusalem had been just a one off. But how to meet? The kibbutz had its own puritan morality. Sure, some of the bachelors went around with the volunteer girls; easy meat, Rami and Shumikeh joked in the garage. But not a married man. A *vatik*, an 'old timer' like himself would just never go across to their huts, or be seen chatting alone with a volunteer girl. Agreeing to do guard duty had opened up a possibility. Now he had to let Kate know. But how?

His head grew hot and his stomach churned as he puzzled. And suddenly, he had it. He'd borrow the Fordson and trailer from Joe and pick up the grape pickers. See her then.

The next morning, Amos turned onto the muddy track and switched off the Fergussson. Mist still clung to the sodden cotton plants and the early sun shone directly into his eyes. Gumboots squelching on the wet soil and prickly leaves brushing cold and wet against his bare knees, he eased his way between the rows of cotton with the workers' lunch box. During the night, Yossi had given the final irrigation before the picking.

'Here. Real coffee!' he called to Nurit and Ilana as they waited by the thorny acacia tree. He set down the box containing a thermos and three plastic cups. 'Snatched from under Aliza's nose.'

'No dinner for you from the kitchen, Amos,' Noorit laughed.

'So,' he poured the coffee, 'what's the count?'

'Here. See for yourself,' said Noorit, handing him her notebook. She clutched her hands around the warm cup. 'Not too good. A lot of *Heliotis*, especially in that patch near the *wadi*.'

Starting at dawn, throughout the growing season the girls walked slowly up and down the rows of cotton plants looking under leaves and on stalks. Searching for eggs or grubs of cotton pests and recording the degree of infestation plot by plot.

Amos ran his finger down the columns of figures, then looked along the rows of waist-high bushes. White puffs of cotton-wool were beginning to break out of the pods. If it wasn't the tiny *Prudenia* moth or the fat green *Heliotis* caterpillar nibbling the leaves, the *Boll Weevil* would be laying eggs in the buds, destroying the tightly-balled cotton fibres.

'God. This coffee is marvellous,' Ilana gasped, sipping the steaming coffee.

'Almost worth chasing the moths for,' smiled Noorit, black curls glistening with dew poking from her head scarf.

'Damn,' Amos snorted as Ilana's notebook had confirmed Noorit's count. 'Shabbat tomorrow. The spray plane won't come until Sunday!' He nodded to Noorit. 'Lucky I booked it for then at least. Must be the same everywhere. I'll telephone to confirm when we go for breakfast.'

He poured himself a mug of coffee and the three of them sat sipping the hot, black liquid, gazing over the dark green mattress of the cotton fields that ended abruptly as if guillotined, where the yellow-grey desert took over and stretched to the horizon.

When they'd finished, the girls hopped up on the drawbar then sat on the rear wheel wings. Amos balanced the box on the three-point linkage, swung into the seat and started the engine.

'Right,' he grunted, 'breakfast.'

The bushes were bone dry when he came back from breakfast and scratched at his legs even more as he walked between the rows in his shorts. Amos picked off a distorted brown pod and crushed it between his fingers and cursed again. With every pilot drafted into the air force for over a month, the cotton too had suffered from the war. And it was a losing game anyway. Each year having to use more and more powerful chemicals, an expensive poison-gas warfare that served only to generate ever more resistant strains of insects. It also made it more dangerous to the workers, yet he couldn't see an alternative.

At lunch time, Amos was parking the tractor behind the kitchen when Joe caught him.

'Hi. Amos. Hear you're on guard duty tonight.'

'Yes. Why?' asked Amos as he climbed down from the seat.

'Don't say I don't do you any favours,' Joe smiled.

'Meaning?'

'Well, I guessed you'd want to finish early this afternoon to rest before guard duty.' Joe beamed, his whole face lighting up, 'so I've arranged for the cowmen to take the Fordson and collect the grape-pickers with the trailer.' He spread his hands. 'How's that, comrade? Won't do it every time!'

Amos didn't react at first. He stood without moving, his head burning and his heart thumping. Bloody, well-meaning Joe. It was as though Fate's little devils were stepping in to mess up his plans to tell Kate.

'Didn't really need to, Joe,' he said blandly, desperately trying to conceal his annoyance while thinking at lightning speed. If he made it too obvious, Joe's Talmudic mind would soon suspect ulterior motives. 'Look,' Amos continued, his mind working in overdrive, 'I need it to set the stopcocks for tonight's irrigation in the alfalfa. The track will be deep in mud from today's watering.'

'Oh heck,' Joe shrugged. 'I've already promised the trailer to Eli in cowshed.' Amos tensed, then relaxed. Eli! He could soon sort things out with Eli.

'Not to worry,' he said. 'Thanks anyway, Joe.'

Amos was hungry, but he knew his stomach wouldn't let him eat until this had been resolved. Jumping back on the Fordson, he shot down to the cowsheds. Eli was throwing hay bales onto the trailer with the Fergusson idling alongside.

'Hey, cowman. Got a licence for that?' Amos called. 'You can't milk it, you know.' He was tense, but like with Nitza, Eli and he went back a long way.

'Listen, mate,' Eli flicked back his long hair. 'We treat it with loving care. Not like you bloody tearaways.'

'Look. I must have the Fordson and trailer at four. Have to take the stopcock wheels out to the fields.'

By the time the irrigation water reached their land, it had come through the two-metre diameter, pre-stressed concrete pipes all the way from the Sea of Galilee, the National Water Grid bringing the life-giving fluid to serve the arid south. The kibbutz was rationed to a yearly quota and every cubic metre cost money. So to avoid wastage, or water being drawn off by the local Bedouin or roadway contractors, the ten-inch stopcock wheels were kept in the garage and taken out when necessary. Now they would be his alibi.

Eli straightened up and wiped his forehead with an old cloth hat.

'Joe said we could have it till six if we agreed to bring in the grape pickers.' His brow furrowed. 'Got to take hay to both cowsheds before that. Yaacov's on night milking and there's only me and that volunteer, Jake.

'Look,' Amos continued, 'I'll pick up from the vineyard

workers on my way back. Just let me have the tractor and trailer at three for an hour.'

'Suits me.' Eli laughed and jammed his hat back on. 'Got enough to do without playing coach driver,' he added, surprised at Amos's tone, as he sharply engaged gear and shot away in a cloud of dust.

As he sped up the hill again, Amos felt his blood pressure returning to normal. But as he parked the tractor by the dining hall, by chance Miriam was coming out of the back door of the dining hall, having brought the food containers back to the children's kitchen.

'*Nu*. What time are you finishing, Amos?' She squinted in the bright sunlight. 'You should rest this afternoon.' They had to be saved from themselves these men, she often joked to Nitza; never stopping unless they were forced to — or their wives made them. Especially Amos, always something: another few rows to pick, another few pipes to move or another few sacks to bring in from the fields. She felt as if the constant 'doing' was their life-blood, distracting them from 'being'; of looking more into themselves.

Amos jumped off the tractor, wiping his hands on his shirt.

'I'm going home to change after lunch. Just a few stopcocks to open at four, but I'll be back for the kids.'

'Can't anyone else do that? You'll be dead beat by midnight.' Then she stopped. She had never been a nagging wife and she wasn't going to start now. 'Anyway,' Miriam continued, 'if you can just get the laundry from the store?'

'Sure. No problem,' he smiled. 'See you later.' Miriam went back to the *Gan* and Amos went into the dining hall, taking his guilt with him.

After lunch, Amos threw off his working clothes on their small veranda and went in to shower, glad that they now had electric immersion heaters. Gone were the days of small cans dripping paraffin into a burner so that you had to wait twenty minutes until the water heated up, while the chimney smoked as if the house was about to steam off across the desert.

By the time he had changed, it was two o'clock and Amos suddenly remembered the laundry. Sometimes he collected their clean clothes and sheets on Fridays, sometimes Miriam. And sometimes neither, and they would playfully argue who'd agreed. Today, conscience made sure he did, but his mind raced as he glanced at his watch to make sure he was on time to pick up the grape pickers.

'Leave the trailer by the dining hall,' shouted Eli as Amos backed the tractor, 'we'll bring it down at evening milking.' Amos waved, and head down, drove to the garage, threw two stopcock wheels onto the trailer and in top gear shot out of the rear gateway towards the fields.

As luck had it, one of the stopcocks was jammed; it took him ten minutes to ease it open. Amos cursed. 'Always turn it back half a turn', he'd told them again and again. Now, it would make him late for the workers -- and the kids. Opening the throttle, he sped along the dusty track to the vineyards, the stopcock wheels jumping and clanging on the flat-backed trailer.

The grape pickers all sat on the side of the track, tired, sticky and scruffy.

'Three cheers!' shouted Harriet as he drew up and braked.

'About time too,' Uzi yelled, as everyone started to clamber aboard. 'Trust the cotton *kulaks* to take their time.' Amos felt his face redden. Kate had risen from a pile of boxes. She walked slowly towards the tractor and looked straight at him. He neither saw nor heard anyone or anything else, until Jill's voice sounded in his ear.

'Any room up front?' she smiled, and eased herself up onto one of the seats welded on the top of the wings. 'Here, Kate,' she called and stretched out her hand. 'Travel first class for a change.'

Kate climbed up on the drawbar, sat opposite Jill and held on to the back of the driving seat. Amos looked round, waited for the stragglers to seat themselves then waved and slowly drew away. When he leaned back, he felt Kate's knuckles against his spine. Neither of them moved.

'God,' gasped Jill, as they drove onto the road. 'I never want to see another grape again. I must have eaten ten kilos today.'

'No wonder the vineyard is losing money,' laughed Amos, though he knew it sounded hollow.

The pickers sat around the edge of the trailer and dangled their legs while they chatted and joked, and after a hot, hard day's work, impatient to have a good soak under showers then relax on the lawns in the cool evening.

'No work today?' Kate asked casually and nodded to Amos's clean shirt.

'Finished early,' Amos replied equally casually. 'I start guard duty tonight. Just a few days.'

Kate tensed. A current ran through her body. She looked straight past Jill and didn't dare to meet her eye; the monkey listened to every word.

'Huh. Bit of a skive, if you ask me.' Jill grinned. 'What's there to guard against now the war's over?'

Amos slowed down to allow a truck to pass, then turned gently into the approach road.

'This isn't Birmingham,' he smiled. 'It's the Middle East, you know.'

'Bloody sight more thieves in Brum,' Jill laughed, glancing at

Kate. 'Anyway. I'll bet it's all those midnight fry-ups of eggs and chips you're after.'

'Sure. Why not?' Glancing right and left at the two of them, Amos smiled. 'Want some too?'

'Only if you bring it,' said Kate softly, her voice almost drowned by the roar of the tractor.

'Special order?'

'Special order,' she murmured, and this time looked Jill straight in the eye.

Amos braked gently by the dining hall and the workers jumped off the trailer to race for the showers. As he leaned back against the seat-rest, Kate slowly withdrew her hand, her knuckles scoring the small of his back. Then she too jumped down, and completely forgot her decision, as she headed for the showers.

Amos climbed back up, and his body tingled as he engaged gear. The drawbar dropped with a clang and he drove down to the garage, his stomach clenched and his mind in a whirl. He willed the intervening hours to fly past; his decision to cut out, and Azriel's advice all blown away as soon as he'd seen her.

The tingling in his chest persisted during the children's time. Noa hadn't been her usual sparky self; kept wanting him to read to her while curling up in his lap with her thumb in her mouth. Miriam thought she might be running a temperature.

'*Eilla Kari*, Aba,' she whined, '*Eilla Kari*, the girl from Lapland, Daddy.' The same story, again and again, until he knew almost every word, could number every damn reindeer horn in the pictures. But it served to keep his mind on an even keel.

It was Friday evening, the first night of guard duty. At eight o'clock, Amos collected the Uzi from Yoram in the armoury and filled two magazines with snub-nosed, 9mm bullets. One magazine, he snapped into the breech and carefully checked the safety catch, the other he slipped into a pouch on his belt. Knots of people hung around on the terrace and across the lawn, came the rattle of chairs and tables being moved; the dining hall was being prepared for the film-show after supper.

In the cloudless sky, a quarter moon hung over the water tower; stars glittered through the clear, desert air. Amos took out a packet of '*Degel*' cigarettes and lit one with a small plastic lighter. All around him was the stillness of the night, but his stomach quivered as he stared into the darkness.

'Why the frown?' It was Miriam, unexpectedly coming along the path on her way to see the film.

'Who, me? I'm fine,' he said quickly and shot her a smile.

'Well, don't forget to pop into Noa on your rounds. I gave her half an aspirin at supper time.' As if he needed to be told, but then she was like that. Sometimes it annoyed him, but this evening he was careful not to let it, and she hurried away to the dining hall.

Amos began his first round and called in the babies' house as was customary, to let the night nurse know who was on guard on duty, and to find out whether he should look in on any of the children's houses on his way.

Ruth warmed two feeding bottles in a saucepan of water. On the wall above her chair, the green eye of the new security fence alarm glowed on the grey cabinet, emitting a faint buzzing sound. It had been installed at great cost about six months before; if the fence wires were cut, the alarm would sound and give the location.

'Shalom Amos.' Ruth brushed back her hair and smiled. 'So you'll miss the film too, eh?'

'I don't mind.' Amos leaned against the marble worktop. 'It's French. '*Jules et Jim*.' I'd have to read the sub-titles.' From the dubbed English films, he knew that many of the subtleties were lost in the Hebrew translation.

'What time will you make coffee?' he asked.

'About eleven,' she murmured, and glanced at the notebook diary. 'Got to feed Orna's baby first and,' she nodded to a closed door to the babies' room, 'Ayalah is still in there, feeding.'

Along the paths, people hurried towards the dining hall and by the time he reached Noa's house, the kibbutz was silent, just a faint sound of music to show that the film had started. Inside him, the tension continued to mount as he walked past and down the track to make his rounds of the cowsheds, the garage and poultry houses. Less than three hours to midnight.

After that round, he came up again and when he passed the dining hall, the catchy tune of '*Jules et Jim*' caught his ear, rising at the end, as though asking a question. He found himself humming it all the way down to the babies' house and gasped for a cup of hot coffee. After that, it was one more round behind the children's houses. Then it would be time to eat. And to see Kate, tell her it had to finish. Had to.

9

As soon as they came back from seeing the film, Kate plugged in the small kettle. Jill took out two cups and their precious, small tin of real Nescafé.

'You look pale, Kate,' she smiled. 'Looks like you need it strong.' Jill half turned her head as she spooned coffee into the cups. 'Think he'll really bring you chips?'

'Bring *us*,' corrected Kate. She slumped back against the wall, head bent. 'Who knows?'

'Hey?' Jill came over and looked down. 'Why so miserable?'

Kate sat on her bed silent while the kettle sang and her loose hair tumbled onto her shoulders.

'God. Wish I hadn't seen that film. Really depressed me. Triangle relationships. No future. Sudden death…'

'Hey. Not so bloody morbid.' Jill stood back. 'It's only a bloody film, Kate. Anyway, only the French carry on like that!'

Kate looked up and shook out her hair.

'I know it's only a damn film. But the horrific end unsettled me. Conscience. Oh, God. You know what I'm on about, Jill. Can't hide anything from you. Don't want to, really.'

Outside, on the patch of lawn behind the huts, some of the other volunteers were talking loudly. But they could have been a million miles away.

'You know Jill,' Kate muttered, 'if I'd any sense, I'd have stayed in Jerusalem, so I would.'

'With Shafik?'

'*No*. He's just a friend. Helps me make sense of the politics out here. No. I mean. Well. Married, man. Kids.' She half smiled. 'Belfast isn't swinging London, y'know. Perhaps I'm still a bit of a provincial hick compared to you lot. I've never been into that kind of thing.'

Jill eased herself down, and they sat together on Kate's bed and held the warm cups between their hands.

'Well, don't jump the gun, Kate? I thought you would tell him it's over, anyway?'

'Up here, sure.' Kate tapped her forehead. 'But here, Jill,' she clutched at her breast, 'every time I see him — and even more when I don't see him. Oh. I don't know.' She turned to look into Jill's face. 'Crazy, isn't it?'

Jill sipped her coffee and was silent for a moment.

'Listen. I don't usually give advice, Kate. But I'm quite fond of you and would hate to see you getting into a pickle.' She paused and laid a hand on Kate's knee. 'Look, this isn't in town somewhere; it's a small, closed community. If it gets public -- as it would, whatever happened with him and his marriage, you would be a pariah. So if he does bring chips, tell him it's been nice, but it's over. You must do that, Kate. You can see that, can't you?'

Kate nodded just as a shriek from one of the girls outside came through the open window, followed by laughter. Probably a king-spider, thought Jill, the gruesome but harmless crawlies that blundered across the ground at night, long white feelers groping out in front of them. The laughter faded as the group dispersed to one of the huts further along. Then everything grew quiet again and they sat in silence, sipping their coffee.

Kate glanced at her watch. It was five minutes to twelve.

'Think he'll come?' said Jill.

'Don't know,' said Kate, staring at her small, framed print of Van Gogh's chair on the wall opposite.

'Well.' Jill stood up and put her cup on the table, 'I'm not playing gooseberry, that's for sure.'

'No. Please. Jill. Wait!' Kate half rose, her eyes wide.

'You'll cope, said Jill. 'I'm going to join the crew in Jeff's room. See if they've still got any wine left.'

Without waiting for Kate's reaction, Jill went out and closing the door behind her, strode along the veranda.

Kate closed her eyes and gripped the cup tightly with both hands. Lines and stars flashed across a purple background. Maybe she over reacted, anticipated too much. Either way, she had made her decision. If he came, she would let him know. It had to finish -- before it started.

Just after midnight, Amos left the kitchen carrying a covered plate of chips. He glanced up at the sky, clear with a crescent moon. Noa had been breathing normally when he had looked in at the toddlers' house. He would drop in again on his next round.

Fronds brushed his face as he made his way through the grove of Casuarina trees. Music came from one of the volunteers' huts. Amos stopped in the shadows and hesitated, his forehead tight while and his heart thumped in his chest. The rest of the kibbutz would be in bed but on Kate's veranda the light was still on. He waited, wary. The volunteers kept late nights and if he was seen, any of them might pass a remark that could be picked up by an eager ear in the dining-hall tomorrow.

At that moment, Kate's door opened. Jill came out to the veranda then walked along towards the next hut. Suddenly she stopped, stepped back and switched off the outside light, then carried on. Amos held his breath, looked right and left, listened, then gripped the plates, stepped out from the edge of the trees and strode quickly across to the huts.

A footstep sounded on the veranda. Kate tensed. A moment later, there was a light tap on the door.

'Room service?' Amos's voice, imitated that of the waiter at his hotel in Nairobi. Kate jumped up and opened the door.

'I – I didn't think you'd take us seriously, Amos. I -- You didn't have to, you know.'

'I know.' He grinned holding out the covered plate. 'Here. They'll get cold.'

Kate backed into the small ante-room. Amos followed, and not wanting to be silhouetted by the room light, quickly closed the door.

'I brought enough for Jill, too. Will she be back?'

'No. I… Not for a little while.' Her heart was pounding against her ribs. 'Went to see if there was any wine left.'

The two of them stood a few feet apart, Kate searching for words while Amos leaning awkwardly to one side. He held out the plates, fingered the strap of the Uzi and wondered whether Jill was about to come back.

'They'll get cold,' Amos repeated. 'Sit down and eat, Kate. I've had my fill.'

'Sure. Thanks.' Kate backed into the larger room and sat on her bed. 'You can sit too, sure.'

Amos settled on the wooden chair by the table, his mind spinning. He was here, with Kate, alone. He felt so good just being with her; her lips pouted as she nibbled at the chips.

'Okay?'

'Great,' said Kate. 'Haven't had chips for ages.' She grinned. 'Perhaps I ought to volunteer for guard duty?'

'Any time,' and adding quickly, 'want to give it a try?'

'Now?' she asked, head cocked to one side.

Amos caught his breath, then winked and shrugged.

'Sure. Why not?'

The brief exchange had sparked a fire that spread out from her stomach, through her chest and up to her forehead -- and burned away any good intentions.

Kate set down the plate and stood up.

'Okay,' she said. 'Fine,' and her hands shook as she snatched her jacket from the hook on the wall, and turned to the door.

'Wait,' Amos called softly. He stepped into the small room and switched off the light before he opened the door. 'Avoids the evil eye,' he hissed. 'All of them!' And his whole body tingled and blotted out his good intentions too.

Without a word, he led the way round the back of the huts and down to the rough ground at the rear of the children's houses. Every few yards he waited for Kate to come alongside.

The night was still, hardly a breath of wind. The moon had sunk towards the west and its fading yellow light vaguely illuminated the fields beyond the perimeter fence that merged into total darkness beyond. Bats flitted and jinked through the fence-lights. Somewhere unseen, a little-owl screeched.

Kate pulled her jacket tightly around her. Goose pimples on her arm told her the night was much cooler than she'd thought. Inside though, she was warm, all her senses heightened and sharpened in the darkness and the silence. And suddenly she realised that despite having been on the kibbutz for several months, this was the first time she had been out alone, or almost alone in the small hours. Now, with the stillness of the desert night around her, she looked up into the huge bowl of the sky that stretched over her then down to the dark horizon, so full of stars, more than she'd ever seen in England.

They walked on into a small grove of young eucalyptus trees, Kate still determined to tell him that this must be their last meeting. At that moment, she tripped on an unseen branch She flung out her hands to break the fall, but Amos swung round and caught her.

'*Le'at, Le'at,*' he murmured. 'Gently, Kate, gently.' And slowly, his arms slid around her and pulled her to him. Her face nestled into his shirt, his lips warm on her hair.

'Okay?' he whispered.

'Mmm.' Kate slowly rocked her head on his chest. Amos ran a finger down her back.

'Didn't hear you.'

She raised her head and looked up into the darkened face.

'We shouldn't be doing this,' she said, not moving.

'I know,' Amos whispered, kissing her forehead.

Kate raised her face, her lips meeting his. 'Later,' she murmured. 'Later.' And they kissed again and again, the tension and pent-up passion at last flowed freely between them while they swayed back and forth, and all their resolutions melted into the night air, before they sank slowly to the ground under the motionless, black silhouettes of the drooping branches.

Amos raised himself on one elbow and carefully laid the Uzi to side on a drift of dry leaves, the muzzle pointing away. Kate's face was pale in the last, low light of the moon and her hair had spread out over the sleeve of his jacket. Gently, he leaned down and kissed her, and his tongue reached inside to engage hers, his hand on her breast. And they lay like that, and kissed and held each other close, the warmth of their bodies keeping at bay the cool night air.

'Millions of infiltrators could be coming through the fence,' Kate whispered. She half-raised herself to looked into his face, and her teeth glinted in the faint light.

'Let them,' whispered Amos, and laid his head back on the dry grass. 'As long as they don't steal you, Kate.' He sounded confident, but at the back of his mind still niggled that the meeting had been to cut out, to finish before it got too deep. Why was he so weak?

'How long can we stay here?' asked Kate. 'I mean -- The other guard?'

'My problem.' He kissed the tip of her nose. 'Don't worry. Kassim is doing the cowshed rounds until three. And anyway, we're guarding the rear of the children's houses, aren't we?'

After a while, Kate sat up. She brushed back his hair, silver fringed in the moonlight.

'We have to talk, Amos.' He half raised his head.

'I know.' He reached under her shirt and slid his hand between her breasts. Kate drew in a sharp breath, clutched her hand over his and pressed it against her chest.

'So?'

'You. Miriam. Family. Oh, you know what I mean, Amos.'

'Like the guard duty,' he said softly. 'My problem. I'll manage it.' He stared past her at the setting moon. 'And you, Kate?'

'Oh God,' she breathed. 'Need you ask, Amos?'

Kate turned and kissed him and they lay back again, while Amos stroked her stomach, his hands running over her skin stretched tight between her hip bones, so smooth against his work-roughened fingers.

Kate sighed and buried her face in his neck. She felt his hand slip inside the waistband of her jeans then between her thighs, and moved her hips gently with the rhythm of his arm. Waves of warmth washed over her whole body and out to the tips of her fingers.

Afterwards, they lay back, their breathing the only sound in the silent night.

'When do you have to go?' she whispered, and pressed her lips against his neck, all her good intentions melting away into the night.

'Soon. Or the night-duty nurse will wonder where I am. We always drop in for a chat and coffee after midnight, to kill time.' He gave a short, quiet laugh, 'even in tense times, after midnight it was always more relaxed. Infiltrators need a few hours to get back over the border before dawn.'

'When can you manage again, I mean?' whispered Kate.

'Well, I've got to make another round, then pick up the early call list, Kate.' He thought for a moment. 'Say in an hour and a half?' Amos stood up, held out his hand and helped her up. He brushed himself down, then picked up the Uzi and slung it onto his shoulder. Kate rested her hands on his chest.

'No. I didn't mean tonight, Amos -- or rather this morning.' She reached up and kissed his lips. 'I want to go to bed now and stretch out between the sheets.' Her teeth caught the last moonlight. 'Just to lay back with this marvellous feeling inside me. And think of you.' She looked straight into his eyes, 'do you mind?'

Amos stood for a moment, silent. Then he kissed her.

'Of course not. I'll miss you, but I feel good that you're happy Kate, and that it was so good for both of us.'

'Until tomorrow night, then.'

'Chips at midnight?' Amos grinned.

'No. No need,' she whispered, 'I'll meet you here, in this spot. I'll find it.'

'Sure?'

'Sure.'

The moon had set and left a faint afterglow. They walked slowly back towards the huts and in the shadows of the trees, they held together for one long, last kiss. Then Kate turned and hurried in.

Amos stood and waited until the door closed behind her, then slowly walked away along the path. In the light of the street lamps he peered at his watch. Nearly two o'clock. How quickly the time had gone. And how marvellous his whole body felt — as though renewed, every limb tingling and his brain buzzing and alive; not for ages had he felt anything like this.

But when he walked on, that feeling in his stomach faded all too quickly. After all, this was the night he'd intended finishing it -– before it started. And how would he face Miriam? Surely she would sense something the moment he walked in the door. And the sense of dread stayed with him all the way to the dining hall.

Taking the early call list from notice board, Amos hurried down to the babies' house. He'd intended to look in on Noa again after his meal, but with his mind on Kate, had completely forgotten.

Was this what passion led to? Neglect of what really mattered?

But she had slept well at ten o'clock, he consoled himself. He'd look in on his next round.

Ruth raised her eyebrows as he bowled in.

'Shalom, stranger. You must have had a busy night.' She obviously meant guard duty, but Amos wondered whether his face had reddened. 'Anyway, I've had coffee,' she said, 'and I've got to warm up these bottles. Fraid you'll have to make it yourself.'

'*Ein ba'ayot,*' no problem, Amos responded quickly. 'Got chatting with Kassim before he went down to the cowsheds.' Which was true, though only for a few minutes. 'His son is getting married next month,' he continued, reinforcing his alibi. 'Wants to invite a load of us up to the wedding.' God. Would he always have to fabricate excuses? And would he always have one?

Kassim was a Druze, from a village in Galilee. Their religious sect having suffered persecution under the Ottoman Turks, the Druze had allied themselves with the early Jewish settlers. So when the State of Israel was created, they received full citizenship and unlike the Arabs were not subject to military administration. They also served the army and now filled many of the Border Police units, as well as making up night-guard numbers as the border kibbutzim grew shorter of manpower.

For some years now, Kassim, tall and lean, with his sergeant major moustache took turns with his son Nazim, living in a small hut behind the volunteers' area. Amos was looking forward to the wedding; the Druze certainly knew how to celebrate.

Ruth disappeared into one of the small rooms and a thought sparked in his brain. Perhaps Kate could come with him. Then dismissed the idea immediately; it was insane. And with that came the realisation that from now on he would be would be constantly thinking like this: planning and scheming so that they could find time alone together. Even if they got away with it — which seemed unlikely, who would he become in the process?

10

In the babies' house, Amos laid the Uzi on the tiled floor and clicked out the magazine; second nature -- removing the magazine when indoors. After boiling himself up some ground coffee, he looked around. The only seat was a low, mothering chair and he creaked down and sat back, looking at the early-call list, trying to work out the best sequence of running between the rooms to wake each one on time. He cursed. Almost indecipherable handwriting covered the dog-eared strip of paper.

The early-call list always started as a new sheet of paper pinned the lobby notice board. As people came up to eat, those on early shifts wrote down their name and call times one after the other, so from the start there was no chronological order. To complicate matters, as the evening progressed the page was constantly being reduced by people wanting a strip of paper to leave a note or make a brief memo, so later additions were squeezed in anywhere there was a space. The end result was a jumble of names, times and room locations — and this night it was no different.

'Borrow your *globus* for a second, Ruth?' he asked. Ruth passed him the ballpoint pen then noting the state of the list, she smiled and tore half a sheet from her night notebook for him. Thanking her, Amos began to re-write the rota chronologically, smiling as he noted some odd rooms next to two of the bachelor's names. He was glad to have something fiddly to do. Helped distract him from the emotional meeting.

When he had finished, sipping his coffee Amos looked up.

'Want me to pop in anywhere special on my way round?'

Ruth nodded. 'Oh, yes. Please. There's mumps in the toddlers. Someone might want a drink.' She glanced up at the flickering red eye of the call system, which listened in to all the children's houses. 'Though it's been quiet so far.'

'Mumps!' Amos grinned. 'Have to look to my fertility.'

Like most children's ailments, it was more serious in adults and could even cause sterility in men. Ruth nodded and half-smiled.

'You'll manage.'

He glanced away, was the guilt making him paranoid?

Ten minutes later, tucking the early call list in his top pocket, Amos went out.

The toddlers were all appeared to be sleeping peacefully when he quietly opened the door to the kindergarten. But as he paced gingerly along the corridor, a thin voice called out.

'Water. I want water.' A second later, the sleepy figure of Irit tottered out into the hallway. Amos went to the sink, half filled a plastic cup and gave it to her. After two sips the girl gave him the cup, turned, and trotted back to bed. Two seconds later, she was fast asleep.

Closing the door gently behind him, Amos walked across the lawn to Noa's house. His daughter was sleeping soundly, thumb to her lips, her fair glinting in the orange glow of the night light. His stomach twisted. The kids. What would they think of him if . . ? He recalled that time Giora left Yocheved; his eight-year-old daughter screaming at him on the path one evening after he had moved out. And with that, as he hurried between the houses, waking all those on early call, the all embracing, warm feeling with which Kate had left him, fading. And as dawn broke, in the cold grey light feeling even more confused.

Miriam grunted as he slipped into bed, then half asleep, turned and slid up against him, her body warm and soft and comforting. In half an hour she would be getting up for work, leaving him to sleep off the morning. He lay absolutely still, as though fast asleep. A few moments later, he was.

Miriam switched off the alarm almost as soon as it sounded. Amos didn't even twitch. She slid out of bed and looked down, his curly hair faintly outlined in the dim light through the slatted shutters. He must be dead-beat, doing guard straight after a day's work. Closing the door quietly, she took her working clothes from the cupboard on the veranda and went into the toilet to get dressed.

The sun rose as she hurried along the path to the kindergarten. Through the faint mist that hung over the perimeter fence, the lights still glowed. She must get Rafi to re-set the time clock. If people cared more about not wasting money, they might have a bit more left for the education budget.

The early breeze that stirred the cypress windbreaks of the orange groves, strengthened through the hot afternoon. Out in the plain, dust-devils rose like miniature tornadoes, whirling and dancing through the parched fields and across the desert. Those on guard duty usually slept until lunchtime, but Shabbat mornings from nine to midday were sacrosanct children's time. So Amos only managed a few hours sleep. Miriam had taken Noa to the sand-pit to let him sleep as late as possible, but the girl had soon wanted Daddy and had dragged her to the room at half-ten, where she insisted on Amos taking her to the children's swimming pool.

Amos dozed on the poolside lawn, his body weary and his mind full of the previous night. In the sun's warmth, his early morning misgivings evaporated and with eyes closed, Kate's upturned face in the faint moonlight filled his mind. And guilt or not, he felt good.

Miriam was working that Shabbat so Amos went up alone to the dining room for lunch, hoping to catch sight of Kate. More than just hoping. Compelled. He had to see her, even if only to exchange glances, to convince him that it really had happened and that she hadn't had second thoughts or regrets. And that she would be there again that night. He couldn't dispel the misgivings that shot through his mind from time to time, but they soon became submerged in the memory of their lovemaking.

Along the path, Eli caught up with him heading for the babies' house. His wife Bilha was nursing the new addition to his family.

'*Nu?*' he grinned. 'How's guard duty, fighter?'

'A great rest,' smiled Amos. 'You should try it some time.' Since they regularly worked nights, the dairymen were excused guard-duty rota.

'Listen,' said Eli. 'I'm on late shift tonight. Might join you for midnight chips on the way home.' Amos caught his breath, but concealed any reaction. Normally, he would have been only too pleased to have company to help pass the time. But tonight was different.

'Sure,' he said casually, 'see you down in the dairy.' His neck grew hot; every little action now seemed beset with obstacles -- with deception.

Amos joined Eli and Bilha at their table, taking pains to sit facing the entrance. Their sons were in the same class and they often sat together.

'Coming to cheer on the kids, this afternoon?' asked Eli. Their school was playing neighbouring kibbutz, Beit Kama in the junior volleyball league.

'Think I'm too beat from guard duty. You know, Shabbat morning, Kids.' The server came round with the trolley and placed a large bowl of soup on the table. Eli was already noshing dry croutons. Ayala tapped his hand with her spoon.

'You want some soup with the croutons, maybe?'

Eli sat back as she ladled the soup for Amos too.

At that moment, Kate came in with Jill and another girl. She paused at the doors and glanced around. For one brief instant their eyes met, before she continued on and found a table where she could sit and see him. Conscious of Eli and Bilha, Amos continued the conversation, glancing over the rim of his spoon towards Kate each time he raised it. And each time, Kate, catching the glance, closed her eyes for a moment in recognition.

When they'd finished eating, Amos rose and went out with Eli and Bilha. But knowing she was so close was compelled to hang around and meet he, even for an instant -- to be sure that she would be there that night and to alert her that he might be late. He strolled across the lobby as if to scan the work rota.

'Want to see who's checking the cotton,' he called. Eli nodded and he and Ayala went out.

Seeing Amos get up, Kate couldn't wait to finish eating. It was midday. Half the kibbutz would be coming in but she felt sure he would be waiting somewhere. Like him, she could think of nothing else other than trying to make some kind of contact. God, how difficult it was even to exchange a few words without arousing suspicion.

When she'd come back to the room last night, Jill was fast asleep. Kate had quickly slipped into bed then lay on her back, re-living those wonderful moments. Now, having the *shabbat* off, she'd slept almost until noon and would have slept on had Jill not woken her.

'Here, sleeping beauty,' Kate turned over and shielded her eyes from the brilliant sunlight streaming through the doorway, 'you look as though you could do with some coffee.'

Kate swung her feet onto the cool, tiled floor and brushed the hair away from her face.

'What time is it?'

'Long past a virtuous woman's breakfast time,' grinned Jill. 'And don't think I've made this especially for you. I'm having one anyway.'

Kate yawned and came to sit on the veranda.

'Haven't cleaned my teeth yet,' she murmured, sipping the thick, black, kibbutz issue coffee.

'Sins of the flesh,' said Jill.

Kate glanced at her watch. 'Holy God. It is that late?'

They sat and drank quietly, Jill bursting to know, but not wishing to pry, Kate thinking she would like to share it but wondering how much of it she would. In the weeks since their first visit to Jerusalem, they'd grown quite close and Kate liked Jill's openness and directness: 'You Ulster lot are so bloody uptight,' Jill once said. 'Don't you ever relax?'

'Excuse me. It's Northern Ireland,' Kate had replied. 'Ulster's bigger.'

In an adjacent hut, the radio was on loud, tuned to the B.B.C. news, from Forces' Radio in Cyprus. The two women strained to listen.

'*In Kharthoum, leaders of Egypt, Jordan and Syria have decided that there will no peace and no negotiation with Israel until...*' In the nearby eucalyptus tree, a black-headed Bulbul chattered as it picked at the flowers.

'Huh,' muttered Jill, 'nothing changes.' After a short pause, she looked into Kate's face and smiled. 'So. How was it for you?'

'Good,' said Kate, looking down into the cup. 'Tell you later.'

Back in her hut, Kate sat on the bed. So many things to do. Wash some underwear -- the kibbutz washing machine shredded anything delicate. Wipe over the floor -- the loess dust got everywhere. Answer her mother's last letter; they seemed to arrive with such frequency. And wash her hair; she wanted to look good for Amos. Then she leaned back against the wall, her eyes half closed; he wouldn't notice anyway, it would be dark. Would they only ever meet after dark?

Just then, Jill's shadow fell through the doorway.

'Say. What's up, Lovesick?'

Kate creaked up and came to sit on the veranda. Jill, sensing her mood, sat down facing her and in the scorching afternoon heat, settled herself in the shade.

'No. It's just that -' Kate began, 'just that everything is so claustrophobic. It's going to be impossible to meet alone, Jill. If I'd thought about it more, I'd never have let it start.'

'Could you have stopped yourself?' Jill half smiled as she rose and plugged in the kettle; this conversation needed strong coffee.

'Probably not.' Kate shrugged. 'Oh God. Why do I get myself into these things, Jill?' She paused and looked down. 'Not the first time y'know.'

'Married men, Kate?' Jill rose and plugged in the kettle, 'a bloody minefield!'

'No. Not that. I mean. Well. Unusual, complex, situations. Holy God. Why don't I find an uncomplicated, unattached man.' She slapped her hand on her knee. 'Even Shafik, platonic more or less, even that's not simple, sure.'

The kettle boiled. Jill started to rise but Kate sprang up and went to the cupboard to get the jar.

'No. Let me make it.' Kate wrenched the plug from the socket, took two mugs and slammed the doors closed.

'Careful how you spoon the coffee,' Jill smirked. 'You'll make holes in the cups.'

Kate poured the water, handed one mug to Jill then took her own and leaned back against the warm, timber wall.

'No. I'm not dramatising, Jill. This isn't the first time.' She paused, 'the reason why I left Belfast.' Slowly, Kate took a sip of coffee then leaned forward.

She set the mug on the tiled floor and went into the room. From her dark blue writing case on the table, she pulled a folded letter and brought it out into the sunlight.

'From Marina.' She held it up. 'Came last week. Wrote that "by the way", Robert got engaged. Didn't say to whom. And after all this time, it didn't much matter really.'

Jill stared out across the sun-baked waste ground. Sure, she knew about the troubles in Northern Ireland, the religious divide, the senseless antagonisms. But it was something quite different to see Kate's personal anguish.

'So,' said Jill, trying to lighten the atmosphere, 'couldn't you find a nice simple English boy at the L.S.E?'

Kate smiled and nodded.

'Well. There was. Nothing serious though. Nothing I wanted to last. But now. Out here. Maybe I have. And it's churning up my inside. Taking me over.'

'Well. My psychology lecturer would have said something about avoidance,' said Jill, 'not that he avoided me, the lecherous bastard.' She looked at Kate. 'So. What now?'

'Don't know, Jill. Just don't know. But when I see him. When we're together, like last night…' She clutched at her stomach,

'God. It's there, you know.' Kate's voice faded almost to a whisper. 'All there, so it is.'

'Look, mate. A quick fling, maybe, but it seems you're getting into something more. Listen. I don't want to be a killjoy, Kate, but he's a leading member of the kibbutz; wife and kids. Just think of the repercussions if it gets out!'

Although Jill had previously made negative comments, her outright disapproval at things becoming more serious took Kate by surprise. Perhaps she ought to think more of what might happen, just savour last night as a lovely memory, and go back to her original decision to cut out before it got deeper.

At that moment, Anthony and Roger, two Aussie volunteers, came along the veranda. When they spotted the two women deep in conversation, they stopped.

'Here you two. Why so bloody miserable?' said Roger, 'the sun's shining, mate.'

'It always bloody well is here,' retorted Jill. The spell was broken.

'Listen. We're going over to see the Beduin,' said Anthony. 'They invited us. Yesterday. Wanna come?'

Kate shook her head at first, then after a few seconds jumped up.

'Sure. Why not,' she smiled. 'Might meet Sheik Valentino.' Anything, she was thinking, anything to take my mind off the heart-searchings and help to pass the time until the night.

'Right,' said Jill, always game for something new. 'I'll grab our hats.'

11

Back in his room after lunch, Amos lay on the bed; Miriam was working this *shabbat*. With the shutters closed and the room almost dark, he wanted to drop off to sleep but couldn't, images whirling in his mind; the drooping eucalyptus leaves silhouetted black against the setting moon, Kate's hair brushing his face.

He began to wonder why he was investing so much in it. Was it all just sex, as Azriel said? No. That didn't explain it. And Suddenly, the scene in St Stephen's street came into his mind; staring towards the Lion Gate and thinking of Ya'ir, of all that his friend wanted to achieve and hadn't; that life could be so short. And with Kate, he had never felt so alive.

Sure, he was treading a dangerous path; like poking his head above the parapet when bullets were flying. But he'd survived all that, and if he took care, he could manage this too.

Amos gave up trying to sleep, lit a cigarette and lay back, staring at the ceiling. At that moment, came the sound of feet running along the path, children's shouts echoing across the lawn; the kids were going down to the volley-ball court. Ran!

Amos swung himself up, pulled on his shorts and hurried out to follow them.

At supper, Kate looked out for Amos in the dining hall, but the volunteers usually ate early to avoid the rush before the parents came up from the children's houses. With no plausible excuse to hang around, she wandered back to the hut and managed to sit herself down at her table to write home.

The blue air-letter was half filled with unconnected sentences, the gaps marking each time she had managed to tear her thoughts away from midnight. Now, as she chewed the top of her pen, she became aware of the stillness of the desert evening that had replaced the stiff breeze of the afternoon. From the dairy a cow lowed, crickets chirped from the gaps in the block-wall foundations to the hut; '*tzartzar*', they were called in Hebrew; how onomatopoeic that word was.

Now and then, the stillness was shattered by an indignant shout. Jill was playing scrabble with the Aussies and someone was obviously trying it on with a quasi-authentic word. The boys had asked her in for scrabble too, but she wanted to let Jill go on her own. Although Jill didn't seem to mind sharing her confidences and taking some of the strain, Kate had begun to sense her strong disapproval, and feared that if things became too heavy, it would dent their friendship.

Kate stared at the blue paper, stuck again; her mind began to wander. It had been so good to get out for the afternoon, the time had sped past. Space. Just what she'd needed. And suddenly, she knew what to write; she'd tell about the Beduin; that would take up the rest of the aerogramme for sure.

Kate took the pen from between her teeth. Yes. Poor bastards, Roger said, stuck out there and not allowed to roam around as they used to. She thought again of Shafik, his bitterness at the Israeli occupation and his pride in being a Palestinian. Yet his life was even more removed from those Beduin than the Israelis in the kibbutz. God. Everything out here was so damn complicated. And she must ask Amos why the kibbutz didn't help to unblock their well -- if the two of them ever managed to be alone long enough.

Through the window, the last purple light faded and the sky

darkened. Three hours to go. Somehow, the time had to fly. She glanced at the letter, and bending her head began to write.

After supper, Kate went back to the hut. Unable to settle, she went across to the next hut to watch the scrabble. Roger had made kibbutz 'mud' coffee and it all helped pass the hours. She also noticed that Roger and Jill were playing at more than scrabble. Jill caught her eye and smiled.

'Don't think you can be the only one,' she muttered as they went back to their hut.

'Our room or his?' said Kate.

'I'll let you have ours.' Jill winked. 'I'm generous like that.'

On his way down to the cowsheds, Amos strolled past the dining hall. It was half-full for the regular Saturday night general meeting. Uri, the farm manager was standing by a blackboard, outlining next year's investment plans.

Miriam was there too, as well as many of the women. Investments also meant buildings and equipment for the children's houses and the kitchens as well. 'If we left all the decisions to you men,' she would say, 'there'd only ever be tractors and cows!'

Down below, Amos walked slowly around the perimeter track some twenty yards inside the security fence, out of the glare of the lights. On the moist, night air came the sweet smell of silage. He stared into the darkness. Beyond the fence lights, the quarter moon cast gentle shadows into the folds of the ground. The longer he stared, the more the black, stunted thorn bushes seemed to quiver and move, each dark shape taking the form of an infiltrator crouching in the darkness ready to fire, or making off towards Hebron. Although he was used to that, he often looked twice to be reassured that it was only a bush.

In the dairy, Eli had finished the milking and was washing down the milking parlour as the last cows sashayed down the ramp back to the cowshed. It was nearly half-past eleven.

'Can you close the far gates for me?' he called, as Amos poked his head through the doorway. Amos strolled across the dusty courtyard and clanged the gates shut, then went back to the milking parlour. Eli would be coming up with him for a midnight supper in the kitchens.

Kate waited in the eucalyptus grove; her watch showed twenty past twelve. The leaves hung absolutely still, outlined black against the setting quarter-moon like a Chinese paper-cut. She sat on a folded blanket, wondering whether Amos would agree to come to the hut. If he wouldn't, at least it would keep the sand out of her hair -- and everywhere else. She glanced at her watch again trying to see the tiny hands on the delicate going-away present her aunt had bought her in Oxford Street. So little time together and even that was being nibbled away.

Perhaps something had happened. In the dairy? Or a children's house? Perhaps he was having second thoughts? Oh please God, no. But how long would she wait? Until one? Half past? And once again doubts rose and clouded her mind; was it worth all the agony? She should have cut out last time as she'd intended. At that moment, a twig snapped; and the doubts vanished.

'Sorry I'm late,' Amos hissed as he loomed over her. 'Eli came up to eat. Then Ruth sent me…' Kate stood up and flung her arms around his neck and they kissed long and close, his hands slipping under her shirt and sliding up her back, squeezing every ounce of air from her lungs.

'Jill has moved out for the night,' she gasped when he finally released her. 'We can use my room.'

Amos pulled back, tense. 'That would be marvellous,' he said, 'But…'

'I know. But the verandah is dark and everyone will be asleep. It's a work day tomorrow.'

Amos kissed the crown of her head. Her hair smelled of sandalwood. To be somewhere comfortable together, instead of out here like a couple of school-kids. His groin grew hotter though his brain was urging caution. But Kate's hands were warm on his chest; her warm lips soft on his neck.

'Come,' he murmured. 'Let's go.'

Amos waited by the edge of the trees whilst Kate went onto the veranda and opened the door. Everything was still and dark and silent. Gingerly, as though scouting a minefield, Amos crept over the rough ground and slipped silently through the doorway.

'So that's what they teach you in the army,' whispered Kate as she closed the door.

'Amongst other things,' Amos murmured.

Carefully he lowered his Uzi to the floor, automatically clicking out the magazine onto the tiles and they clung together for several minutes, their breathing becoming more regular. Slowly, Kate disengaged and, holding his hand, led him into the back room and they quickly undressed.

The bed creaked as they sat down, seeming so loud in the silence, and creaked again as Amos rolled over to lay full stretch on Kate, and feeling their bodies against one another, relaxed. Cocooned in their own world and cloaked by the silence and darkness of the desert night, slowly they made love.

Within the hut it grew hotter, the sun's stored warmth radiating from the timber walls and adding to the heat of their lovemaking, soaking their bodies with sweat. Amos rolled over and lay on his back, his chest heaving and sounds of his breathing filling the small room.

'Amos.' Kate leaned up on one elbow. 'I feel so alive, so good, more than I've ever felt, ever.'

Amos cradled her head in one arm and stroked her thigh as it lay across his stomach.

'Me too, Kate.' He kissed her. 'When we're like this…'

Kate raised her head and put a finger on his lips, then rolled over and straddled his hips. She felt him harden and raised herself, then pressed down, a searing heat entering with him and spreading through every organ in her body, and out to the tips of her fingers and toes.

Afterwards, she lay easily along his broad body, her head on his shoulder, rose and fell with his breathing. It was so wonderful just lying there in the darkness, the closeness, his heart throbbing against her breast. His fingers slowly rippled up and down her spine.

'I just feel so great, Amos,' she murmured. 'More than I've ever been.' She raised her head to look down at him. 'You too?'

She wanted to say more. To know more about him, things that only such intimacy would allow; get to know the real Amos under that brash exterior.

Amos reached up and kissed her then lay back, silent for a moment, as though sensing the moment of complete intimacy in the silent night. Then he began to speak, softly, slowly.

'It was Ya'ir, going like that, Kate,' he began. '*Shalom, shalom, ve'ein shalom . . ,*' he would say. *Peace, peace, and yet no peace.* And now he is at peace -- forever. And I suppose I still haven't got over that.' He reached up and kissed her again. 'It made me realise that life is short – too damn short, and that we only live once.' He paused and took a deep breath. 'And you know Kate, I fear I never shall get over his going like that…'

Kate wrapped her arms about him and held him to her like a small child; her world shrunk to just the two of them.

A door slammed in another hut and Amos jerked apart. He stretched out his arm and peered at his watch. Half past two? Couldn't be? The luminous hand seemed to have spun round the dial. Luckily he had popped in to see Ruth again beforehand. He didn't want to move.

Kate opened her eyes and saw the green glow of his watch-face.

'Stand still you ever moving spheres…' she murmured. 'I'm like old Faustus, wishing time would stop.'

Her whole body willed him to remain there, but her head told her he had to go. Slowly, she sat up, turned over and leaned back against the wall. Amos slid his feet onto the tiled floor and dressed mechanically, he couldn't think of anything else. If he did, he would have thrown them off again and jumped back on the bed. But he had to go. For both their sakes, he had to leave.

'Till, tomorrow,' he whispered.

'Here?'

'No. Better meet in the trees, as before. Might be someone mooching around.'

'Uhuh.'

They kissed, long and hard then with his body glowing and head still fuzzy, Amos reached down and picked up his Uzi. Slowly opening the door, he peered out and listened. Nothing. He crept out to the veranda and turned. Kate stood in the doorway, her pale, naked body faintly outlined in the soft glow of the starlight. He leaned forward and kissed her, then turned away, the vision indelibly imprinted on his brain. He would remember her like that, always.

In the shadow of the trees, Amos waited for a few seconds to accustom his eyes to the darkness and listened. Not a sound nor movement anywhere. He hitched up the Uzi and strode across the rough ground to the path, then hurried along to the dining hall to pick up the early- call list.

Ruth looked at him quizzically as he came in to the babies' house. Or was he imagining things?

'Hi, stranger. I'm already on my third coffee.' She took a plastic cup from the shelf.

'Good timing,' Amos grinned as took the cup and poured from the *kumkum*. 'Made another round behind the children's houses,' he excused.

He slipped the Uzi from his shoulder and instinctively he pressed the magazine-release catch. It was slack. He tensed and looked down; the breech was empty. Where the hell was the magazine? He tried not to betray his panic; felt in his trouser pockets, then his jacket.

'Here,' said Ruth, throwing him a pen, 'you guards never have one on you.'

'Thanks.' Amos forced a grin and sat down then spread out the crumpled list on his knee. 'We're an illiterate lot.' But as he started to write out the early-call names in sequence, his hand trembled and his forehead burned. The magazine couldn't drop out; it was failsafe. Perhaps he left it on the dining hall table after the midnight snack? But Eli would have noticed. Then where? How?

While he appeared to sort out the list, Amos desperately tried to recall where he had left it, thankful that one of the babies whinged, sending Ruth into the side room. Suddenly, a cold sweat broke out all down his back. The hut! He must have left it in the hut! Instinctively, he had slipped it out when he laid the gun on the floor of Kate's room. Yes. He must have left it there. '*Khamor gerem*, Amos,' he cursed under his breath. 'You stupid idiot!'

For an instant, he thought of going back to pick it up. But the early workers were beginning to stir; he might easily be seen, and anyway, he had to wake the morning shift for the dairy in five minutes. His head ached. What an idiot! Then he tried to calm down; surely Kate would find it and get it back to him somehow. But what if someone else did? He visualised Roger walking into a packed dining hall, and holding it up to ask whose it was! Oh God. It would be the end. Somehow, he had to see her during the day. But how? When?

Amos managed to conceal his panic from Ruth until he went out. But once alone, out in the cool night, he began to tremble, the terror churning his stomach as he ran between the rooms waking those on early call, and it grew ever stronger as the first fingers of a grey dawn reached out from the east.

Back in his room, when he lay in bed, Azriel's caution echoed in his head again and again: 'Is it is worth it, Amos. Think what could happen, mate. Is it worth it . . ?' It took him a long time to fall asleep.

Jill returned about an hour after Amos left. Kate didn't even hear her come in. As she quietly closed the door, she trod on something hard in the ante-room. It was unlike Kate to leave her shoes all over the place. Gently, she tapped it to one side.

The following morning as they dressed for work, Jill nudged Kate.

'And next time don't leave your shoes all over the bloody place. Nearly went arse-over-tit when I came in last night!'

'I didn't,' Kate protested. 'Where?'

'There. I kicked it under the table.'

Kate looked then snatched her hands to her mouth.

'Oh, God. From Amos's gun!'

She bent down and grabbed the black metal case, the tiny copper snub nose sticking out from its brass cartridge-case at one end. She held it tight. It was a piece of him. Of Amos. But did he know? And how to tell him?'

'That's a bit of a fuck-up, Kate, isn't it? You'll have to be a bloody sight more careful, mate,' Jill muttered. 'And him!'

Kate couldn't say anything. She opened the wardrobe and tucked it under a sweater.

'C'mon mate,' said Jill, 'we'll miss the bloody tractor.'

When he woke, Amos could think of nothing else apart from that missing magazine. All through the day he went about as though on automatic pilot, his stomach turned and his brain overheated. He ought to think about firming up the cotton-picking schedules, but the image of the magazine intruded and he struggled to hide his agitation even during the kids' time.

That evening before he started guard duty, when he and Miriam went into the dining hall lobby for supper, Amos caught his breath. Half-hidden by Aviva who was arguing with Joe and Motti, Kate stared intently at the notice board. She had hung around in front of the volunteers' work rota board and hoped that Amos might come up early.

'Just a minute,' Amos said to Miriam. 'See you inside. Want to check who's down for work in the sugar beet.' Miriam nodded and continued across the lobby towards the dining hall doors.

Amos came up beside Kate and ran his finger down the work list as though to look for someone's name.

'It's okay,' she murmured, 'I've got it.'

His whole body relaxed. He was safe! He wanted to laugh out loud, but just whispered.

'Thank God. Thank God.' Suddenly he felt light headed and barely audibly, added, 'see you later.'

Just before he moved away, Nitza came out of the dining room, having brought the children's food containers back to the kitchen, and bumped into Miriam.

'Noa get to sleep okay?' asked Miriam.

'Yes. Fine. Seems to have got over her temperature pretty quickly,' she said, smiling.

Miriam had her back to the notice board, but Nitza was facing into the lobby. By chance she noticed the auburn hair glinting in the fluorescent light. What caught her attention though, was how close it was to Amos's shoulder — almost touching. A woman would usually move away slightly, leave space. Unless. Unless… At that moment Amos turned and came over to join them.

'Nu. How was my beautiful daughter?'

'Beautiful as ever,' said Nitza, her eyes narrow. 'Like her father,' then carried on out to the path, but her mind buzzed.

Ever since their teen-age fling, she could read Amos like a book. And he had been really odd ever since coming back from the war. Since Yair. As if constantly preoccupied, remote even. Reminded her of that time Azriel had been badly wounded. God! Azriel and Gila. Gila! Yes. That was what it reminded her of -- of that time!

They were a great couple, Miriam and Amos, contributed so much to the kibbutz. It would be an earthquake if… But was she jumping to conclusions, making something out of one fleeting impression? Yet she was an attractive girl, Kate. No fool either. And they had been to Jerusalem recently the two of them. It stirred a tinge of jealousy from their teenage past. And when she carried on down to the children's house, it stayed with her.

12

It was Sunday, last night of guard duty. The moon had swollen to a full quarter and hung in the cloudless September sky. After that scare, throughout afternoon and evening Amos had realised that next time he might not be so lucky. Yes, it had to end. But he had to tell her face to face. Tonight.

At midnight Amos had no appetite and gave up on frying chips, merely ate cold chicken and munched a hunk of brown bread and margarine. God, it would be painful. But had to be.

He went to see Ruth. On the first night he had explained his not dropping in more by saying he had dozed off. The second night she hadn't mentioned it. But she would certainly think it strange for a third night. He had to keep up appearances. A quick cup of coffee and a short chat, and all the time his pulse raced, knowing that Kate would be waiting.

In their room earlier, Jill had been in a foul mood all evening. Roger had joked about a large bra she'd left in his room. Now all the volunteers knew.

'Bloody uncouth Aussies,' she snapped. 'Should have known.' And with the abrupt end of that brief relationship, Kate hadn't the heart to ask her to move out for the night. So it was the eucalyptus grove again.

Kate waited, a folded blanket under her arm and yet again doubts floated through Kate's mind. Yes, it had been fantastic, but it was getting too heavy and was bound to blow up if they continued. She had to cut out. Sure, it would be painful, for both of them. But it had to be.

Just then, the dry leaves rustled. She turned and he was there, and as they embraced all her good intentions -- and his, melted into the dark summer night. They sank down together on the blanket and lay still, folded into one another, and yet again both their resolves folded too.

'My last night, Kate. But we must meet soon somehow, somewhere.'

A momentary breeze ruffled the leaves overhead before they settled to hang motionless again. In the distance, a jackal wailed. Desperately, they talked of places in which to meet. Walks where they could be alone.

'What about Jerusalem?' asked Kate. 'You go there anyway.'

'Possible,' Amos murmured, 'but not often. Most of the agricultural agencies and government departments are, in Tel Aviv.' His brain raced and he stared into the darkness. 'Look, Kate. I'm not much good at this,' he said after a while. 'It's okay for those idle bastards in the Hollywood films; time and money and a list of hotels.' He flicked her nose. 'You shouldn't have got involved with a penniless *kibbutznik*.'

She clutched his hand then kissed it.

'Ah, sure. And I was only in it for the money!'

They dragged out the final minutes, suggested dates and places, but the illuminated hands on his watch showed it was time to go. With a last, long kiss, they rose and walked back towards the huts together.

Kate stepped onto her veranda. She turned and blew a kiss, then went in and closed the door behind her. Amos stood in the shadows and body still glowed. It was as though a part of his very being had gone in with her. Tomorrow, it would be back to normal, checking the cotton, sort out the picking schedules and all the other hundred and one things he had to arrange. And for the next four weeks, a twenty-four-hour-a-day job.

Amos began to walk away and wondered how he would manage to concentrate on that vital work. He knew that his mind would be in a whirl, desperately trying to arrange the next time they could be together. At the same time he questioned whether it could continue for any length of time until someone saw them together, or before Miriam caught on. Women sensed things so quickly.

He turned towards the path to go back towards the babies' house and fingered the magazine in the breech, reassured, but as he did, he heard someone running. Instinctively he slipped the gun from his shoulder and drew back the bolt. Someone was running towards the fence. He opened his mouth and shouted '*Atzor!*' The figure stopped, turned and walked back towards him.

'Hey. Didn't you see him?' he called. It was Rami. 'Bloody Beduin,' he snapped as he came up. 'Probably be on the scrounge.'

Together, they hurried to the fence and sure enough a few strands of wire had been parted enough for someone to slip through, but the figure had disappeared.

'Lucky we were here,' said Amos.

'Uhuh. But it's way off your patrol route isn't it,' said Rami, as they walked back to the path.

'Sure,' said Amos, thinking quickly. 'Like you. Thought I saw someone slipping away from behind the children's houses.' It was a lame excuse, but the best he could think of. And what if really it had been an infiltrator while he was with Kate?

His head burned from the impotence of his situation; guilty over what he should be doing on guard and hadn't. But as they each went their own way, more worrying was that Amos was sure he had been seen coming from the direction of the volunteers' huts. And it had to be that loudmouth Rami. Wouldn't take him long to tell Motti, and for them to put two and two together and broadcast it.

Amos hurried towards the dining hall to pick up the early call list, then went to Ruth in the babies' house, all the time his mind full of nothing else. And it remained with him until he dragged his weary body back to his room.

A dim, grey light filtered through the shutters when Amos slid into bed. Miriam turned and nestled against him. He lay on his back and put one arm around her shoulder. And when she got up for work, although his eyes were closed and he didn't move, Miriam sensed that he was still awake. She had felt the tension in his body as he lay beside her. So many years together, she could tell his every mood. He must be getting worried about the cotton picking. Leaning over the bed, she lightly kissed his neck then went out to get her working clothes.

At lunchtime, hoping that Amos would come up early for lunch, Kate hung around in the lobby of the dining hall, barely managing to jump on the trailer as Joe opened the throttle and moved off. For Joe, half-an-hour was thirty minutes and no longer.

'Bloody hell,' said Jill. 'You're cutting it fine, Kate. You nearly had to walk it!'

The afternoon sun bore down from a clear blue sky. Any day now and clouds could herald the *Yoreh*, the first rains, though being at the edge of the desert, when they did come it would probably only be a brief shower. But even that, thought Kate as she dragged the box of grapes along to the next vine, would be a relief for the intense dry heat. There was no romance in grape picking. Like most agricultural work, it was repetitive and boring and only congenial company made it bearable. She and Jill often tried to work together and chat about anything, to make the time pas more quickly.

Today was no different. The dry edges of the vine leaves scratched at her arms and legs; grape juice trickled and congealed on her hands and arms. And all the time she couldn't stop herself thinking of Amos and last night, of his body pressed against her and the wonderful feeling afterwards as she lay in bed before she fell asleep. Now there was the only pain of his not being here and even worse, of not knowing how and when they would be together again; thoughts of having to end, it lost in the night.

'Come on dreamy.' Jill's voice cut into her thoughts. 'We finished that vine last year.' Kate looked round and saw that she had been crouching in the same spot, whilst the others had progressed down the row. At that moment, Roger came along in his broad-brimmed Acubra hat, high boots and khaki shorts, taking the full boxes to the to the packing area.

'Look Jill,' he began, as he crouched by her gripping a loaded box, 'sorry about --'

'Get lost,' she snapped. 'Come back when you've grown up mate.'

He winced then straightened up, lifted the box onto his shoulder and marched away down the row.

'Bit hard on him,' said Kate.

'Sometimes you got to draw clear lines, Kate. Be an adult.' Kate knew that Jill was referring to her too…

Amos rose after midday. He went up to the dining hall for lunch and hoped to see Kate, but the wish to know if he had been spotted now nagged most at the back of his brain. The last thing he needed was for someone to gossip and it get back to Miriam.

Although he wanted so much to be with Kate, Miriam, the family, the kids were still the most important to him. He should have cut out after last night as he intended, yet still he was thinking of a way to be with her again, especially when he spotted Kate in the lobby that evening. Unable to acknowledge her, only intensified the frustration.

Kate looked at the work schedule with Jill and saw that she was working only half-day in the vineyard. In the afternoon, for two hours she would be cleaning in the kindergarten -- Miriam's kindergarten!

'And you can wipe that smirk off your face, so you can,' she said to Jill as they made their way back to the hut.

'Me. Didn't say anything,' said Jill. 'Must be losing your sense of humour, Kate. Watch out for that!'

'Uhuh. It will be strange, sure,' Kate murmured. But within, she felt it would be more than strange. Awkward even. And wondered how she would manage.

Miriam was cajoling the children to change into pyjamas for their afternoon nap when Kate came down the steps into the kindergarten.

'Ornit! Not those pyjamas,' she called across the hall. 'The short sleeved ones from your shelf. You know!' The girl trotted to the wardrobe and Miriam turned to greet her.

'Shalom Kate.' She smiled, and added, 'there's always one who gets it wrong, no matter how many times.'

'*Shalom*,' said Kate, glancing around the room to avoid looking straight at Miriam and trying to stay calm. 'Where shall I start?'

Walking across to the sink, Miriam nodded to the pile of

dishes.

'If you could start on these, Kate. Meanwhile, I'll get them into bed so you can clean up the dining room.'

Every children's house had similar afternoon help. The *metapelet*, the children's nurse, had to work in the evenings when the children came back, so she was usually replaced in the afternoons. It was always a welcome change from sweating in the sun. Kate, like some of the other volunteers, quite liked this half-day shift in the cool and calm. It also gave her a chance to try out her few words of Hebrew: '*bevakasha*': please; '*todah*': thank you; and '*Mah ata rotzeh?* What do you want?' If she made a mistake or the pronunciation wasn't up to scratch, the kids giggled, but Kate didn't mind. Now, close together with Miriam in her kindergarden, was something she'd never contemplated.

Kate began to wash up the dinner things. From time to time she glanced at Miriam as she bustled about in the hall, and in and out of the rooms from time to time. She glanced at the trim, neat figure, the black hair tied back with a shoelace, full breasts tight in the check shirt and full hips, not plump yet but perhaps on the way, like with most of the kibbutz women, from eating too much starch. Above all, there were the sharp, dark brown eyes and firm nose. Character.

With her hands in the soapy water, Kate absently stared down at the plates and dishes. The soap-suds climbed up her arms, soaking the cuffs of her sleeves rolled up to the elbows.

'Okay, Kate?'

Kate jumped. Miriam was standing just a few feet away. 'Oh, Yes. Sure.'

'Just that you looked a bit, sort of, worried,' Miriam continued. 'If -' she hesitated, 'if you ever want to chat, just pop over to the room one day.' She smiled. 'Okay?'

'Oh, thanks.' Kate smiled back. 'Just weary from the grapes,' she lied.

'Anyway. I'm off now.' Miriam came up to her. 'No real problems with the kids, Kate. Just Nadav. He's in that last room. Has to stay in bed until the nurse comes at four. Mumps probably.' Kate nodded and half-smiled. Miriam stepped away and walked towards the doorway, then turned and looked back. 'Sure you'll be okay?'

She paused on the threshold, recalling how, at first, many kibbutz members had tried to make the volunteers so welcome, inviting them to their rooms and forming friendships, hoping also that some would stay. But as they all moved on, back to home countries or continue on the hippy trail to Nepal, it became too draining to offer close friendship again and again.

Now, most of the volunteers were just left to get on with it, living almost as a separate community within the kibbutz. A few however, obviously looked for something other than what they had back home, and with these, friendships still flourished in the hope they would join. And to Miriam, Kate seemed one of these.

'Listen Kate. Why not come round for coffee later?'

Kate jumped and her face flushed.

'Oh. Yes, sure.'

'About five?'

'Fine. Yes. Thanks.'

'*Tov.*' Miriam nodded. 'See you then.'

'Miriam had suggested this yesterday, as she and Amos had coffee. 'What do you think? Will you be home in time tomorrow?'

Amos swallowed a gulp of coffee, his stomach churning as Noa slid off his lap.

'Depends on the cotton,' he said. 'Try to.'

He'd tried to sound nonchalant, but it only made Miriam puzzled. Being indifferent to the prospect of an attractive girl coming for coffee just wasn't Amos. And she wondered about that...

The next day, Amos was out in the cotton field as the red Farmall tractor hauled the loaded trailer up the slope and onto the road, then backed to the other trailer. Yossi slipped in the pin, hitching the two together then snatched off his hat and ruffled his black curly hair. Amos watched, hands on hips, hat pulled down to his eyebrows against the glaring sun.

'That's it!' Yossi called to Amnon. 'Away you go.'

The tractor pulled away, taking the two trailers to the cotton gin; they would be just in time before it closed for *Shabbat*.

'Not bad eh? War or no war,' Amos said as he looked at the bulging load of snow-white cotton inside the wire mesh cages. 'Reckon nearly 400 kilograms to the *dunam*. At least.'

Yossi climbed back down the bank and pulled a wet-sack-covered churn from the shade of bush. That lunch-time, they'd taken the churn from the cooler tank in the dairy. Now, in mid-afternoon, it was lukewarm but still refreshing amidst all the heat, and dust and Yossi drank two full mugs. Dipping a ladle into it again, he called over to Amos.

'Here, worryguts. Have a drink and relax. It's going well.' Yossi couldn't help but notice how pre-occupied Amos had been over the last week, and supposed it was about the cotton schedules. Sure, each cotton harvest was a strain, always trying to beat the first rains, but he'd never seen him so tense.

Amos walked across and took the mug of diluted orange-juice and the two men sat on an upturned box. They watched the huge, red cotton-combine as it crawled the last few yards of its final run. And Amos's mind wandered to tea-time -- and to Kate.

Whenever there was a pause, or a lull in the furious activity of the cotton-field, his mind drifted and thought about her, and made it ever harder to concentrate, as the day wore on.

Since finishing guard duty, he and Kate had caught only passing glimpses of each other at lunch or outside the dining hall, but no more. So many eyes and ears that would immediately latch on to any longer exchange, as though an invisible purdah separated her from him. And now, Miriam had asked her round for coffee!

Amos tried to think how it would be after those three nights, so near to each other but together with Miriam and the kids; to seem at ease, while inside he would be keyed up, and she probably too. Yossi threw the churn into the back of the jeep, the two of them climbed in and set off for the kibbutz.

and down the rows after rain. Like Mum's red hair-drier. Only bigger.'

Amos ruffled his hair.

'Good idea. Can you work on that for us, son?'

The wind continued to strengthen, buffeting and hissing across the desert, heralding the deepening depression that had swept through the straits of Gibraltar a few days before. Picking up moisture along the Mediterranean, it brought relief and hope for a spring harvest to the coasts of north Africa and Sicily. Now, as the eye struck the coast of Israel and Lebanon and swept inland, it was bringing with it the *Yoreh*, the blessed 'first rains' of the Bible. Like everyone else, Amos wanted the blessing, only he desperately wanted it to hold off for a few more days.

Yusuf was sitting in his usual chair by the brass-tray table as Kate walked in; there was no point standing outside hoping to entice tourists, in this rain.

'Ah. Miss Kate.' He rose and clutched both her hands. 'Come in. Dry yourself.' A small charcoal brazier glowed by the wall. Kate took off her cagoule, leaned over the glowing charcoal and fluffed out her hair, the warm air drifting past her face and neck. Yusuf hurried out to order hot *shai*.

'So. Tell me how you are,' he asked when he returned, his whole face beaming at the welcome break in his dreary day.

'Fine,' said Kate, coming over to sit by the table, thankful of the hot tea, the glass warming her hands. 'This is the first time I have been here in the rain.' She laughed, 'I always think this is a hot, dry country.'

Yusuf smiled, showing his yellowed teeth.

13

In their hut after work, Kate was dithering over what to wear; how to look. Whether to tie her hair back, or leave it loose — a loose woman? She tied it back. She half thought of wearing the blue dress she had bought in Jerusalem.

'But that might be too dressy. Make Miriam wonder,' she said to Jill. 'But I can't go over like a tramp'

'For God's sake, Kate. Just go fuckin' naked,' stormed Jill, after Kate had turned over her small wardrobe for the third time. So she settled for a light green blouse and jeans. They were getting tight. She would have to watch her appetite or she'd end up like the kibbutz women.

Kate sat down on her bed.

'I really don't want to go?' she moaned. 'But I can't refuse either. If only it hadn't come so sudden.'

Jill was at their small table, trying to write a letter. She looked round.

'Well you could develop a bad flu, break a leg -- or something like that.'

Kate thought for a moment.

'You know, Jill, the problem is that I want to see him so much. And it will be a chance to be close to him, even if… Otherwise we'll never meet at all!'

'So go and enjoy it,' muttered Jill.

'Yes, but I'll also feel such a bitch. His wife. The kids. Happy family. And me, trying to play the sweet innocent little volunteer. Holy God, Jill. Why do I get into these jams?'

'Sex!' muttered Jill. 'Gets you like that.'

'No. It's not just that, Jill. It isn't so!' Kate snapped and went back to sit on the bed.

'I know. I know, Kate.' Jill sighed. 'Just me trying to lighten up again.' She put down her pen. 'I'm not very good at this sort of thing. That's why I gave up Social Work. Low empathy register!'

For a few moments, the two women looked at each other, silent. Then Jill got up and went to sit by Kate, and their hips touched.

'Look mate. This kind of situation sorts out the women from the girls.' She laid a hand on Kate's knee. 'You've got to face up to it Kate. Either you tough it out and be prepared for what might, or might not happen. Or, or like I told you last week, give it up and get out of here fast.'

'I know,' murmured Kate, staring at the floor tiles. 'I know that's what I ought to do, Jill. That's just it. I can't. I just can't!' Jill sat for a while, hand on Kate's back, silent, then shrugged, got up and went back to her letter the table.

Kate finished dressing and went out.

After his shower, Amos's brain still whirled as he sat on the bed with Ran while they sorting out Arabic numerals the boy had been learning in school trying to concentrate while wondering whether Kate would actually come. Being close to her again even in this awkward situation, being better than not meeting at all.

'It's the dot for the ten and nought for the five that mixes me up,' Ran complained. 'And the two is like the six, just the other way round.

'So is our six and nine,' said Amos.

'Anyway. Why do we have to know,' the boy muttered. 'They should write figures like we do. It's our country!'

'The Arabs invented the nought, Ran. And also working things out in tens. Why should they change, eh?' He paused for a moment then looked into his son's face. 'And it's their country too, you know.'

Amos sighed. All his son had ever known was that the Arabs were the enemy. His dad and the other dads going off to fight. Never having known Arabs personally, all the younger generation was the same.

'Never mind what people like Motti say, Ran,' he would say, again and again. 'Always remember. The Arabs are people. With families and kids. Just like you and me. And one day, we shall all have to live together in this land.' It was an uphill struggle. But just now, more he was more anxious that Kate might not come, and suddenly he felt uneasy -- spouting about universal values to his son, while at the same being so devious with Miriam.

Miriam was helping Noa embroider cross-stitch on a handkerchief, the child's tiny fingers struggling with the needle. She'd baked a small fruit-cake on the little stove in the kindergarten. It lay on aluminium foil on the veranda table; she had just managed to prevent Amos and Ran finishing off all the *challah* when Kate knocked on the open door.

'*Shalom*, everyone,' Kate smiled awkwardly as she stood on the veranda. 'Thanks for inviting me over.' Amos tensed and glanced up. For a split second, their eyes met as Kate turned to look at Miriam, who had stood up.

'*Shalom*. Come in Kate.' Kate entered and sat in the plastic webbing easy chair. 'So,' asked Miriam, 'how did it go?'

'Just the usual problems,' said Kate, 'trying to keep the boys neat and tidy until it was time to run home.' She had noticed that equal education or not, the girls sat and played amongst themselves, or combed and re-tied their pony tails, while the boys charged around, or clambered up the climbing frames, and threatened to look like a load of urchins. Somehow, she had just about managed.

'Yes, The kids were fine,' she said, as she sat on the bed.

'Show Kate your embroidery,' Miriam called through the doorway as she made coffee. Noa hesitated for a moment, then came over to Kate and lifted up the handkerchief.

'*Yaffeh. Yaffeh me'od,*' smiled Kate, practising some of the words she had learned from the kids. Deftly, she helped the girl complete a line of cross-stitch in blue. Noa held up a spool of red silk and Kate threaded the needle. Proudly, the girl took everything into her own tiny hands, went over to sit on the corner, her nose almost touching the cloth as she started to sew again.

Miriam served the coffee then offered round the cake. Ran reached out.

'Wait,' snapped Miriam, smiling. 'Guests first.' Remembering the tight jeans, Kate took a small piece and nibbled it with her coffee. Ran took the largest slice, then excused himself and ran out to play with the kids on the lawn.

'So. Working in the children's house is better than Joe's grapes,' joked Amos, trying to sound as normal as possible.

'You can say that again,' Kate grinned. 'But why do they call him "the *Yecker*"?'

Miriam laughed. 'Where did you hear that?'

'Oh. From Yossi when he came to pick us up one day.'

Amos took another piece of cake and spoke as he munched. Miriam wanted to tell him not to talk with his mouth full, but they had a guest. Through his cake crumbs, Amos explained how the

German Jews arriving from Nazi Germany in the Thirties, were noted for their puritanical work ethic and drive.

'And because they had nearly all been professionals, whatever work they fell into here, they still wore their tailored jackets. So Jackets — no J in Hebrew, became '*Yeckets*', so you have *Yecker*s.' He grinned. 'True. Joe's a New Yorker, but he works like a *yecker*.'

From then on, Kate helped Noa with her embroidery, the conversation flowed easily and she even managed to relax. To play at pretence was less of a problem than she had feared. Amos too seemed to be relaxed, so if it meant at least being able to be near him, then from time to time this was how it would have to be.

Just before the children were due to go back, Miriam looked across the room at Kate.

'Tell me, Kate.' She held up her hand. 'How would you like to work more permanently in the Gan?' Without waiting for a reaction, she continued, 'we are short of reliable girls to work with the children and you seem to manage so well.'

Kate was dumbstruck. The volunteers were used mainly as 'canon-fodder', as Roger put it. Some had more permanent jobs in places like the cowshed or orchards. But to be trusted with the kibbutz children? That was unusual -- an honour in a way, and in Miriam's kindergarten of all places.

'Look,' said Miriam, noting the hesitation. 'I know it's a responsibility, Kate. Think it over. Take your time and let me know.' Apart from wanting a responsible worker in the Gan, Miriam had her own reasons for wanting to keep Kate close.

Kate's stomach clenched. To keep-up a pretence for tea-time was one thing; to work together nearly every day would be quite different. A steel band seemed to tighten around her head, but it would be strange and even arouse suspicions, if she were to refuse this steady place of work, instead of being shuffled from one place to another.

'It's very good of you to offer, Miriam,' her voice rose as if to overcompensate. 'What can I say?' she added. 'I'm flattered. Sure. And thank you.

At half past seven, they stood all up to go.

'I'll take Noa for a change,' said Miriam. 'Perhaps you'd like to see Ran's school, Kate?'

'Shall we show Kate your school, Ran?' said Amos. The boy had just come back in. He shrugged, smiled at Kate and nodded.

It was almost dark and the pathways hummed with parents and children going back for supper. After Ran had shown Kate his room, a few of his books and the classroom, the boy said goodnight, broke away and hurried over to his friends. Outside, the school patio was brightly lit, with parents coming in and out and with just her and Amos, Kate felt exposed.

'I told Jill I'd see her for supper,' she said, deliberately loudly.

But as they left the lights and crossed the dark lawn to the toddlers' house, their hands touched and Amos managed to whisper: 'Miriam will take Noa to the Zoo on Tuesday week. They stay overnight at her parents.'

Amos turned and went to pick up Miriam. Kate carried on up to the dining hall. Overhead, a half-moon hung in the night sky. She clenched her hands and looked up -- and hoped the guilt would allow her to keep on an even keel until then.

On Tuesday morning, Miriam stood with Noa by the roadside. They waited for the early bus from Beersheba to Tel Aviv. A stiff breeze from the west made it feel quite cool. Amos had come back from the fields to run them out to the main road. It wasn't a long walk, but Noa loved to ride in the jeep.

The girl hopped and skipped along the verge of the road.

'Don't get all dusted up, Noa,' Miriam said, reaching out and gently taking the girl's hand. 'Let's try to keep nice and tidy for *Savta.*' The grandmother always made such a fuss of her. Chocolate cake, sweets, a new hair ribbon and a storybook.

The evening before, Miriam had wanted to phone her mother to put-off the trip. She couldn't fathom why -- or if she had, didn't want to admit it. It was very first time ever she was reluctant to leave Amos on his own. She and Amos had always trusted one another, he going on archaeological field trips, she on courses at the educational institutes. And their first night in bed together afterwards had always made the time apart worth it.

Until now, she'd put it down to the war -- his coming back preoccupied, less sociable and less willing to take on responsibilities. For days after the kibbutz remembrance evening for Ya'ir, he had hardly spoken.

'Lots of the boys have come back like this,' Nitza had tried to reassure her. 'It's the first time we've taken so many casualties.' Yes, the victory was swift, but the cost had been high.

'I know,' Miriam said. 'But Amos was always so independent. Perhaps he never realised how much he and Ya'ir relied on one another.'

'Sure. Since they were kids,' said Nitza. 'Still. Give it time, Miriam. It'll pass.' She smiled, 'Make 'em tough in Haifa!' Unlike Tel Aviv with its business and commerce atmosphere, Haifa with its docks and hinterland of heavy industry always prided itself on being the 'workers' city'.

Nitza was Miriam's closest friend on the kibbutz, but even so it was an ambivalent friendship. Despite her three children, she was still quite attractive and, more to the point, still seemed to have a soft spot for Amos.

Miriam looked down and stroked Noa's hair. Nitza was also her daughter's *metapelet* and a very good one at that; if only there were more like her. All the women who'd wanted to work in education were now spoken for. But now, with more and more children, they'd begun to scrape the barrel to find women prepared to work with them. It was why their last education committee meeting had been so difficult, as they tried to find a new nurse for the kindergarten, and also why she had asked Kate.

Miriam raised her head and looked up to where the road disappeared over the horizon then glanced at her watch; the bus ought to be due.

A young Beduin boy strolled past. He drove half a dozen sheep along the dirt track just back from the road, and dust rose from their hooves and drifted away across the yellow stubble. The boy caught her eye and smiled, large yellow teeth and shiny black eyes. Miriam nodded and smiled back, but as Noa clung close to her jeans and looked away, she found her mind had wandered back to Amos.

Her thoughts were cut short as the bus came round to bend and stopped with an angry hiss of brakes; Miriam and Noa had been the only ones who waited. Noa ran up the aisle to kneel on the back seat and look out of the big window and Miriam held her hand against the girl's back.

Miriam's mother met them at the bus station. Her car was parked in a side street. After giving Noa a hug and a big kiss, she tied cuckoo plaits in the child's hair with two new blue ribbons. In a red plastic bag were sweets and a storybook about Nissim the policeman. For Noa, a kibbutz kid, he was almost as exotic as a pilot or a mountaineer. Mrs Swartz knew that Miriam was careful about presents, always something small and not to upset the delicate balance of equality amongst the children.

'You are your principles,' her mother sighed. Miriam just smiled. She hadn't gone to live a different way of life out in the desert only to throw away her ideals after a couple of years. If an increasing number on the kibbutz didn't care, so be it.

Kate had replaced Miriam that day in the Gan, and by chance when she brought the food containers back to the kitchen that lunchtime, she met Amos. He had come to collect lunch for the cotton workers out in the fields and was in the jeep.

'Come at half past nine,' he murmured. 'Just knock and call out that you want to leave a message for Miriam.'

As she went into the dining hall, Kate bumped into Nitza, with her containers from the toddlers.

'How's it going in the Gan without Miriam?' she asked. Everyone referred to the kindergarten as the Gan, even when speaking in English. Nitza spoke it well but with a much stronger *sabra* accent than Miriam.

'Oh. Fine. Fine. Hannah is helping and she knows the routine anyway,' she replied.

'Good.' Nitza grinned. 'You'll want to replace Miriam before you know it, Kate.' She paused for a moment. 'Completely.'

Kate started.

'Oh God, no. Replace Miriam? Oh no!'

Nitza didn't seem to notice. Like Miriam, she hoped that some of the more serious volunteers would stay on the kibbutz, especially capable ones like Kate. But then most of the likely bachelors were spoken for and she couldn't see any of the few that were left being a match for someone like Kate. Yet if she stayed alone, well, someone like her could… and there were certainly a few shaky marriages around. As she dumped the aluminium containers into the sinks, through the window she saw

Kate striding confidently across the lawn, her hair tied neatly in a green kerchief. Yes, she mused, even the not-so-shaky.

Hannah, a heavily pregnant, dark haired woman was trying to get the children undressed and onto their beds for the afternoon nap when Kate came in. Yaniv and Oren chased each other around the table, and laughed and pulled out chairs as they went.

'Stop it you two,' Hannah yelled. 'Into your rooms now,' her voice rose in exasperation. They had dodged her outstretched hands, but Kate darted across the room and caught Yaniv by the arm.

'*Azov!* Leggo,' he yelped.

'*Lamittah*! to bed,' Kate snapped, imitating Miriam's decisive tones. The boy shook his hand free, dug his chin into his chest and scuffed his bare feet across the tiles to his room. Yaniv, with no one to play, trotted to his room too.

'Huh. I had two groups before this one. Six years,' Hannah said in halting English. 'Enough.' She rose slowly, holding her lower back. 'I come back this evening for supper. Okay?'

After the woman went out, Kate walked slowly along the doorways, looking into each room. Some of the children had already lay down under a sheet. Oren had his thumb in his mouth, finger curled around his nose. Others sat quietly, leafing through storybooks. She sat on one of the small beds staring ahead, unfocused.

The kids paintings on the wall opposite, dissolved into a blur of bright colours. Children. Families. The kibbutz social life revolved around them: birthdays, parents meetings, celebrating the festivals. Now it was *Sukkot,* he eight-day Festival of Tabernacles, celebrating the Israelites journey through Sinai. She had helped Miriam and the children build their *sookkah,* a lean-to of poles and branches, roofed with eucalyptus branches and elephant grass collected from the orchard windbreaks, symbolising the ancient sojourn in the desert.

The previous week, they'd invited her to join the parents and children as they sang, read passages from the Book of Ruth, and noshed goodies from the children's kitchen. It was a secular Israeli and kibbutz agricultural celebration, but it was also a Jewish festival. And she wondered what that would all mean to her if she ever settled down on a kibbutz?

Thinking of that, Kate also wondered whether she would ever be able to bear her children not sleeping with her, and brought-up by others right from up from birth -- though she could also see the advantages of their collective education. Children. Yes. She had like to have children. In time. With someone she really loved. Her stomach moved. To have children with Amos? Fantasies. Fantasies.

The coloured blurs opposite dissolved as her eyes focussed more clearly. Above each bed, the children's own paintings depicted brightly coloured tractors and trees; ships on dark blue seas. Above Dror's bed, a huge red combine harvester; his father Motti worked in the arable crops. But next to it, one of crude black tanks firing red streaks into brown, square houses, matchstick men running up a hill, firing red and yellow bullets. Over Noam's bed, were two pictures of aircraft in dogfights, one spiralling out of a blue sky, trailing red fire and black smoke. War. Kate dimly remembered her father talking about Malaya. Men. Boys. War.

She stood and went back to the sink to wash up the dinner things. As the suds climbed her suntanned arms, she wondered how long it would take for them to pale now she worked inside all the time.

Beside her, on the dining room wall, was a beautiful collage that Miriam had created with the children. Why couldn't Amos's wife be some stupid nobody - a real bitch who made his life a misery? Instead, Miriam was a woman with whom, in time, she could have developed a really close friendship. And Kate suddenly shivered, feeling herself so close to the woman whose role she might play -- replace her completely? *Could* she?

Kate glanced through the window. The Chillean Poplar trees by the school were bending and whipping in the wind. Amos said there might be rain.

14

In Tel Aviv, the mother took Miriam and Noa to have lunch at the zoo café. Afterwards they wandered around again, but by mid-afternoon Noa began to loose her enthusiasm and said she felt tired.

'You know, Noa looks a bit green,' said her mother and suggested go back to her house to stay the night as planned. Miriam said it would be better if they went back to the kibbutz and after a short discussion the mother agreed. Strangely, although she had been looking forward to staying and chatting with her mother, Miriam felt more content with that, as though it was what she wanted -- wanted to get back, although she couldn't fathom why. Her mother drove her to the bus station and they waited for the next bus to Beersheba. They would get back late, just as the children were going to sleep, but if Noa was coming down with something, better she was in her own bed.

Amos came back from supper, closed the rear shutters and part drew the curtains, leaving a large gap by the door. If Kate was there when anyone came, he didn't want it to appear that he was hiding anything; she'd just come to leave a message about the Gan for Miriam.

He sat on the bed and twiddled the knob on their small radio. The strains of the BBC overseas' service '*Lilli bolero*' suddenly blasted from the set, followed by the announcer reading the headlines:

'…and President Nasser repeated today that he will not allow the sunken ships to be removed from the Suez Canal until Israeli forces have withdrawn from the whole of Sinai. In response, the French foreign minister stated that…'

So what was new? He gazed at the bookcase opposite and his eyes caught the red spine of a small selection of Tchernichovsky's poems that Ya'ir had given him one birthday.

'Life's not an insurance policy,' Ya'ir used to laugh. 'Doesn't promise you anything.' No, mused Amos, not even life itself. And now he knew it could be all too short. Too damn short to be routine anymore -- family, kids, kibbutz, cotton, sugar beet, committee meetings. The kibbutz wanted him to be the next farm manager. No way could he get his head around such a responsibility now.

Amos had long realised that his archaeology bug had been an escape valve. Now, after the war, and Ya'ir, it didn't seem enough. Soon, it would be reserves' service again for a month, and the year after, and the year after. Until when? The next war? Because this one hadn't resolved anything -- and with the hubris from the swift victory, the government was lacking any kind of peace initiative.

Then there was the kibbutz, the relentless struggle amidst a growing general apathy to kibbutz principles of sharing, equality, no hired labour, battles with Motti and the like. And now Kate had come into his life, and when he was with her it was as though he had become re-charged, ready to spark and glow.

Amos glanced across to a Gaugin print Miriam had bought long ago, then rose and stepped closer to look at it: large dark eyes, red hibiscus flowers, soft brown rounded shoulder and full breasts. His crotch grew hot as he looked then imagined himself lying next to Kate and by chance as he raised his hand to scratch his chin, he saw his watch.

'*Le'azazel.* Hell,' he snorted. Standing up, he hurried along the path say goodnight to Ran.

Coming back from the school, he passed Noa's house. And abruptly stopped, and caught his breath. Chatting to Nitza by the door, was Miriam!

'Hi,' she called as she saw him. 'Had to come back early. Noa sicked up after the zoo.' She came up to him and gave him a kiss. 'At least Mum drove us to the bus station.'

'A nice surprise! But Noa must be upset,' Amos managed to say, and despite his body trembling and his head spinning, added, 'I'll just go in and kiss her goodnight.'

'No. Don't go in now,' said Miriam. 'She's had some medicine and we want her to sleep. She must be coming down with something.'

Amos's head was spinning. *Elohim*, Kate was coming at nine! And suddenly he remembered the shutters closed and the half-drawn curtains.

'Had a rough day,' he said. 'Was planning an early night.' He was rambling. 'Anyway, you must be hungry. Come. Let's go and eat.'

'I'll just go and say goodnight to Ran,' she said. 'See you up there.'

All the way up to the dining hall, Amos's head burned and his stomach churned. By the path, some kid had left a ball. Damn it. Damn it, he swore as he gave it a fierce kick into the bushes.

Kate walked along the path towards the new houses, head up, stride firm, as if any other evening. But within, everything quivered. Her hair was tied back and in her pocket, a woollen hat. For later. In her hand was a note for Miriam as an excuse for going to her room. Luckily, there were things to report: Ori had developed a temperature; Rina was being taken to town tomorrow.

The evening was cool; third week of October. Above, a thin wafer of the new moon peeped in the dark sky. Here and there black wisps of cloud that had been scudding east all day obscured some of the myriad stars of the clear desert night. The kibbutz was anticipating rain.

She glanced towards the lighted windows of the dining hall. Around one of the tables, sat half a dozen people, some committee or other in session. But already, at just gone nine, elsewhere the kibbutz was quiet, everyone in their rooms and most of the children asleep.

To her left, bright security lights illuminated the white walls of the children's houses. Could she ever consider her own children sleeping away from her, if… God! He wasn't going to marry her. A meteor suddenly streaked across the sky for a split second and disappeared down towards the horizon. Rubbing her arms, Kate carried on along the path between the oleander bushes.

Amos's room was one of four in the long, concrete house facing east and backing west against the prevailing winds. Three rooms away, Sha'ul, bald head and long grey shorts, was watering his garden patch with a hose.

'*Erev Tov*,' he called softly. Kate knew him a little. Like Joe he was an American, but from San Francisco. The kibbutz philosopher, Amos called him. No fear of gossip there.

'*Erev Tov*,' replied Kate boldly. 'I have to leave a note for Miriam.

She turned onto the approach pathway -- and stopped short to catch her breath. Amos was on the veranda holding the kettle, and through the open doorway she saw Miriam; Amos had had the nous to draw back the curtains when they'd returned from supper.

'Shalom Kate,' he said, adding loudly, 'trouble at the Gan?'

Miriam came out, unable to hide her surprise.

'Hi, Kate. Problems?'

'Shalom. Miriam.' She smiled, though her whole body was pulsing. Guilt, shame --

and for a moment, anger. 'Come to leave a note about the Gan for when you came back. I'm not working tomorrow.'

'Oh thanks, but you could have come and told me when I got back.'

'Well, I'm going to Kiryat Gat on the lunchtime bus.' Kate laughed, but it came out a bit choked. 'Jill wants to buy a cheap pair of sandals.' She held out a folded sheet of paper Thank God she had prepared that. 'Just says Ori is in bed with mumps, and Margalit is taking Rina to town in the morning.'

'Oh, thanks for that.' Miriam flicked her hand. 'Look. Amos is making coffee. You're welcome to join us.'

'Thanks, Miriam, but I'm tired. Another time. Thanks.' She raised her hand, turned and walked away up the path.

Miriam watched Kate's pace quicken until she was all but running.

'Come,' Amos called from inside. 'Coffee's ready. Let's have some of your Mother's biscuits.' Miriam turned and went in, thinking…

The next day, a stiff breeze blew across the fields, raising a haze of fine dust. Amos sat on an upturned box and took the wad of crumpled delivery tickets from his pocket that Itcho had brought back from the cotton gin.

'What's the score, fighter?' Yossi called down from the tractor as he manoeuvred another empty trailer into the path of the combine.

'Not bad.' The tickets flapped in the breeze as Amos spread them like a fan. 'Two, a bit on the dirty side but not that bad. And all with medium to long fibre.' He looked up at Yossi. 'Just need the rain to hold off a few more days, eh?'

Yossi glanced up at the thin cloud scudding across the sky.

'Pray!' he grinned.

Amos shrugged. 'Forgotten how.'

Yossi engaged gear and drove away towards the combine. Amos stood up and looked across the field; over two thirds had now been harvested. Close by, scattered tufts of white cotton fluttered in the wind and the parched, grey soil was covered with the brown debris of broken stalks and crushed leaves. What they had already sent would just cover the costs. Over on the far side was their profit, a cloud of white cotton waiting to be picked. It had survived the war and the pests. Now, the mad rush to beat the first rains.

Tucking the paper slips back into his pocket, Amos strode across to the jeep. He wanted to check how many loads the gin could take tomorrow. Rain threatened and all the local kibbutzim and farms would be screaming at the manager. The gin was a co-operative, set up by the settlements in the area, but now as each grower competed to increase their daily quota to beat the rains, there'd be precious little neighbourly co-operation.

Parking the jeep behind the dining hall, Amos hurried across the courtyard to the office hut. Ayalah looked up from her ledgers as he came in and adjusted her glasses.

'Have to phone the gin,' he explained, dialling without waiting for her nod of permission.

'Hello. Mikhal?' he grunted as an answer came. 'How many loads do we have tomorrow? What do you mean, four? Only four?' He slapped his hand on the desk. Ayalah looked up, frowning. 'Can I speak to Nahum? No? Why not?' he snapped, glancing through the small window. To the west, a watery sun shone pale yellow through the thickening cloud and haze. The rains were on their way. They would fall first along the coast, but would soon work their way inland. 'I must speak to Nahum,' he said. The manager was the only one who could change the schedules. The voice replied that he was out in the sheds. Amos tried charm. 'Look Mikhal, I'll hang on. Can you get him for me?'

'And for everyone else,' came the reply. 'It doesn't only rain your way, Amos. Everyone is driving me up the wall. It won't help.' Amos glanced at Ayalah as he put down the phone.

'There go our profits. The first third covers the costs, the second goes for interest to the bloody banks. And now, the damn rains could wash the rest away.' He breathed out. 'I ask you: who invented agriculture?'

Ayalah shrugged and half smiled. 'Some *meshuggah*, I suppose.'

Amos waved and hurried back to the jeep. Starting the engine, he backed away from the dining hall, his forehead hot. He glanced up at the sky again. The clouds suddenly seemed closer. And heavier.

In the Gan, Kate started washing up, feeling wretched. All that anticipation and then, nothing. She ought to be angry and hate Miriam, yet found she couldn't. She tidied up the kids' dining table, thinking. It was all getting too heavy; she ought to get away leave and go home. But when she went through the rooms, picking up the kids' discarded clothes and tidying up, she knew she wouldn't. Couldn't. Something that had been aroused had to be consummated first -- her devout grandmother's 'the devil within'? And Miriam? She would have to live with that.

At four o'clock, after the last children had run out and away to the parents' houses, Kate finished cleaning dining area. Without the noise and chatter, it was eerily silent. She sat on one of the small beds staring ahead, unfocused. The kids' paintings on the wall opposite dissolved into a blur of bright colours. Children. Families. The kibbutz social life revolved around them: birthdays, parents' meetings, celebrating the festivals.

Now it was the last day of the Sukkot festival. The previous week, she'd joined the parents' and children's parties as they sang and read passages from the Book of Ruth, and noshed goodies from the children's kitchen. It was a secular Israeli and kibbutz agricultural celebration, but it was also a Jewish festival. Kate wondered what that would all mean to her if she ever settled down here…

The wind that had been blowing all afternoon grew stronger as evening came. Pale grey loëss dust, raised from the dry fields and the desert, hung in the air. Despite closing all doors and windows, a thin, white layer soon settled on tiled floors and furniture. Miriam was wiping the bookshelves and the children were having tea when Amos came home, face grey with dust and wisps of cotton-wool in his hair.

'Sorry I'm late,' he smiled. 'Bloody cotton!'

Miriam came out onto the veranda and kissed his nose.

'I'll put the kettle on.' After a perfunctory return kiss, he went in to shower. Back to the family routine. As the hot water cascaded from his body, washing away the day's grime and weariness, with the frustration from the missed tryst, he couldn't rid himself of the thought that Miriam had invented Noa's sickness. That in the way she could read him, she had begun to suspect. He was annoyed, but realised that now he had to take even more care.

Amos drank his coffee and munched a jam sandwich trying to concentrate, his mind a seething caldron: cotton, Kate and Miriam, and the threat of rain. He tried to transfer his annoyance to the cotton.

'They've only given us four loads of cotton tomorrow,' he muttered, looking at Miriam, 'and it looks like rain any minute.'

'Didn't your heart-throb at the gin help?'

His being attractive to other women had never really bothered her — after all, would she have wanted someone who wasn't? But now, as she grinned room at him across the room, she wondered why her voice sounded a bit hollow. Amos flicked his wrist.

'She's everyone's heart-throb at the moment,' he said. And it's Nahum who's fixing the quotas. I must drive over to Mishmar Hanegev to see him tonight.' He sipped his coffee. and wondered whether he could take Kate with him. It would be dark. He could turn off into the orchards. No lights. Even for half an hour. But then he dismissed it.

'Be careful, driving.' Miriam's voice cut into his thoughts, 'you're tired, Amos', adding, 'most road accidents occur near to home. Then, after a short pause, added, 'Perhaps I'll come with you? Make sure you're awake.'

'No. I'll be okay. I'll go after supper. Won't be long.' And she didn't.

Amos hardly said a word all the way back from seeing Nahum, his lips tight. Despite their friendship from way back in the Sinai campaign, he hadn't got increased quotas. It was ten o'clock by the time he drove home up the deserted road. White cylinders of light from the headlamps thrust into the dust haze ahead, no stars above and all around an empty blackness. Within five minutes, even the fence lights of Mishmar Hanegev had disappeared in the gloom. He slowed down to turn into their approach road; two drops of rain splattered on his windscreen and trickled down through the dust. No more. But it was enough, and Amos remained taciturn even after he got back.

'I'm whacked, Miriam,' he said throwing his jacket onto the veranda table.

Miriam stood by the door.

'Didn't get any more quotas?'

'No. None. And now with the damn rains threatening… think I'll go to bed.'

Amos had always taken his work to heart, but she had never seen him so tensed up like this. And again, couldn't avoid thinking that it wasn't only the cotton.

'I've just got to go round to Hannah to check the kindergarten arrangements for the weekend.' She took her jacket. 'Be back soon. Perhaps we'll have coffee.'

As soon as she had gone out, Amos undressed, and leaving only the small side-light, lay back in the bed, eyes half closed, thinking of Kate. Then he thought about Miriam. He loved her too didn't he? And there was nothing wrong with their relationship. Sure, it had become predictable and she was a little overbearing at times. So what? But try as he might, his thoughts kept wandering back to Kate. Then, quite suddenly, overcome by weariness and the accumulated tension from the day, he dropped off.

Miriam was surprised to find Amos so fast asleep. The first time before eleven o'clock that she could remember. She undressed and slipped in beside him. Automatically, his arm came around her then he was still.

Miriam lay there in the dark, wide-awake and staring up at the ceiling. Yes, Amos was going through a difficult time, from farmer to fighting man then back to the fields all within the space of a few weeks; the trauma of Yair's death, the watermelons' fiasco, the cotton, everything piling up at the same time. She wanted so much to talk to him, make him share it with her as they always did. But she didn't want to add to everything; she'd wait until the cotton was in and his anxiety had gone. Yes, after the cotton they would talk — must talk.

With his regular, deep breathing echoing in the small room, Miriam's mind wouldn't rest and she couldn't sleep, wondering again and again, if it wasn't the cotton, then what?

15

When Amos rose for work the next morning, a lingering smell of summer-dry dust hung in the air, but the sky was heavy and the cool wind from the west had brought a worrying dampness. And over the next three days, while the red combine sailed back and forth along the rows of white cotton, the wind continued to blow in more clouds. It could only be a matter of time before the rains came. The only question was how much would fall this far inland, and what area they would manage to pick before they did.

The hectic cotton schedule had kept thoughts of Kate at bay, but whenever there was a lull, she entered Amos's head with an increased intensity. He sought plan after plan to meet and talk with her, only to discard each one like the crushed, brown stalks that carpeted the field.

'Cheer up mate,' said Yossi, as another load went off to the gin. 'Nearly three quarters picked — and still no rain,' puzzled that it didn't improve Amos's mood.

When he got to the room, Miriam had taken winter sweaters out of the cupboard. Noa smelled the mothballs as he'd dressed after the shower.

'*Phooyah, Aba.*' She wrinkled her nose. 'You smell like a wardrobe.' And while he sipped his coffee, she spread out a painting she had completed that morning.

'*Yaffe. Yaffe,*' he said, almost automatically, then stood up.

'Got to phone the gin,' he muttered. 'Make sure our four loads are secure for tomorrow. Won't be long.'

Borrowing the office key from Ayalah, he phoned the gin. There was no change; the loads were agreed. Just the rain to worry about. He locked the office hut, then and stood outside for a moment, thinking. The sky was still a hazy grey and evening was coming in earlier because of it. Suddenly a raucous laugh came from his right. Through the trees, lights shone from the huts of the volunteers. All he could do was to look from a distance.

In her hut, Kate was having coffee with Jill. After leaving the kindergarten, she deliberately she had taken the long way round behind the babies' house, through the eucalyptus copse -- where they'd first met that night. A stiff breeze was bending and tossing the young trees, branches whipping and hissing, leaves fluttering. These were their trees; their moonlight. Already, those nights felt in another century.

'Got so used to the bloody heat,' Jill muttered, when Kate came in, 'the least wind makes it seem chilly.' She was curled up on her bed with a book and a blanket over her feet.

'Cup of coffee help?' smiled Kate. Jill grinned back.

'Thought you'd never ask.'

Kate sat on her bed sipping the coffee and gripping the warm mug tightly. Then began in a monotone;

'So, Jill. What now?' she began. 'Snatched moments together; the odd night? After all, I'm only "the other woman" -- the mistress!' Kate half-laughed. 'God. I'd never imagined myself as that. Okay in town perhaps, but here in this small village, bloody ridiculous.' She sipped her tea. 'And the tension is driving me doolally, Jill.'

'You can say that again. Me too, Kate.' She sat up. 'So?'

'I need a break, Jill. Need to get away; think things over.'

'And?'

'I'll take the *Shabbat* days owing me and go to stay at the hostel in Jerusalem.' She sighed. 'And maybe he might just manage to come up for a day. Either way, I have to do it, Jill.'

Jill came over and put her arm around her.

'Getting that serious?'

'Uhuh.' Kate gripped the mug, 'and bloody impossible. And I have to let him know. Explain.' She glanced at her watch. 'Time for walkabout, as Roger would say.'

Coming away from the office, Amos turned down the path and made his way to the dining-hall lobby to look at the work rota for the next day. Repeatedly now, he found excuses to go up to the lobby, or the office telephone. And suddenly, there she was. Stifling a shout, he willed her to look up and see him coming -- and in that way that people sense someone looking at them, she did.

The lobby was empty at that hour and almost dark, families in their rooms with the children, the single ones resting after the day's work. They clung to each other for a few seconds then broke apart.

'Amos,' whispered Kate, 'I need to get away for a while. I... I'm thinking of going to Jerusalem on Sunday.'

'Second thoughts?' he murmured, his hand reaching for hers.

'Oh, God. No. No! Please, Amos. You know how I feel.' Tears began to form in her eyes. 'But it's so... so impossible. I can't stand it, I -' Kate looked up, his pained face blurred through her tears. 'No. I'm not leaving you, Amos. But we have to talk, need time together.'

As they stood there, clutching hands, Amos had an idea.

'Listen, Kate. In a few weeks time there's a Prehistory Society meeting in Jerusalem. I've put my name down. I go every year. Two days. We can spend real time there together. Please Kate. Can you wait 'till then?'

'Oh yes. If that's so, of course I can.' And with that, any thoughts of leaving for good flew away. She gripped both his hands. 'But I still need a day or two away now; the tension, Amos. Please. Can you understand that?'

'Sure, sure. But if I know we'll meet in Jerusalem soon, I'll manage.'

At that moment, children's voices sounded from across the lawn.

'*Le'azazel!*' Amos gasped. With a final squeeze of her hands, he hurried into the dining-hall and slipped out through side doors. He hurried through the bushes onto the path, and walked swiftly down to his room.

Kate stayed by the notice board, as though studying next day's work list and fighting to remain calm as Joe's two boys thundered in, with Joe following. He smiled as he saw her.

'Hi. Thought I saw Amos coming this way.'

Kate shrugged. 'Didn't notice. Why?'

'Oh. He wants the extra trailer for tomorrow. So do I.' Joe grinned and half crouched as if pointing a six-gun. 'Uri says we have to fight it out.'

Kate smiled then went out, clutching her arms around her stomach, her mind spinning as she walked back to the huts. Either way, she had to get away for a day or two. And if they really would meet during his seminar, they had to talk seriously. Very seriously. Kate glanced up at the grey sky. Yes. In Jerusalem they would have to decide; one way or the other.

On Sunday morning, Kate took the bus to Jerusalem. It had been a miserable weekend. And not just the weather. On Friday night, the kibbutz held the usual communal meal, everyone eating together. All the tables were set out in two rows, and covered with white sheets and set with flowers, the older children sitting with their parents. It was also the only regular occasion that the volunteers all ate at the same time together with the kibbutzniks.

As usual, before the meal there were songs and readings, creating a wonderful *Shabat* atmosphere and a real feeling of community. Kate had once looked forward to it. But these days it was torture. Amos would be sitting with his wife and Ran, laughing and chatting to friends while on the far side, she sat with Jill and the other volunteers, desperately hoping to catch his eye -- or a fleeting smile.

This Friday, he had ended up sitting with his back to her so she hadn't even managed to make eye contact the whole evening, then having to watch him go out with Miriam and down to Ran's schoolhouse, while she went back to the huts, the cold wind gusting against her.

The *shabbat* was no better, the wind and dust and the threatened rain and kept everyone indoors; the kibbutz was built for summer. She made sporadic forays across to the dining hall. Once even to the kindergarten on the pretext of having left a book there. But he was never amongst the huddled figures hurrying along the pathways. Yes, for her sanity, she had to get out and away, even for a day or two.

Rain spattered on the side windows as the bus sped north, and by the time they left Masmiyya, it was raining hard. It was the first real downpour she had experienced since coming here and on the road climbing up to Jerusalem, the window streamed with water.

Kate stared through it, seeing only a blur of white limestone terraces on the mountainside and bright green patches of young pine trees. Winter in Jerusalem was real winter they'd told her, three thousand feet up and all that. Now, she could see what they meant -- and she didn't even have an umbrella! Who the hell thought of such things in the blazing months that had just passed?

Outside the main bus station, Kate sheltered under the rickety, steel bus-stop, waiting for the local bus to Kikar Tzion. How she'd cursed the sticky heat and the sweaty crush of people during the summer. Now she would take it all back just for a few rays of warm sunshine.

The hostel in East Jerusalem was half empty, the stone corridor echoing to her footsteps as she checked in and walked to her small room. It was really cold and reminded her to go and buy a cheap sweater in the old city and an umbrella; luckily she had hung on to the bright green cagoule from her hiking days.

Inside the Damascus gate, Kate haggled with a vendor and bought a small expanding umbrella, then decided to go and visit Yusuf. Instead of going the short way through El Wad road she turned left, wanting to go the way she had walked with Amos their first time. Half-way along, the heavens opened again and remembering her favourite cafe, she ran like mad down the Akbat Darwish and in through the small doorway.

The cafe was almost empty, just two old men playing Shesh-Besh. Still the pink plastic-covered Formica tables and the sleepy barman with his huge moustache, and the smell of spices mingling with the dampness. But now she was alone, nibbling a sweet, sticky cake and sipping hot Turkish coffee with the smell of cardamom in her nostrils. Despite the cold and the rain, Kate was glad she had come to Jerusalem. God, how she had needed to get away; be able to think rationally about where she was heading.

She looked across at the empty chair where Amos had sat, his broad, tanned face, the unruly fair hair and his strong hand over hers. Kate stared down at the small cardamom pod and the coffee grounds in her empty cup. Her grandmother used to read the tea-leaves. Could you do that with coffee? Foresee what would happen? Anyway, at his Pre-history conference, painful as it might be, yes, they would have to have to decide -- one way or the other.

That Friday evening, Amos kept looking up at the dark sky. No moon. No stars. And a freshening, threatening wind that hadn't died down with nightfall. His only relief was that they had managed to get five loads of cotton to the gin before the Shabbat shutdown.

On Shabbat morning, he drove out to the fields in the jeep, taking Ran with him. A brief squall overnight had soaked the fields; straggly tufts of cotton hung from the plants, fluttering and twisting in the stiff breeze. Ran watched.

'Bad, Dad?'

Amos jumped as if stung. 'Lost some, that's for sure.' He walked up one of the rows, boots crunching on the sodden stalks and leaves. Ran jumped out and followed.

'See that?' Amos pointed to a bedraggled twist of cotton wool. 'The combine can't pick it up. Lost.' He fingered a split, swollen brown bud from which white cotton was just about to burst. 'If it doesn't rain again, that will be ready tomorrow or Monday.'

'And if it does rain, Dad?' Ran squinted.

Amos shrugged. 'Another load will have gone.' He turned and ruffled Ran's hair, half smiling. 'Only crazy people try to make a living from farming, Ran.'

They drove back, silent, Ran staring out at the grey sky. Suddenly, he turned to Amos.

'Perhaps they will invent a drying machine that could run up

'Oh. It does get cold. Snow too.' He waved his hand. 'But it soon passes and the sun is here again. Even in winter.'

They talked on and off for a long while, and Kate was about to go when the doorway darkened.

'Oh. Hello, Kate. Long time, no see.' Shafik's voice was easy and calm; showed no trace of resentment. Relieved, Kate stood up and held out her hand.

'Nice to see you.' She smiled. 'Just popped in to see Yusuf.' He took her hand and shook it gently. Like Amos, he too had a strong hand. Strangely, it felt comforting, his calm demeanour spreading to her as they both sat down. Yusuf went to the doorway to call for more *shai*. For the few seconds they were alone, Kate felt Shafik's eyes on her face, though she deliberately looked towards the doorway. Comforting, perhaps, but she had to be careful. No misleading signals this time.

'How long are you in Al Kuds?' he asked as Yusuf came back.

'Oh. Just a day or two.'

Shafik sipped his tea. 'Perhaps I could show you more of the Old City, Kate. If you have time, that is.'

'Well, I can't just now,' she said, 'I've got to buy some things for Jill.'

'Well, tomorrow then?'

'If I can make it, Shafik,' she said, hesitating, her mind spinning. 'But I'm not sure.'

'I'll wait, then,' he said. 'About ten.'

Afterwards, Kate wondered why she had agreed. Didn't she have enough on her plate? But she did know why. For since she had arrived in Jerusalem, being alone with her thoughts was proving more depressing than she had imagined. For the very first time in her life, she was afraid of being lonely.

Kate nodded and said goodbye, and went out. She wandered back through the Souk, which, despite the fine rain was busy, and bought a plain, thick sweater on the way.

16

On Sunday morning Amos drove Uri out to the fields.

'*Nu*. What do you think?' Further rain had fallen overnight, but the strong wind was drying out the plants.

'Depends on tonight,' said Uri, squashing one of the sodden cotton bolls in his hand. 'Can't risk getting the combine getting bogged down in this lot.'

Amos nodded and they stood and looked along the rows, then out to the grey desert beyond.

'Boys from the Falkha are pleased, as least,' said Uri. 'Give the winter barley a chance.' Amos shrugged.

'Glad someone is happy.'

'Look, mate,' Uri slapped his shoulder. 'Done as much as you can. And Shmuel reckons we're making some profit now. Anyway,' he pointed to the few tight bolls still clinging to the nearest plant. 'Still a few more loads when it dries up.'

'If it dries up,' muttered Amos.

Uri looked at him sideways.

'That's not like you. What's eating you, mate?'

'Oh. Nothing,' Amos muttered. 'Just the damn cotton,'

Uri didn't press. Yes, obviously Amos was anxious. A whole season's work could be washed out. But he was puzzled. He'd known him since they were boys; that just wasn't Amos.

Miriam had lit the incandescent 'Fireside' paraffin heater for when the kids came home. Amos was in the shower scrubbing the grease from his hands, he'd been in the garage all afternoon preparing the sugar-beet drill for the sowing next week.

'Toast?' she called out as he dried himself.

'Uhuh. Please. What an awful day.'

Like most houses in Israel, Kibbutz rooms had terrazzo tiled floors, wonderfully cool for the hot summer months, but so cold on winter days. Only a few years before, they were still using the old *p'tiliot* paraffin heaters, good for boiling coffee but filling the rooms with fumes. Now, they could make toast from the glowing red element of the more modern heaters.

'More toast, Mum?' mumbled Ran through an unfinished mouthful.

'In a minute,' she said. 'Let your sister have hers first.'

'Don't know where you put it all,' muttered Amos, his son's insatiable appetite still leaving him as thin as a rake.

The four of them sat and played Memory, with cards made up from scraps of glossy magazines.

'You're not concentrating Dad,' said Ran, Amos having gained the least cards of all, in each of the three games. 'Never seen you win so few.'

Amos ruffled his son's hair. 'Just you wait till the cotton's over!'

After they had taken kids back and ate supper, Miriam went off to an education committee meeting. Amos sat in the room, restless, unable to concentrate on anything and went outside and looked up at the sky. Here and there, a star twinkled through gaps opening up in the cloud.

He went back inside and stood in the middle of the room,

hovering. Suddenly, he went to the bookcase, switched on the record player and took out the Bach double concerto, one of Yair's favourites too. The music filled the room, blotting out everything except Kate. He'd intended listening to the record with Kate, the night Miriam was going to her mother's. And the longer he sat there, the more miserable he felt.

When they went to bed, Miriam nestled against him, sweet smell of shampoo from her hair, her soft hip in his side. And he still found that easy and strangely, still satisfying. Perhaps, he thought as he lay there before dozing off, he would be able to manage like that: '*al shtei khatunot*' as the sages said: riding on two weddings.

He slept until the gutter overflowing and cascading onto the path outside woke him. Heavy rain was drumming on the concrete roof. Amos slid out of bed and went to open the door. In the half-light of dawn, he glanced back at the luminous hands of the alarm clock. Quarter to five. So much for the cotton.

'Raining?' Miriam mumbled.

'Uhuh.'

It was a cold morning. Shivering, Amos slipped back quickly into bed. As he turned on his side, Miriam backed against him, her rear into his belly. She liked to lie like that. Security, she would joke to him. By chance, her night-dress had ridden up and with the bare bottom against him, his crotch began to feel hot, hardening and stiffening against the crease of her buttocks. As though on its own, it slid between her legs and into the soft moist opening beyond.

Miriam breathed out and still half asleep, pushed against him, feeling him coming in and out, his hand sliding round her belly and in to the cleft, playing and fondling, making her move with him. She felt good, but strange — they hadn't done this kind of thing in the morning for… for, she couldn't remember how long.

Quite quickly, Amos climaxed, pushing into her hard and strong, almost violently. And then a few moments later she gasped and trembled too, his arms pulling her against him tighter and tighter, until eventually they both relaxed.

'It's alright for you,' Miriam murmured. 'I've got to get up in half an hour. Kids are kids, rain or no rain.'

And as he held her close, again Amos wondered why he was seeking anything -- anyone, elsewhere. Then, sated and drowsy, immediately fell asleep.

With the rain, they couldn't get onto the fields so when he got up, Amos called for Yossi and they went down to the garage; there was always something to do to the equipment. Motti and Rami were already in the garage, fixing a drill. With a brief nod between them, each got on with their own work, but again Amos felt Motti's knowing glances from time to time.

Rami's boasting of his amorous exploits with this volunteer girl or that often made Motti envious. Fearful of Orna finding out, he would never dare, but after what Rami told him, it seemed that Amos might have, and with that volunteer girl, Kate. Good looker and real sexy arse in her tight jeans. He wondered if Miriam suspected? Or anyone else?

The rain ceased that evening and the following afternoon, under a watery sun, Amos took the combine out and they managed to pick two loads from the higher ground. On Wednesday it was windy but still dry and the last three trailers went off with everyone's blessings, especially Shmuel's. It was a bonus, he had already discounted them as lost to the rains. And on Thursday evening, the cotton crew and wives and girlfriends crowded into Uri's room. Beer all round with pretzels and two cakes from the kitchen.

'God was on your side,' grinned Ilan.

'That's what the boys from the *falkha* were moaning,' said Yossi. 'They were praying for the rain to continue but evidently Him up there didn't listen.' He grinned. 'The Beduin said it wouldn't rain again either.'

'So Allah was with you too,' coughed Ephraim, munching a fistful of pretzels. Everyone laughed and for a moment, Amos felt a schadenfreude that Motti was adversely affected. Then came a twinge of conscience: Motti or no, *falkha*, the cereal crops were an integral part of the kibbutz.

Kate came back on Tuesday evening. She had kept the meeting with Shafik to a brief coffee in the Old City, but it had helped to break up the time in Jerusalem. She had used the two days to think. And decide. And had made her decision. She wanted Amos, wanted him more than anything else. Now, it was up to him.

Somehow, she would get through the week on automatic pilot, sustained by the anticipation of spending two days with Amos in Jerusalem when he went to his conference. And there, they would have to decide one way or -- Oh God no, the other, in which case she would go straight back to England.

On Tuesday morning, Amos caught the bus to Jerusalem. That evening would be the opening session of the Prehistoric Society annual meeting. Time to book in and arrange his room at the teacher's seminar in Katamon.

Like most Israeli archaeology fanatics, Amos had started with the Biblical period: Israelite, Philistine, Late Bronze, Canaanite. He had a shelf-full of shards from one *Tel* or another. But gradually, he and Eli had gone back further after finding a cache of flint tools on one of their trips near Nitzana, and encouraged by an enthusiastic woman professor from the university. 'You and your stone-age men -- and woman!' Miriam would joke.

Kate had worked the last two *Shabbat* days to store up time in lieu. She would work the afternoon shift tomorrow, then take the early evening bus. 'Visiting a college friend in kibbutz Nakhshonim near Petakh Tikva,' she would tell everyone. But he couldn't dispel the anxiety that something might screw things up.

Amos checked in at the seminar office, then left his pack in his room and took the number four bus into town. Time to find a cheap hotel. With tourists flooding into Jerusalem, finding a hotel room was no easy feat. He had to settle for an old, converted thirties hotel off Queen Helleni Street, and booked two nights.

Two others were in the room when Amos arrived back, a boy from kibbutz Afikim and a man from Haifa, short, lined brown face and stiff grey hair, an old-timer.

'Your kibbutz.' The man smiled, 'know the area well. Was in the Givati Brigade in '48. After the battle of Huleikat, our unit drove across to that military road and down to Beer Sheba. Just empty space then. Must have changed now.'

Amos nodded as he prepared his bed, hoping the man would sense that he wasn't the talkative type.

That afternoon the conference opened with lecture on the latest Palaeolithic discoveries in the Jordan valley; bone fragments, flint tools and evidence of fire over a hundred thousand old. He felt an irrational continuity stretching back from him to these Palaeolithic inhabitants, a strange pride, that together with the Mount Carmel Neanderthals and others, his country -- this tiny piece of the continent, had yielded so many important clues to human evolution.

This time though, preoccupied with whether Kate would make it or not, he found it difficult to concentrate or engage in the friendly discussions over coffee that were so much a part of every conference. And after tea, and the closer it got to evening, he grew more and more anxious at a possible hitch to their plans.

Kate worked in the Gan that afternoon, her body here but her mind already on the bus winding up the road to Jerusalem and anticipated two whole wonderful days and nights with Amos together.

Again and again she wiped down all the basins until they gleamed and tried to keep busy. She glanced at her coat on the rack and holdall tucked beneath every time she passed, and waited impatiently for the kids to go home at four o'clock.

Kate had told everyone that she was going to Tel Aviv, and then on to meet her friend at the Petah Tikva bus station. Instead she would then take the express from Tel Aviv to Jerusalem. The Tel Aviv bus came at half past four. She would have to hurry out to the road to catch it, but the parents usually came on time, and some even a bit before so that shouldn't be a problem. She could have left earlier to catch the Jerusalem bus at three, but that would have made it too obvious.

At half past three Kate woke the children, and one by one they were collected, leaving only Gil, and Ronit, Batya's child. Kate began to feel anxious. Oh God. No latecomers. Not today. Please.

At five past four, Shula came for Gil.

'Have you seen Batya?' asked Kate. Shula shook her head.

'Saw Ronit's sister going home from the school. Perhaps Batya's sick?'

Kate's stomach sank and her heart began to beat faster. Batya was never late. Oh, God. Just today. Why? Why? She glanced at her watch. Four fifteen! It would be a mad rush down the main road. Ronit leaned against the door-jamb, thumb in mouth, one foot scraping on the mat. The seconds ticked away. Suddenly Kate slipped on her coat and snatching up her holdall, took the girl's hand and closed the door behind them.

'Come,' she snapped. 'Let's go to *imah*!'

Half-way along the path, they met Batya running towards them, hair all over the place, face red and puffed.

'Oh Kate, I'm sorry. I really am sorry.' She panted to catch her breath. 'I lay down a few minutes, after work. Must have fallen asleep.' She knelt down and kissed the girl. 'What a bad mummy you have, eh? Come. We've got some cake.' She stood up, her head to one side. 'Sorry, Kate. I really am.'

But Kate had already hurtled away and ran past the dining hall and down to the road. Just as she reached the gate, the bus stopped out on the main road and two people dropped off. She started to run, desperately she called out and waved one arm but no one was looking. It took off again and the noise of the engine drowned her cries.

Kate stopped half-way down the road, panting and sweating; she had missed it. Oh, God. She had missed it! Not another for three hours. And that would arrive too late to get a fast connection to Jerusalem. And Amos would be waiting, and think she wasn't coming. She was about to burst into tears but the two who'd got off were almost up to her. Unable to face them, Kate turned and hurried back.

She hurried round to the courtyard behind the kitchen, her throat like sandpaper and her head a furnace. There might be a supplier's truck going out, or a visitor leaving for town. But there was nothing. Tears of frustration welled up in her eyes.

Suddenly, she straightened up. Uri! The farm manager. He would know if any other transport was leaving. She snatched up her bag, and made a made dash back down the path to the houses.

Uri was on the bed, playing chess with his son.

'Hi! Kate!'

'Oh. Uri. Look. Sorry to trouble you. I -,'

'What's up?'

'Well, I was catching the Tel Aviv bus. But the parents came late. You know. In the Gan,' Kate panted as she caught her breath. 'So -- so I missed it, and I wonder. Well. Look. Is anyone going out? You know. I -- My friend will be waiting in Petakh Tikva. And if I don't turn up, she'll be really worried. Oh. God. I don't know what to do, Uri, honest.'

At that moment, Uri's neighbour Nitza stepped onto their veranda. 'Shalom, Kate. Thought you were going to Petakh Tikva?'

'She was,' said Ayalah. 'Dear Batya collected Ronit late for the first time in her life and made Kate miss the bus.'

Nitza shrugged. 'Well, there's another one to Tel Aviv at seven thirty.'

'No. No. It will be too late,' Kate snapped, her face flushed, then caught herself and abruptly lowered her voice. 'I mean, Jane is meeting me in Petakh Tikva to take me to her kibbutz. She'll think I'm not coming and go, sure. Or that I've got lost or something.'

Uri stood up.

'No problem, Kate. Here,' he called to his son, 'want to buy ice cream in Kiryat Gat? I've got to see Moshe, the sugar-beet marketing man sometime anyway.'

Uri went out to the veranda, took his jacket and checked the keys.

'Oh. Thanks. Thanks so much, Uri,' said Kate following him out. 'I'm sorry to cause all this trouble. I -'

'*Ein Ba'ayot*,' said Uri. 'There's bound to be a bus from Kiryat Gat to Tel Aviv.' He ruffled his son's hair. 'Come Nadav. Let's go.'

Taking the pot of jam, Nitza went out to the path and watched the two as they hurried away, Uri with his long firm strides and Kate in a dark green dress and neat leather jacket, body tensed, and tightly clutched the holdall. How desperate and frantic she had been to get out.

Back on her veranda, Nitza paused for a moment, and her fingers stroked the lid of the jar. 'A friend? Petakh Tikva?' Maybe. She had not the slightest doubt just who waited to meet her. And where...

The jar grew warm in her hands. If Kate really was going to meet Amos, Miriam wouldn't forgive her for not telling. Then again, if she did, Miriam might think that she had an interest. No. She couldn't say anything yet. And the more it turned in her mind, the more she felt a keen resentment towards Kate.

Kate stood by the doors as the bus from Tel Aviv turned into the Jerusalem bus station. As soon as they opened she jumped down the steps and sprinted across the concrete apron and out to the main road to catch the number four bus to Katamon. It was after eleven. She had never travelled this late in Israel before, and didn't know if there would be any buses -- or even if she'd be able to find Amos? And then what would she do in Jerusalem in the middle of the night on her own? Oh, it was impossible! All this planning and calculating just to snatch a few hours together. She really had gone crazy.

Just then a No.4 bus pulled up. Kate clutched some small change and jumped up the steps.

It was nearly midnight and Amos's head was a cauldron. Something must have happened in the kibbutz. His stomach ached yet his mind refused to accept that Kate wouldn't come. He hadn't wanted to leave the hostel in case she did and now he was really hungry. The grocers' shop at the end of the road -- the last place to get something to eat before morning, would soon close.

He crept back into the room, switched on his bedside lamp and tore a page from his notebook. The boy in the corner-bed twitched and half turned. Amos held his breath then relaxed as the sleeper slumped back again, breathing heavily. 'Back soon. A', he wrote in English capitals and made a hole in the paper; he would leave it on the door handle.

He clutched the paper and glanced round again at his two sleeping room-mates, then opened the door slowly lest the hinges creaked, and backed into the hall. It was in semi-darkness, with only the emergency lighting at the far end.

As he turned, he froze. There, in the half-light, about to tap on an adjacent door, was Kate!

Quietly, he closed the door. Kate dropped her bag, turned and fell against him and they hugged each other until it hurt.

'Amos. Amos. I missed the bus… I wondered what to do…? Which room?' The words spilled out. 'Wondered if you'd given up… Oh Amos.' She clutched at him, tears wetting her cheeks.

They kissed and clung together, then after a few minutes, Amos slipped back into his room, rucked up his bedclothes, took up a small bag he'd prepared and closed the door silently behind him.

'Come,' he said. 'We might just catch the last bus into the centre. Or it'll be a long walk!'

On the way, Kate told of Batya coming late; of going to Uri's room. Of the neighbour. Amos tensed. Nitza! Then relaxed. To hell with them all. Kate was here and that was all that mattered.

They hardly talked during the ride into town, just held one another, as if to make sure it wasn't a dream; nor on the walk to the hotel, when Amos darted aside to buy snacks at a late-night kiosk. Nor when they threw off their clothes and fell into bed and made love again and again, for the first time without fear of discovery. And finally fell asleep tucked against one another. They woke at dawn to make love again, then slept until the sunlight crept through the roller shutters.

Kate raised herself on one elbow. How marvellous it was to wake up beside him. She had never felt such exhilaration before. She tweaked his nose. 'Don't you have to put in an appearance with your Stone-Age men?' unwittingly, using the same expression as Miriam.

Amos reached up and kissed her nipple. This was how he wanted to wake every morning.

'Glutton,' she grinned. 'You've had all night.'

'And tonight,' he whispered. 'And I could stay here all day, Kate. All day as well.'

'With the chambermaid too, I suppose?'

'No. Just you, Kate. Just you,' he said and pulled her over, onto him.

It took them a long time to get dressed.

17

They arranged to meet at three in the Old City. Amos had to catch the end of the morning session and at least part of the afternoon session. Eli was bound to ask him about the proceedings; he could fill in the rest. The evening session was a social gathering with the Archaeology faculty at the university. Dr. Elisheva might ask about him, but he would risk skipping that.

Despite Kate's favourite Jerusalem pastime of browsing the English bookshops in Ben Yehuda Street, the hours dragged. She wandered around the alleyways of the *Suk* in the Old City, sustained by the warmth surging through her whole body as she thought of Amos. Never had she wanted something so much in her whole life.

They met up at the cafe in the Aqbat Darwish; over three months since that first hesitant meeting. But now, they openly gripped hands across the table, talking softly, with the aroma of cardamom rising from the tiny coffee cups and an intimacy that blotted out the same pink plastic table covers, the same surly barman.

Afterwards, the sky was a pale blue and a cool wind blew between the high stone walls, when they strolled over the damp cobbles towards St. Stephen's Street where Yusuf was sitting at his small, round table. Despite possibly meeting Shafik, Kate still felt obliged to see the old silversmith and Araf each time she came. Amos didn't mind; reminded him of how they had started. And anyway, they had all evening -- and night.

'Ah. Miss Kate.' Again the long, two-handed handshake, the wide smile. Araf was at school so the man went out himself to call for coffee, the letter from the Sufi lady still on the table. Business had only slightly improved. A few more Christian pilgrims coming through Jordan. Then, as they were about to go, Shafik came in, and almost bumped into Amos.

'Nice to see you, Kate.' Shafik was stiff, his smile thin.

'Hello,' said Kate, instinctively holding out her hand. He shook it warmly, glanced at Amos and nodded. Amos nodded back and smiled and they briefly shook hands. Shafik glanced back to Kate, his forehead creasing. 'But you're leaving, Kate?'

'Yes,' said Kate. 'We have to go, I'm afraid.'

'*Maalesh,*' said Shafik. 'But we'll see you again I hope.'

Kate moved into the doorway to go out. Yusuf hurriedly came forward and the little group stood bunched in the half-light.

'Oh. Yes. Sure.' Then she turned to the silversmith. 'Goodbye, Yusuf.'

'Goodbye, Miss Kate. You're always welcome.' The old man looked up and smiled at Amos. 'And you too, of course.'

Shafik stepped aside, expressionless, and with relief spreading through her whole body, Kate led Amos out into the street.

'Wasn't that pleased to see me, was he?' said Amos as they turned left. Kate just shrugged and squeezed his hand. At least Shafik would know her true situation.

Across the Via Dolorosa, the Souk was beginning to pack up but here and there, bright lights still shone on coat hangers of brilliant coloured scarves, and blue Hebron glassware glowed in the windows. Arabic music blared from a dozen small transistors, and everywhere the aroma of cumin and cardamom mingled with the acrid smell of kebabs grilling over charcoal.

They sat in a small, arched alcove, chewing minced *shishlik* on blackened skewers with chopped green salad, and slices of enormous onions, which Amos loved.

'Won't stop me kissing you, y'know,' grinned Kate, her chin greasy from the grilled meat.

Amos winked.

'Adds to the passion!'

After the meal and two cups of strong Turkish coffee, renewed, they strolled up the Street of the Chain and out through the Jaffa Gate where Amos led her up a steep pathway to a row of old, low, red-tiled houses.

'*Yemin Moshe*,' he said, 'the first Jewish houses outside the Old City.' He nodded to a stumpy round tower nearby, 'with their own windmill.' His hand stroked the back of her neck. 'Can you imagine it Kate? The Eighteen Nineties, just the city walls over there, this row of houses and nothing. Nothing but bare rocks and a few olive trees outside the old walls.'

'Weird,' she murmured, glancing round at the lights of the modern city behind them. And under the orange city-glow on the low cloud that had gathered at nightfall, they walked up narrow road into the New City. 'Like going up the Falls Road to the Shankill,' she'd once joked to Jill.

Leaning on the low concrete wall that ran along Independence Gardens, they gazed across to the floodlit ramparts of the Old City.

'Strange to think, Kate,' Amos murmured, wrapping his arm around Kate's shoulder and pulling her close, 'that only a few months ago, all you could see across there was pitch darkness. And with the chance of a sniper's bullet from those ramparts, so this wall used to be head high.' Kate remained silent, not wanting to break the spell that was holding them so close.

Amos was staring out to beyond the Old City, where Ammunition Hill was hidden in the darkness.

'It was Ya'ir going like that, Kate, that made me think,' he began softly, 'that life is too short.' Looking over her shoulder he added, 'and the war isn't over, Kate. A battle maybe. But not the war. No,' he continued after a short pause, 'like with your friend Shafik, the Palestinians will never accept the occupation, Kate, and none of our politicians have the balls to use this opportunity for peace. So it will go on, Kate, one way or another. And if so. Who knows?'

Amos hugged her against him, his voice resonating in her chest.

'And the same in the kibbutz, Kate, arguments with the Motti's and the like, fighting to preserve our ideals and way of life. And those of us who want to keep all that becoming a diminishing minority.' He suddenly reached down and kissed her, with a passion that was almost violent. 'So I'm fed up with fighting, whatever the battle. I want to live to the full, now. Now, Kate. And to live it with you.' He pulled away, his face half in shadow. 'Whatever has to happen.'

She looked up. His broad face glowed softly in the reflected light, his fair hair standing out against the dark night sky.

'Amos. I -. Oh God, Amos. I love you so much.' She threw her arms around him and hugged him to her, his warm body seeming to wrap around her completely and both oblivious to the passers by along King George Street. 'I didn't… I don't want to push you, Amos. Just that like I said, as we were we couldn't go on.' She leaned away and looked up straight into his eyes. 'But I want you to be absolutely certain, Amos, because if not, painful as it will be, I will understand. And that after this, I have to get away.

For good. Okay?'

Amos tensed and again his stomach clenched. Despite the guilt at the pain he would cause, he was certain now that he wanted to with live Kate. He closed his eyes for a moment. Very soon, tomorrow, next week latest, he would have to think of what to do and when; and how.

'Listen Kate. My mind is made up,' Amos said firmly. 'But I have to do it in my own way and in my own time. What I want you to know is that from now on Kate, it is us, you and me.' And for a while they stood hugging close together, gazing across to the floodlit ramparts of the Old City.

Rain spotted the pavement as they walked down the broad avenue of Lincoln Street. Neither wanted to talk, Amos feeling light headed at having made his decision and having told her; Kate relieved, knowing at last which way they were going, despite the problems she could see, yet at the same time wondering whether Amos had seen them too.

Wanting to lighten up after that conversation, as they turned right into King David Road, Amos nodded to a tall, phallic tower of rose-tinted limestone that rose from a domed building, all glowing in the soft floodlight.

'This is *Imka*, as we call the YMCA.' He pointed across the road. 'And over there is the King David Hotel.' He laughed. 'In the old British Mandate days, the Jewish establishment met over there, and the Arabs with their British advisers, in here, both scheming against one another, just a hundred metres apart!'

Inside the lobby, Kate looked up at the domed ceilings with their intricate marble and mosaic inlays.

'My old art teacher always urged us to come here,' Amos grinned. 'Said it was the only building in the whole damn country without square, straight lines!'

At that moment the short, thin doorman came towards them, dressed in colonial, white suit and red *tarbush* on his head. Amos nodded, then turned towards the door.

'Come, Kate. Too expensive for us - even a cup of coffee!'

The wind had changed to blow from the west and it began to rain for real, so they took the number four bus into town and had coffee in the fluorescent lights of a Ben Yehuda Street cafe. Half-way to the hotel, the heavens opened up and they were soaked by the time they reached the lobby and the one radiator in their room was just luke-warm.

'Only one place for it,' hissed Amos.

'Could have fooled me,' said Kate, wriggling out of her sodden jeans. 'Come.' She gasped when their cold skins touched under the bedclothes, then clung to him, still and silent, as the bed warmed up. And now, in the darkness, with all the time in the world, they made love and rested, then again, until they fell fast asleep.

Amos woke. A grey morning light filtered through the roller shutter slats. Kate lay on her back, eyes wide open and stared up. He lightly kissed her.

'Interesting ceiling?' He smiled, raising himself on one elbow, and his other hand smoothed her hair across the pillow.

'Oh. I'm looking far beyond that, sure. Far, far away into space.' She turned to look into his face. 'Just us. And nothing.'

They lay close like this, their bodies almost one, at first Amos felt confident. Yes, it would work out. Yet as he lay there longer, his head on her breast and his eyes half-closed, in the grey morning the realities began to pile in on him. How to tell Miriam? When? The kids? The break up? The scandal. He and Kate in their own room in the kibbutz. Recriminations. He breathed deeply. The kibbutz would just have to accept it; make allowances for

Kate. After all, he was a founder member. It was his home. He was respected, well liked.

Opening his eyes, Amos lifted his head and ran his fingers around the small breast, then down to the angle of her hip bone.

'Sure you could you live on the kibbutz, Kate?'

'Now, he comes and asks me.' She grinned. 'I could live with you anywhere, Amos.'

'Seriously, I mean.'

Kate drew her head away for the smallest of moments. 'Well, truthfully Amos, to live there permanently, I'm not sure. It's a small community and some of them won't hide their feelings.'

Amos knew she was speaking true; yet his heart told him he had to fight like a lion for what he wanted.

'At first,' he began, 'maybe you're right, Kate. But soon, people will see our love and understand. Sure, there will be problems, but we have so much going for us together. Isn't that what's most important: our lives, our love? And people in the kibbutz like you, Kate. How could they not?'

Kate didn't respond. When they were together like this, she too felt so wonderful. Where would she find another love like this. Yet nothing exists in a vacuum, especially where people are concerned. And although she could see all the problems ahead, she wasn't sure that Amos had, but they had talked enough. She rolled over and lay on him, their bodies as one and breathing together, before the daylight strengthened and they had to get up to go back.

After breakfast at a cafe in Agrippas Street, Amos left Kate at the hotel while he went to pick up his things from the Seminar. The rain had ceased but the air was still damp and drizzly. The old man from Haifa was just leaving his room as he came in.

'Huh. Was wondering what to do with your gear. The cleaners are coming round.'

'No. It's okay. Thanks anyway.' Amos saw the quizzical expression on the man's face. 'Met some boys from the unit,' he said. 'Haven't seen each other since the war.' Didn't sound convincing.

'Pity you missed the reception last night,' the man grinned. 'That idiot was still hawking his Essex hand-axes theory around.' He started to walk away then turned. 'Oh. Elisheva sends her regards. Said to tell you she wants to come down and see your collection again some time.'

'Thanks. Sure. I'll contact her. And regards to my dad if you see him.' The man had told him they were in the same Union.

'*Beseder*,' the man nodded. '*Shalom*.'

'*Shalom*,' said Amos and went into the room, wondering why he felt so tense. It would all soon be out in the open anyway. Yet he wanted to do it with his timing, in his own way; the possibility of it leaking out before he had prepared the ground still made him anxious.

He went back to the hotel to meet Kate, and they took the number twelve to the central bus station. Their plan was to travel down to Masmiyya Junction together. He would stay on Beersheba bus, arriving as expected from Jerusalem, but Kate would get off and catch a bus up to Tel Aviv. Then she would come back later as though from Petakh Tikva. Planning. Plotting. Soon, it would all be over.

Amos and Kate managed a find a seat together, and all the way down the winding road from Jerusalem pressed against each other, clutching hands while watching the pine trees and white rocks fly past, each kilometre, nearer to their parting.

As they drew into the roadside at Masmiyya junction, Kate

raised his hand and kissed it. Amos stood up to let her pass, and after she alighted with a few other passengers, he sat down again to watch her through the window.

Motti was on a bus going to Tel Aviv to pick up a set of bearings for the new sorghum drill then staying overnight at his parents in Ramat Gan. The sudden rain yesterday had set back sowing the winter wheat for a few days but he was pleased. The grey skies were promising more to come; with the arable crops, rain was everything.

It was still raining slightly when his bus drew into Masmiyya Junction and stopped. The door opened and people started to climb on, closing umbrellas and unzipping their coats. Suddenly a mop of red-tinged hair caught his eye. Motti looked again, and his mind started to buzz; it was that volunteer, Kate -- the one who'd caused all the fuss with the Arab boy. She must have just come on. What was she doing in Masmiyya?

At that moment, a bus from Jerusalem alongside them began to pull away going, south, and as it did, the girl leaned down and pressed her face against the window. Curious, Motti followed her gaze. And caught his breath. Staring back from a window of the other bus as it edged past into the main road, was a man. Amos! He was sure it was. Yes. Hadn't he been at an archaeology meeting in Jerusalem? He looked again as the girl sat down a few rows in front of him, fluffing out her hair. Suddenly he remembered what Rami had told him about that night behind the volunteers' huts.

Motti sat back, a warm glow creeping through his body as his bus edged out onto the road and took-off north towards Tel Aviv. So. Amos was with that girl in Jerusalem. Well, well, well. Amos, the man of principles. Knocking it off with a volunteer. 'Yea, how the mighty have fallen...'

At the central bus-station, Motti watched Kate as she hurried down the steps and out. He was sure she hadn't noticed him was sitting two seats behind her, and after she crossed over to the next bus stand he got down, and keeping in the crowds stood on the other platform, watching. Sure enough, as he'd guessed, Kate went to join the queue for the Beersheba bus, as though she was coming back from Tel Aviv. He waited until it took off then headed out of the station to catch his local bus to Ramat Gan, his stomach warm. He couldn't wait to get back tomorrow and tell the boys in the garage. If the clothes store was the kibbutz women's radio station, the garage was the men's.

18

As Amos got off the bus and hurried up the side road, it started to rain again. Having noticed Motti staring from window of the other bus, his head was spinning. He tried to console himself that that big mouth couldn't prove anything. And anyway, everything would be out in the open soon enough. But he wanted to do it in his own way — and in his own time.

His stomach clenched, wondering what that big mouth would do, and making those wonderful two days in Jerusalem feeling now a long way away. Turning up his collar and shouldering his pack, Amos strode in through the gateway and glanced at his watch. Time to pick up the kids.

Miriam got to the room late. Amos had already picked Noa up from the children's house and was making her a warm orange squash. Whatever the weather, the kids were always thirsty.

'Sorry I'm late,' Miriam wiped the rain from her face as she hung up her jacket. 'Preparations for the *Hanukah* party.' She came in and kissed him. 'How was the conference?'

Amos plugged in the kettle again.

'Great. Bit of fun too. Some English *shlemiel* arguing with old Yerucham about animal-faced hand-axes.' He spooned coffee into two cups. 'Tell you later.' The kettle hissed, then boiled. How time was flying. December already, and Hanukah next week. Celebrations, kids' parties and helping with decorations in the kindergarten all became jumbled in his mind, mingled with an unsettling apprehension.

Amos looked across the room. Ran was making a cut-out model of Yehuda Maccabee's sword and shield for the school, Noa was colouring in a paper candle to wear on her headband. Suddenly his stomach heaved as he pictured the room without him.

His stomach tight, he handed Miriam her coffee.

'I'd better see Reuvkeh after supper,' he said, sitting on the bed with his. 'He'll want a hand with the *Hanukiah* lights on the water tower as usual, I suppose.'

Kate came in on the Tel Aviv bus at six. Shulamit and Hanokh had got off too -- good for her alibi.

There were no surprises on the work rota board; she was working in the Gan the following afternoon. But as she strode along the narrow, rain-pooled path to the huts, so the anxieties and doubts surfaced again.

Jill was enjoying a cuppa.

'Made with real 'Brook Bonds', she laughed, 'cadged from a new arrival,' and made Kate one too.

'Y'know, Jill,' said Kate as she dried her hair with a pink towel, 'when I'm with him, it's so perfect. Everything so clear. That we'll be together. That we're -- Oh God, I know it sounds naff, that we seem made for each other, sure.' Kate took a few sips then clenched her hands around the mug, in her lap. And it's what he wants too. I haven't pushed it. Honest I haven't.'

She closed her eyes for a second.

'And hell. I know I'm selfish. But I love him so much Jill.' She looked into Jill's face. 'I'm no chicken, you know. I'm nearly twenty five. And he's the first man I've ever felt for like this. Can you understand that, Jill?'

Jill leaned back against the wall and rubbed her chin with her knuckles. They were both sitting on Kate's bed. In the silence, rain drummed on the tiled roof and the wind scraped eucalyptus branches against the wall of the hut.

'Sure, I believe you, Kate...' she paused and sipped her tea, 'and I don't want to be a wet blanket...'

'But?'

'Well, you'll be breaking up a family. Have you thought about that, Kate? And then the logistics. You'll have to move into the kibbutz; he won't move out -- won't want not to see his kids. She spread her hands. Heck. You know the score. And look mate, if he does break it up for you, it will stir up a beehive the kibbutz. And we'll all be dragged into it.'

Kate gazed into the bottom of her mug then looked up.

'Sure. The practicalities, Jill. I know, and I haven't stopped thinking about them too.' Her eyes began to water. 'But I know we can. Together, we'll manage it.' Kate gripped the mug, her knuckles turning white. 'We'll find a way, Jill -- we will, so.'

Jill sipped her tea, silent, remembering Sean. That Celtic stubbornness...

After taking the children back and supper, Amos and Miriam went back to the room, and later that night when they made love, Amos found it still surprisingly easy. But as he lay back in the darkness, Miriam's warm body beside him, nagging doubts pricked again at the back of his brain. Was what he had so bad, that he had to break it all up?

With the wind moaning through the trees and rain pattering against the closed shutters, Amos couldn't sleep, his mind buzzing. Suddenly, he got up and went out to the sink. Pouring a glass of water, he stood staring at the wall, taking small sips. The logistics. How? When? He and Kate in their own room and he still near the kids. They'd come round, or he'd go to see them in Miriam's room. True, Kate would have to find a different place of work, but she was capable and confident; that shouldn't prove difficult.

Amos lay on his side, Miriam's bottom pressed against him. God. Miriam. She would be so hurt. He would have to live with that. But she was still attractive. There was Eldad. And others. She was strong, would make her own life.

Just that he had to make the break carefully, in his own way. But when?

Next week were all the Hanukah parties with the kids. It would have wait until after Hanukah. Kate would understand. Yes, after Hanukah.

The week passed and the eight days of *Khanukah* arrived, the Festival of Lights. After *Khanukah*, Amos had said in Jerusalem. Kate found herself counting the days, but wouldn't push. It was for him alone to decide. And the waiting was as agonising as she had foreseen.

The December wind continued was still blowing when Shabbat dawned, but the rain clouds had been driven across the Jordan and up into the mountains of Moab. Kate rose at six to a blustery but bright sunny morning and hurrying to the children's house, her hair tied back, she clutched her sweater around her against the wind.

She called in at the kitchen to pick up breakfast for the children. Orna, Motti's wife was on early shift. Kate didn't know her well, but nodded and smiled.

'*Shalom* Orna.' Rubbing her hands from the chill wind she added, 'no rain at least.'

Orna finished putting cream cheese and fresh vegetables into the bottom container, a dozen fresh eggs and sliced *khallah* in the top one and closed the lids.

'Miriam on Shabbat?' she asked, still looking at the containers.

'Yes. Sure,' replied Kate.

'Uhuh. Well, this is yours,' murmured Orna, still looking down with a faint smile on her lips.

Brown leaves skittered across the path as Kate hurried to the Gan.

Opening the door to the kindergarten, she went in and clanked the containers on the marble worktop. Immediately, children ran out of their rooms and clustered around her, waiting for breakfast. And Orna's knowing smile went from her mind.

'*Boker tov, Ket*,' they chorused, pronouncing her name as though it was spelled with a short 'e'.

'*Boker tov, koolam*,' she replied in Miriam's sing-song voice, adding, '*Hitlabesh, bevakashah*,' the litany of Miriam's child-care words and telling them to get dressed. Through work and from the children, she was picking up a smattering of the difficult language.

It was cold inside the building and she lit the two 'Fireside' heaters, pointing them towards the tables.

'*Koom*,' she called through the doorway to Netta. There were always the two or three who didn't get up and had to be coaxed. The girl lay on her back, sucking her thumb and waggling her knees from side to side. Kate sighed and sat by her for a moment. If only she knew enough Hebrew to ask the girl what was troubling her. 'Broody, mate. Getting all maternal,' Jill would laugh. Kate had never thought much about having children — too busy charging around the world. But now that she contemplated living in the kibbutz…

The children running back from the toilets shook her from her daydreaming and she went back to the dining room to fry their breakfast eggs.

'I want an eye,' shouted Gil. Sunnyside up, Kate had called it in her holiday waitressing job.

'An eye upside down,' called Taliah, 'but not hard.'

'*Khavitah. Khavitah*,' Shlomit pulled at Kate's jeans, demanding an omelette. One by one, at her own speed, Kate fried the eggs and sat the children down at the tables, cutting tomatoes and cucumbers, ladling out yoghurt to those who wanted it, wishing she had three more pairs of hands.

After breakfast, it was Shabbat and once again the struggle to keep them all clean and tidy until nine o'clock when they dispersed to their parents' rooms.

When the children had all gone, Kate took the containers back to the kitchen. Afterwards, she had a two-hour break until the kids came back at lunch time. When she strolled back to her hut, two men were on top of the water tower struggling with a huge, metal *hanukiah* candelabra.

'*Le'at. Le'at*,' one shouted. She stopped and looked up. It was Amos. At the foot of the tower, his son Ran was holding a coil of electric cable. She tried to catch his eye, glancing up again and again as she walked slowly past, yet trying not to attract attention to herself. Amos didn't notice and Kate walked on to her hut. Nothing had changed; they still couldn't even speak to one another in public. The euphoria of Jerusalem had blown away in the cool, damp breeze.

Having fixed-up the candelabra, Amos cursed as he went down to the garage; rain was threatening. Tonight was the first night of the festival: switching on the lights on the water-tower, then the children's torchlight procession down to the volley-ball pitch to begin the celebrations.

Rami and Shumikeh were in the tractor shed, bolting discs onto the harrow. Motti was fitting the new bearings into the seed drill.

'Need some paraffin for the kids' torches,' Amos called to Moshe, the chief mechanic. 'Got a key for the pump?' Amos could still remember the days when there was no such thing as a padlock in the kibbutz. Nor locks on the doors. Everyone was trusted. But as the population grew and more traffic came in and out the front gate, so came the petty thefts and things needed to be secured.

'Key's in the top drawer,' he replied, nodding to the work bench.

As he walked across the yard, Amos felt the other three watching him. Defiantly, he turned and stared. Motti looked down at his spanner, smirking. No. None of them would say anything to his face. It was the whispering behind his back that concerned him. And who else had Motti told?

At six that evening, it was already dark and in small groups, parents and children congregated behind the dining hall. Each child carried a tin can of paraffin-soaked hessian nailed to a short stick, to serve as a flaming torch. At half past seven, Reuven tickled the accordion and some of the smokers went along with cigarette lighters. One by one, flames flickered into the stiff breeze and the long crocodile began to snake down towards the basketball pitch, all singing at the tops of their voices while treading to the rhythm of the song that even the tiniest knew;

'Sevivon sov sov sov,

Hanukah hoo khag tov…

Spinning top, spinning round, Hanukah is a wonderful festival…'

Miriam walked with Ran. Amos with Noa, shielding her

burning torch from the wind. Suddenly, a strong gust blew it out, sending acrid smoke into her eyes.

'It's gone out. My torch had gone out, daddy,' she cried. 'My torch has gone out'. Crouching down, Amos took a lighter and tried to re-kindle it, but the wind was too strong. Noa started to whimper.

Kate heard the crying and recognising Noa's voice, she looked across. Amos was crouching by the girl, soothing her as he tried to re-light the torch. Then came the cry of joy as it burst into flame and Amos hugging the child. Kate shivered. All she could do was stand and watch Amos with his family while she was alone, the chilling wind in her face. She slipped in beside Jill, consoling herself that at least here, she could see him.

A small stage of planks on orange boxes stood at one end of the pitch. The choir, in white shirts, opened the festivities, hurriedly putting on their jackets and coats as soon as they stepped down. Yaacov followed with a short piece on the significance of the festival: the struggle for freedom and for Jewish independence, linking it to the recent war, still fresh in everyone's minds. Behind them, high on the water tower, the electric lamps of the large candelabra blazed into the night across the fields and out into the arid plain, points of lights from distant settlements answering, each sending its message of freedom and renewal into the winter night.

On the stage, Ran lit the first flame of a large Hanukiah, followed by other children, one by one lighting the eight branches of a candelabra, each reading a short excerpt from the Book of the Maccabees by the light of the flickering torches. And then with the flames gusting in the stiff breeze, the choir mounted the stage again and everyone joined in to round off the opening ceremony.

'Community,' murmured Jill. 'You can feel it.' She rubbed her arms. 'And talk about talent? Less than two hundred adults and there's a choir, a dancing group, dramatics, committees, and God knows what else.'

'And doughnuts,' hissed Roger.

'Shut up, peasant,' she snapped.

Kate nodded. Community. It was what she too liked about the kibbutz, and had found nowhere else -- except perhaps in her short time in working with Mairead in the Falls. She glanced around the faces of the kibbutzniks, illuminated and shadowed black and yellow in the flickering flames of the torches, reminding her of one of Goya's black-and-white paintings. But how would that community react to her and Amos if and when he broke with Miriam?

Miriam had outlined the history of the festival to her as they helped the children hang up decorations on their walls. Now, as she watched and listened, Kate caught snatches of the songs she had heard in the Gan. But as she stood there, she was gripped by a feeling that even with the friendship and warmth, she was still a stranger, an outsider. Something, that despite Robert and the many sincere friends at Uni, she had also felt in the Protestant areas of Belfast.

The throng began to make its way up to the dining hall, the children's torches spluttering and some fizzling out. In the semi-darkness Kate edged her way towards Amos. Soon, she was walking beside Miriam.

'Shalom, Kate.' Miriam smiled, her teeth white in the reflected flames. 'So. Now you have seen our Christmas!'

''Noa's paper-candle band suddenly slipped over her eyes. As Miriam bent down to straighten it, Amos reached across in the darkness and touched Kate's hand. Instinctively, Kate glanced sideways -- and sensed the pale outlines of two faces looking towards them, one immediately turning its head away as she looked back.

Soon everyone had gathered in the dining hall. Pancakes and doughnuts were laid out, together with bottles of orange juice and wine and beer, for the *Hanukah* party. Then Reuven tickled the keys on the accordion and soon the huge circle of the Horra filled the centre; round and round, hands on shoulders, feet stamping, heads thrown back in a spirited rendition from The Song of Songs:

Yonati bekhegveh hasela, yonati beseter hamadrega…

Oh. My dove in the clefts of the rock

Hidden amongst the terraces… the dancers beating the time with the steps: one, two, three, kick, swing and turn, back kick, one two three… On and on and round and round, singing and dancing that would go on until midnight.

The *sabras* danced easily with the rhythm of the song, legs loose and nimble, bodies swaying this way then that. The volunteers joined in too, ungainly in comparison but swept along in the ecstasy, singing la, la, la, with the tune, hour after hour the dance would go on, the songs changing, people dropping out, others joining in, but the circle continuing, round and round, on and on.

Kate, wearing her blue dress positioned herself in the circle opposite Amos, hair loose and flowing, eyes darting at him from time to time and he returning just brief winks and hint of a smile.

When the *horra* ceased and the couple dances began, Amos. Amos danced with Miriam. He ached to sweep Kate up in a wild *kravkoviak*. Once he could have and everyone would have taken it as a joke; now he knew he daren't. Instead as Miriam dropped out laughing and gasping, he grabbed Nitza by the waist and swung her into a furious *tcherkassia*.

'*Khamor!*' ass, she hissed. 'Think people haven't noticed. Come to your senses yet?'

'With you, always,' he laughed - a choked laugh.

'Idiot,' she puffed. 'I hate you.' They whirled around the floor, Reuven's fingers flying across the keys, the music faster and faster until not even they could keep up and they crashed against the tables and out of the dance.

After a moment, when his breathlessness had subsided, Amos stood up looked around for Kate, but she was nowhere to be seen.

He sat down, breathing heavily, the energy ebbing from his body, but it wasn't from the dancing. Miriam stood up again and held out her hand.

He shook his head. 'I'm getting old!' he said, not sure if she heard him against the music and his thumping heart. Kate had vanished.

19

Taking advantage of a dry, sunny day Amos was out in the cotton field, the tractor whining in second gear and behind him and rotovator flails macerating the dry cotton bushes. Following in his wake, hooded crows pecked at the disturbed soil and a flock of red-faced goldfinches flitted amongst the bare stalks.

Amos was glad to get out into the open air, on his own. Whether imagined or real, the pressure of wagging tongues and sly glances was getting to him. He was worried about Kate. She'd looked so gorgeous at the Hanukah party then suddenly disappeared, and he hadn't managed to talk to her since.

At the end of the field, Amos glanced at his watch; four hours to lunch. And if he didn't see Kate then, it would be almost another week since the party. He had to see her, to reassure her. But how to do that without them being seen together.

When he came in after work the following day, his room was strangely empty. Miriam wasn't there. The children's houses had a well-worn pattern and rhythm; Kate should have been working the afternoon shift to give Miriam her afternoon break.

He was drying himself after his shower, when Miriam's footsteps sounded on the veranda. Half opening the door, he peered out.

'Trouble in the Gan?' he smiled.

'You can say that again. Kate's sick. I only heard at breakfast time. Aviva couldn't find a replacement so I had to carry on this afternoon. God, I'm tired.' She untied her headscarf and threw it on the table. 'Anyway. At least Hedva will work this evening.'

When he'd finished and Miriam went in to shower, Amos plugged in the kettle and took out the cups, his stomach tight and hand trembling as he spooned out the coffee. He was imagining all kinds of dreadful illness but couldn't help but think that whatever it was, he was to blame.

At supper, Eli and Bilha joined him and Miriam at the table.

'Nu. So the conference was great, eh?' Eli grinned. 'And how was Elisheva? Still coming to see our collection I hope?'

'Aha!' Bilha wagged her finger. 'And who's this Elisheva?' She turned to Eli. 'And we all think it's just a load of old stones you lot go to see.' She turned back and winked at Miriam. 'Men. Can't trust them anywhere!'

'Doctor Elisheva, if you please.' Eli nudged his wife. 'Head of the Prehistory department. And she's forty-five if a day!' They all laughed, most of all Amos, relieved of having to fabricate his time at the conference. Then Bilha turned to Kate.

'*Az.* So, Kate's sick?' Like most of the Sabras, nearly all her questions started with *Az.*

'Yes,' said Miriam. 'Jill came down to the Gan to tell me.' She glanced at her watch. 'Reminds me. I have to see Aviva after supper for a replacement and let Kate take a *shabbat* and get over it.' As the two women discussed Kate, Amos sensed Eli watching his reaction. Eli wasn't the type to tackle him just on the strength of idle gossip, but he seemed to know something -- and if he did, others must too.

After supper, Miriam buttonholed Aviva by the roster board. Amos left them to it and went out into the cold, moonless night.

At that moment, Jill appeared out of the darkness, holding some plates and a small plastic container. She must have brought food to Kate. Glancing round to check that they were alone, he asked softly: 'How's Kate? Miriam said she didn't feel well.'

Jill stopped and turned to him.

'Nurse says it's just a bad cold,' and looking straight at him, added quickly, 'but she hasn't been herself since the party!'

'Wish her well, from me.'

'Sure.' Jill walked on a few paces then suddenly stopped. 'Oh,' she called softly over her shoulder, 'but I'm not going straight back to the room,' and carried on through the doorway.

Amos stood for a moment, his brain whirling. He stood at the edge of the patio, swaying forward and back, fists clenched and his brain seething. Miriam was with Aviva, and was probably going back down to the Gan afterwards to see Hedva. Perhaps…

Three people came out of the dining hall, laughing. Amos strode away down the path as though to Noa's house. But instead of going in, he continued around the back, then between the babies' house and the deep shelter, and along the track through the trees.

Standing in the shadows, he looked towards Kate's door. The veranda light was on, but it was quiet, all the volunteers up at supper. He remembered standing here on guard, that first night. Was it only a few months ago?

Moving quickly from tree to tree, he stepped softly onto the wooden boards, hurriedly opened the door and slipped inside.

The small room light was on but the large room was dark.

'That you, Jill?'

Amos's heart thumped at Kate's voice through the dividing doorway.

'No,' he said softly. 'It's me, Kate.'

Kate was sitting on her bed, dressed in jeans and an old brown sweater. Her hair hung loose, her face pale. As he came close, she leaned up and hugged him to her, burying her face in his stomach.

'Oh, Amos. Amos,' she murmured. 'Amos.' Tears trickled down her cheeks and soaked into his shirt.

They clung together, Amos tense and starting at each footstep on the path behind the window, or a door slamming in an adjacent hut.

'Just a little longer, Kate. Then we'll be together. Soon.'

'Oh, Amos. You don't understand. You have your work, your family. You're busy all the time. And I'm stuck here. On my own. Thinking. Wondering…'

Kate straightened up and wiped her eyes.

'Oh God, I sound like a right bloody neurotic and it's just not me. I'm never like this, Amos. It's not me at all and I hate it.' She sniffed and after a short pause continued. 'And then there's Motti. And Orna. And those boys from the garage looking at me all the time -- like I'm an easy lay.'

Despite the cool night, Amos began to sweat.

'Oh, Kate. Kate. I just wanted to get the Hanukah week over. The kid's parties. You know.'

'I know, Amos. I know. And I do trust you. I do.'

Kate fell against him, and they lay back together on the bed. Slipping her hand into his shirt, Kate rested her head on his chest.

'I love you so much, Amos, but I've got to get away from here, until something changes. If we lived together it would be different. But like this, not able even to meet -- to be the only people in the whole kibbutz who can't dance together!'

Amos looked across the room. Van Goth's yellow chair glowed dimly on the light green wall.

'Please, Kate. Don't go,' he whispered. 'With the *Hanukah* parties over, next week I'll settle it; tell Miriam, go to Eliezar for a spare room for us. I will, Kate. I will. And we'll be together.'

Kate snuggled into the shape of his body. She didn't want to go, either. But she had to have some respite, even for a few days despite her own fears -- that if she went, he might delay the break; not manage it at all…

Each with their fears and doubts, they lay there in the semi-darkness, their bodies close and warm — and completely oblivious to the passing minutes.

'You won't get anyone as good as Kate at this short notice,' muttered Aviva in the dining hall lobby. She rubbed off another name and transferred it to the 'sick' column. 'Looks like we're starting a bout of flu.'

Eventually, Miriam did get Hedva. Someone else would travel with the school to the area sports competition. Miriam heaved a sigh of relief and walked out into the cool night. It was later than she'd intended but she would go down to the Gan for a minute.

Hedva was washing up the supper dishes.

'Any problems?'

Hedva shook her head. 'Good as gold. All asleep.' She nodded to Eyal, who was reading a book by the table. 'Nearly all.'

Miriam went and sat beside him on a small chair. He always took the whole evening to calm down, especially now that Brakha had just another one.

'Come, Eyal.' Gently, she closed the book and led him across the room, then sat beside him on his bed for a few minutes until he was still.

When she came back to the room, Miriam was surprised that

Amos wasn't there. It was nine o'clock. Yapping with Eli about the conference? But then she'd seen Eli going to the babies' house. She stood in the centre of the room, strangely restless and happened to glance in the small mirror on the bookcase. Was that a grey hair? Suddenly, she thought of Kate; she had never been sick before. She ought to find out how she was, see how long she would be off work.

A footstep sounded on the veranda. Amos tensed; perhaps Jill was coming back. Suddenly there was a tap at the door.

'Hi, Kate?' It was Miriam's voice! Then another tap -- stronger. Amos started. Here! *Elohim!*

The door handle turned and the door opened.

'Kate. It's Miriam. Are you okay?' With three short steps, Miriam crossed the ante-room and poked her head through the doorway. And froze.

Kate was too muzzy and didn't move, but Amos had managed to sit up, his mouth open, as though seeking for something to say. In the faint light from the ante-room, Miriam saw only his shocked face -- and the supine form on the bed beside him.

'Amos. You --? You pig! You…' She wanted to say more, but the words stuck in her throat. Clenching her fists, and with her whole body quivering, she spun round and ran out, leaving the door wide open.

Running away down the path, and between trying to catch her breath, Miriam started to cry, but approaching the dining hall, she knew she couldn't be seen like this. Beside the laundry, she turned aside and in the shadows, leaned against the corrugated sheet, shaking and sobbing, tears streaming down her face.

After a few minutes, she braced herself and stopped. She was Miriam. She was strong. She would show him the bastard. Taking a handkerchief from her pocket, she straightened up, wiped her eyes and blew her nose. Then breathing deeply, she turned and with clenched fists, walked on swiftly past the dining hall and down to the room.

Amos held his head in his hands for a few seconds then stood up, his legs trembling.

'*Elohim*. Oh my God, Kate!'

Kate sat up, and hunched forward.

'Oh, Amos. What now, Amos?'

He leaned down and kissed her.

'I'd better get back to my room.'

Kate clutched his arms.

'I love you Amos. Always,' she said in a whisper -- though there was no longer any need. They kissed.

'I love you, Kate,' Amos whispered and kissed her again. And with his head burning and his body trembling, he hurried out leaving the door wide open.

Kate sat forward, her stomach turning and her head aching. It was cold and she clutched her sweater about her, feeling as though she'd been punched. And suddenly her mind flipped back to that day in school when the teacher had hit her with the heavy ruler, and she'd run home to her mother, crying.

When she'd burst through the door sobbing out her tale, her father was there. 'No one is going to treat my little girl like that he'd snapped,' and grabbing his jacket, took her back to have it out with the teacher. But Dad couldn't help her now. In this she was on her own.

Amos cut swiftly through the trees behind the school and made a beeline for the room. Finding it empty, he stood in the middle of the floor breathing heavily, hands limp at his sides.

After a minute or so, he grabbed a magazine from the bookshelf and sank down in the easy chair, his body quivering. He didn't have to wait long.

Miriam burst into the room and stood over him, fists clenched, her face white and taut.

'Just what the hell do you think you're playing at?'

Amos looked up, trying to avoid her eyes.

'Playing at what?' he said lamely.

'Screwing around. In Kate's room, *Nokhel!* You stinking cheat!'

Her whole body was shaking but it was with anger, black anger. Her eyes were slits, her face hard and her mouth tight, jaw jutting towards him.

'All this time, I've been patient with you Amos. Your damn moods; your silences. Thinking it was from the war; from Ya'ir. And all the while it was because you were messing about.' Tears formed in her eyes. 'And with someone I trusted, someone who worked with our kids, Amos!' She lashed out and caught him across the side of his head. 'Bastard!'

It was the very first time either of them had ever been violent. Amos jerked his head back, the shock hurting much more than the sting.

'Damn you! And that bloody girl!' Miriam felt her voice rising and abruptly stopped. The neighbours would find out soon enough -- and the rest of the kibbutz, but for the moment she wanted to keep it between them. 'Tell me,' she hissed, *'Mah khaser?* Is our marriage that bad? How could you do this? Me. Us. The kids. You lousy pig!'

Turning away from him, she slumped down onto the bed, tears running freely down her cheeks.

Amos was thinking, fast. No point in denying anything. He

had rehearsed in his mind over and again what he would say, and this was the chance to tell her. But now, faced with it, he couldn't find the words, or the courage.

'Look, Miriam,' he began, unable to look at her -- he never could handle tears. 'Yes. I went to see Kate. I thought she was upset.'

Miriam sat up.

'Upset? *She* was upset! God! And me? What about me? Me, thinking all the time you were still upset about Ya'ir, the kibbutz, the arguments with Motti…' She took out a handkerchief and wiped her eyes, then blew her nose. 'So. How long has it been going on?' Miriam leaned towards him, shaking her fist. 'She was in Jerusalem with you, wasn't she. Wasn't she?' Miriam let out a deep breath then sat back, arms folded tightly across her chest. '*Nu*. So where's it all leading, Amos? Tell me.'

Amos continued staring along the zigzag lines, up to the fringes and then back again. Yes. He should tell her all about him and Kate. Everything. This was the opportunity. But try as he might, he couldn't, his mouth like parchment, the words sticking in his throat as he suddenly imagined Noa sitting on that carpet, her wide brown eyes staring up at him.

'I don't know. It's difficult; complicated. I… Yes. I have been thinking about Ya'ir; the state of things here…'

'No, Amos,' Miriam cut in and shook her hand at him. 'It's quite simple. This is your wife. And here is your family. That's all.' She thumped her fist on her knee. 'Damn you. I love you, Amos. And I won't let you ruin our lives. I won't.' Footsteps sounded along the path outside, then died away. Amos looked down. Silence. 'Amos. Look at me.' He looked up again. Their eyes met, but he said nothing. Miriam breathed out.

'I'm exhausted, Amos. I just don't know.' She stood up. 'I'm going to bed.'

Miriam went out to the shower. When she came back, she was in her long winter nightdress. Until now, she had always changed in the room.

'And just keep your distance,' she spat, '*Khazzir:* you pig. You and your early morning tricks! I don't know why I don't just throw you out!'

After she switched out the lights, Amos remained sitting in the chair, his head throbbing and his stomach churning. Once and for all, he ought to tell Miriam everything now. Whenever he told her, it would be painful. He tried to console himself that he had taken the first step, but he knew it was a lie. She had.

The room was growing cold. There was only the one bed and he had to get up for work in a few hours. Taking off his clothes, Amos groped his way into pyjamas. Slipping slowly into the bed, he kept well to the outside, a cold, empty space between them.

In her hut, Kate lay staring at the wall. She was drained, completely empty, the image of Amos's face as he ran out, engraved on her mind; pained, frightened. Was it the end? And for whom? Miriam and Amos. Kate and Amos?

At that moment, heavy footsteps clomped onto the veranda.

'Early night.' Roger's hoarse voice. 'Gotta get up early for the cowshed, mate.' Then Jill giggling.

'Me too. Sleep well.'

'Never a problem,' he laughed. Silence. A goodnight kiss. Then the door opened.

'Bloody hell,' snapped Jill as she came in and switched on the light. 'It's cold Kate! You should get undressed and into bed.'

'Can't feel it,' muttered Kate, still facing the wall. 'Can't feel anything.'

Jill sat on the bed beside her and gently slapped her thigh.

'Know what they say: No sense. No feeling.'

'And no joking.' Kate sat up and looked at Jill. 'Amos was here.' Adding, after a short pause. 'So was Miriam.'

Jill stared at her, dumbstruck.

'And?'

'Well she ran out. Then Amos ran out in a panic.'

Holy smoke. Well. Anyway. That will blow it, won't it? Make him decide one way or the other.'

Kate sat forward and clasped her hands around her knees.

'I wish I knew, Jill. 'Oh God. I wish I knew. And I have to find out, sure. Somehow, I must know.'

Jill stood up and pulled Kate off the bed. Gently, she shook her shoulders, then pulled back the covers.

'Get in,' she snapped. 'If you don't get under those fucking covers mate, all you'll ever know, is fucking pneumonia!'

20

The next morning, leaving Yossi to continue ploughing up for next season's sugar beet, Amos drove back in the jeep to pick up the breakfast box. But instead of going straight into the kitchen, he engaged the four-wheel drive and whined round the rough perimeter track to park by the fence. It was the quiet of mid morning with everyone out at work, as he cut through the trees to the rear of the huts.

Kate was sitting on the bed, fully dressed but wrapped in a blanket, writing a letter. The nurse had called and given her some Paracetamol. It was Shabbat tomorrow and she could start work again on Sunday. Work! And again, she felt a panic gripping her. Where would she work? How could she stay?

The door suddenly opened and quickly shut again. Three steps and he was with her, clutching his cloth hat and looking down.

'Your breakfast call.'

'Glad you can smile,' said Kate as he sat beside her. 'What happened last night?'

'Not a lot,' muttered Amos. 'Blew up when she came to the room.'

'And?'

'Well, she was upset. Went straight to bed.'

'Oh God, Amos, of course she was upset. But what are you waiting for? Either we're doing this or we're not.' She looked up. 'I love you so much, Amos. But I can't stay here like this. Not after last night.'

Amos leaned down and kissed her neck.

'Look. We shall do it Kate. It's *shabat* tomorrow. We'll have time and I'll tell Miriam. Trust me. Please. It's not easy.'

'God. I know it isn't easy. It isn't easy for anyone.' She rested her forehead on his chest, the smell of diesel oil in her nostrils. 'I love you Amos, but the uncertainty. I just can't…' She looked up into his eyes. 'I'm catching the midday bus to Tel Aviv and going on to Jerusalem. I'll just make it before the *shabbat* comes in.'

In the nearby bushes, birds fluttered. Out in the field beyond the fence, the caterpillar tractor chugged and clanked as it turned into a new furrow.

'Please, Kate.' He gripped her shoulders. 'It will soon be okay. I promise.'

'I hope so Amos and I do believe you. But I have to go.' She broke away and looked into his eyes again. 'You know where to find me. A letter only takes a day. And Jill and Roger are going to Jerusalem on Sunday. Send a message with them and I'll come. Or you will come. I'll wait for you, Amos.'

Amos knew there was no way he would dissuade her. He remembered their very first argument — last spring, in the potato field; it was about equality. She wouldn't give an inch. Determined, decisive, just like now. Was that what he envied in her, what so attracted him, that decisiveness he seemed to lack? He pulled her against him.

'I'll come, Kate. And you'll come back with me. And we'll be together. I promise,' and they clutched at each other, kissing again and again until they broke apart.

Kate guessed he had taken advantage of the breakfast-run to come in.

'Poor Yossi,' she whispered, managing a thin smile, 'he'll starve to death.' Amos kissed her nose, walked to the door then slowly turned, raised his hand and blew a kiss.

Kate stood up, and went to the open door, watching him go, the broad shoulders hunched, right hand gripping the car keys and the dry grass crackling as he strode towards the fence. A *khardon*, one of the large, scaly lizards, scuffled past her feet and across the boards and disappeared under the veranda. Suddenly, everything around seemed so dry and desolate. She glanced towards the small grove of eucalyptus trees: their grove, the cradle of their love. The narrow, silvery leaves fluttered forlornly in the breeze.

Jerusalem would be no respite. But if he came and they talked, they'd find a way. What she wanted and what he wanted. 'Nuts and bolts, my girl,' her father would say. Dad! And Mam. Oh God. They'd go spare! And suddenly she thought of Mam. Poor Mam. Having to put up with her father and his wild drinking, always worrying something would happen to him.

Auntie Clare had written that Dad had had a nasty fall, and although she didn't spell it out, Kate knew it was probably him rolling home late one night in the dark – or from one of his drunken fights. Kate had grown close to the aunt when she was still at convent school. The aunt's house had been round the corner, before she had moved over the water to Kilburn. On the way home from school, especially after she had had a run-in with one of the nuns, Kate would pop in for tea and sympathy. Kate had sent her the address of the kibbutz and the phone number -- though she'd probably never need it, and was glad they had kept up the contact.

Back in the jeep, Amos stared ahead, his head spinning. Kate leaving, even just for a day or two, twisted his guts into a knot. He couldn't care now whether anyone saw or heard. *Le'azazel!* To hell with, the lot of them. Starting the engine, he grated the gears and drove round to the kitchen. He had lost all appetite for himself, but picking up the box of food from the kitchen, he sped out to the fields, almost overturning on a bend he'd taken hundreds of times before.

Miriam was packing a holdall when he came to the room after work. Before he could say anything, she straightened up and faced him.

'Rivka's parents are driving back to Tel Aviv tonight. I'm hitching a lift with them. After the children go back.'

Amos plugged in the kettle and grunted. Either way, he needed a cup of coffee before the kids came home.

'I need a bit of space,' Miriam continued. 'I'll be back Sunday afternoon with the bus.'

Amos poured coffee for both of them, then took out the bread tin and slipped two slices into the toaster, having to keep doing something to keep on an even keel. She was probably going to her mother. Would she walk out on him? It would make it so much easier. '*Fighter*', they called him back in the unit. If only they knew!

When Ran went back to the schoolhouse with his friends, Amos and Miriam took Noa back together. Nitza was sitting the children down for supper.

'When will you be back, Mummy,' asked Noa as she sat at the supper table.

'Sunday. Just one day, *Khamoodi*. I've got to see *Savta*.' Miriam knelt by the chair. 'What shall I bring you from Tel Aviv.'

'*Pezim!*' grinned Noa. 'An orange one with a Goofy head.' She loved the tiny sherbet sweets in their small plastic-animal dispensers.

Amos deliberately avoided Nitza's questioning glances as she sat down and served out the children's supper things. And when Miriam turned and hurried out alone, he felt the other parents glancing at him. Kissing Noa on the head, he hurried out. It was going to be more awkward than he'd imagined.

After saying goodnight to Ran, Amos went up alone to the dining hall, and spotted an empty space at Eli and Bilha's table.

'Miriam coming up later?' asked Bilha, when he sat down.

'No.' Amos took some sheep's cheese and spread it on a slice of brown bread. 'Gone to town to see her mother.'

'So sudden? Is she ill?'

'Don't think so.' Amos shrugged. 'Just said she wanted to visit her.'

For a moment, the three of them sat in silence. Eli reached out and picked up the stainless steel jug.

'Anyone for coffee?'

Amos nodded.

'None for me,' said Bilha. She got up. 'Have to see Aviva about an extra person for the babies' house. Rachel comes back with their new addition tomorrow.'

'All she needed,' grunted Eli. 'As if we haven't enough problems with their first two.'

After Bilha had gone, Eli looked across the table.

'*Nu.* Want to give me a hand feeding the new calves after supper? Only half an hour.'

'Sure,' said Amos, Eli 'I'm a bachelor tonight. Why not?'

After supper Amos loitered in the dining hall lobby waiting to see Jill. There was no post or transport on Shabbat, but she and Roger were going to Jerusalem on Sunday. When she came out from supper, he gave her the sealed letter he'd scribbled for Kate; 'the deed was done and he was coming up on Monday morning'. He would tell Miriam as soon as she came back on Sunday afternoon.

After she promised to deliver it, Amos thanked her then crossed the courtyard and walked down the slope and across the road. A smell of silage and musty hay rose from the light mist that hung over the cowsheds. Sharp, black angles of roof-lines stood silhouetted against the yellow glow of the fence lights; a cow lowed from the dark yards.

By the whitewashed walls of the milking parlour, half-a-dozen young calves jostled and clattered on steel-slatted floors of a narrow open shed, a patchwork of black and white, shifting in and out of the fluorescent lighting.

Amos glanced around the cowsheds, then at the young calves Eli was feeding. Perhaps Kate could work here. Eli wouldn't cause a fuss. Along with Nitza and the others from Haifa, the two of them went back a long way.

'So,' said Eli, as he washed out the milk buckets and stood them upside down on the rack. 'Just you and me, Amos.' He dried his hands. '*Mah Holekh?*

'Coffee first,' said Amos.

'Uhuh,' said Eli. 'Reckon we'll need it.'

They walked across the small office attached the milking parlour. Most of it was taken up by two large green filing cabinets holding the herd's record cards. A small desk and two chairs occupied the remaining tiled floor space. Eli plugged in the kettle and sat on the edge of the desk. Amos flopped onto a wooden chair and looked across at him.

'So. What can I tell you, Eli? You seem to know something already.'

'Only what the rumours say,' Eli smiled. The kettle began to hiss. 'You and Kate. Jerusalem.' He brushed his hand across his forehead. 'Motti saw you both at Masmiya. And a mind like his would have made something even if there was nothing.' He stood up, spooned out coffee into two cups and poured in the hot water. Then sat in the other chair, waiting.

Amos gripped the mug and sipped, collecting his thoughts, then began with the incident of the Arab boy, and how the friendship had grown and deepened, his whole body growing warm as he described how alive he felt when he was with Kate.

Eli sat silent, nodding, his tanned face taut, from time to time ruffling his hand through his thick black hair.

'So. It's a matter of deciding which way I'll be happiest,' said Amos. 'It's my life, Eli. I only have one.' He looked down at the mud-soiled tiles. 'And it's so short, Eli. Look at poor Ya'ir. Gone. Too bloody short!'

'More coffee,' said Eli. Amos nodded and as he rose to plug in the kettle again, Eli leaned forward, half smiling. 'Sure it's not just sex?'

Amos shook his head. 'No. I've sorted that one out, Eli.' He spooned out the coffee. 'Sure. At the beginning. But not now. Not for a while. No. It's everything.'

'And Miriam?'

'Difficult to explain.' Amos paused, not having completely sorted this out in his own mind. 'Look. I still like her. Respect her as much as I ever did. But, *Nu*. Compared to when I'm with Kate Eli, it's just predictable.' The kettle began to boil. 'Sure. I know the sadness and hurt I'll create.' He stopped for a moment then raised one hand. 'Listen Eli. If I don't do this, I'll regret it for the rest of my life. And how would it be for Miriam to live with me then?'

Amos made the coffee then sat down again.

'Look. Perhaps I'm not the steady type like you and Avram, and Uri. You know me. I've always had ants in my pants. Made me leave home for agricultural school when my parents wanted me to continue studying. Joined the tank corps when you all went into *Nakhal* units. Went out to teach cotton in Kenya that year.'

They sat and drank in silence for a while. From the milk-tank room, the compressors purred.

'And Miriam's still young. Still attractive,' he added. 'She'll find someone else.'

Eli half smiled.

'Trying to absolve your conscience?' He took a sip. 'Women are different, Amos. Marriage, home, kids. It's all one thing.' He leaned forward. 'And what about the kids, Amos?'

Amos sat up.

'I'm not leaving the kibbutz, Eli. I'll always be here. I love them to bits.' He paused for a moment, turning the cup around on the table. 'Sure, they won't be happy. But in a few years they'll be at high school, then in the army, making their own lives.'

'And meanwhile, you think you and Kate can live here together, playing happy families, eh?'

Amos sat back, eyes wide. He set down the mug with a sharp click.

'Sure. Why not? It's personal!' He picked up the cup again. 'Nothing to do with kibbutz principles. Do I enquire into what goes on in other families as long as it doesn't affect the kibbutz?' He raised his cup. 'Yoram had a fling with Hedva that time. Did it matter?'

'Maybe,' Eli smiled. 'But that was, as we say, "in the family", and just a fling.' He paused. 'Look. I like Kate, Amos. So do many others. But she is an outsider. And Miriam; well, she is one of us, popular, highly respected.'

Outside, a cow lowed in the darkness. Somewhere, a metal gate clanked as a beast rubbed itself against the fence rails. He looked up at Amos's face. The unruly mop of fair hair, the wide brown eyes, suddenly seeming so boyish.

'Listen, Amos,' Eli continued, 'I can't help thinking you're being more than a little naïve. Me, Menakhem, Uri, maybe Nitza -- all our lot from Haifa, sure, whatever happens, it makes no difference to our friendship, our comradeship. But for others, those with a grudge, your Mottis and Ramis and Shmuels, then those with their own shaky marriages – "there but for the grace of God…"' Eli wagged a finger. 'Look. We pride ourselves on being liberated, progressive, revolutionary and all that.' He glanced at the door. 'But just remember Amos, despite all that, we are a village too. Just a *kleiner shtetl!*

Amos frowned and pursed his lips.

'I can't take account of petty minds, Eli. The people I respect and care about will get used to it. They will take me for what I am and always have been.' Amos raised his mug and finished the last drops. 'And anyway, Eli, in time we won't be the only ones.'

'Sure, and right now, Kate is liked. But if you go ahead, for many she'll become 'the scarlet woman'.' Eli shrugged. 'And it's not just petty minds, Amos. Many people will find reason to oppose it.' He took a gulp of coffee and leaned forward. 'And what if Kate doesn't want to live here? Wants to live in town. Abroad, even?'

'But she agrees with kibbutz,' Amos protested. 'She's been searching for a society like ours. Feels at home here.'

They sat silent for a moment, then Eli rose, took the cups and rinsed them, and they went out. Locking the office door, he slipped the key under a nearby concrete block and they walked up the rise together.

At the rear of the dining hall, Eli slapped his hand on Amos's shoulder.

'Look, mate. If you've thought it right through, if you're absolutely sure, then best of luck.' He leaned forward and they hugged for a second. 'Because you're going to need it, my friend.'

Amos went down to Noa's house and looked in. In the faint, orange night-light, she lay on her side fast asleep, her thumb by her mouth. Gently, he pulled the covers up over her shoulder, then eased a stray strand of hair from her face.

In the schoolhouse, Menakhem was tidying up the classroom.

'Don't you teachers ever rest?' smiled Amos.

'Lifetime job,' he smiled, nodding.

Amos went through and glanced in at Ran's room. It was dark but his son was still awake.

'Hi, Dad.' In the faint light from the corridor, he raised his head. 'Mum get away okay? Is *Savta* ill?'

'No, don't think so.' He came up to the bed. 'It's nearly ten, Ran. You should be asleep by now.'

'I was reading in bed.' The boy lay back and pulled up the covers. '*Shabbat* tomorrow anyway.'

'See you tomorrow.' Amos ruffled his hair. '*Leyl menucha.*'

'Night, Dad.'

As he came out, Menakhem was waiting, a pile of books under his arm.

'Like to come over for a cup of coffee? Two of the kids found some Bronze Age sherds in the *wadi* this morning. Could even be Chalcolithic.' Together with Eli, the three of them were setting up a small museum.

Amos thought for a moment. Sudden hospitality. Everyone seemed to know that Miriam had gone to town. And all his close friends trying to talk to him -- make him think again.

'Thanks, Menakhem. I'm a bit tired. Perhaps I'll come over with Ran tomorrow.'

The room felt cold. And empty. Amos sat in the easy chair,

staring at the incandescent red glow of the 'Fireside' element. Miriam would be talking with her mother. They were close, the two of them, much closer than he had ever been to his parents, his father always busy at meetings, planning strikes, organising demonstrations; against the British, against the orange-grove *kulaks*. And Mum, organising infant welfare amongst the worse off, as well as with the Arabs, in Haifa.

Amos glanced at a photograph of the two of them, taken last year. Dad, thin and bald. Mum, lined face and frizzy hair. Dad and his old comrades were now functionaries in the fossilised *Histadrut* trade unions, out of touch with the oriental Jews who now made up the new proletariat, yet imagining that they were still on the barricades. Mum and Dad. God. They loved Miriam.

It wasn't late but he was tired. And he would have the kids on his own tomorrow; morning and afternoon. They always joked that the *shabbat* rest-day was the parents' hardest day of the week.

Amos unbuttoned his shirt and pulled back the bed covers. Almost twelve years they'd shared the bed together. It was supposed to be a seven-year itch. Yes, there was Gila. Didn't seem to need it. That, and loyalty to Azriel, perhaps.

He sat on the bed and imagined himself walking with Kate over the cotton fields' stubble, talking, laughing, the wind blowing in their faces. He would take her down the Arava to Eilat and swim in the Red Sea; up to the icy springs at Tel el Khadi, the source of the river Jordan. Rediscover his whole beautiful land together with her.

A little owl screeched, searching out voles and field mice. His mind churned; he wouldn't be able to sleep. Jill would give Kate the letter on Sunday. She would know he was coming on Monday. And on Monday he would go. Meanwhile, he must make arrangements for a room and arrange a day off to go to Jerusalem, and wait for Miriam to come back on Sunday, and he'd made it final.

At that moment, he heard laughter coming across the lawn. He stood up and slammed his rear window shut. And couldn't sleep after that, and felt he had to do something -- and decided to go to see Elieazar who was in charge of accommodation; he was on night shift loading broilers for market. Buttoning up his shirt, he hurried along the path -- and caught him just as he about to go down to the poultry houses.

'Hi. Glad I caught you.' And continued with a pause. 'I need a spare room.'

Eliezar took off his cloth hat and scratched his balding head.

'We've only got two guest rooms and one I have to keep for emergencies, like someone ill. Or isolation.'

Amos looked straight into his eyes.

'It is an emergency. Eliezar. I'm moving out!'

Instinctively, Elieazar glanced at his watch. Dudik would already be down in the chicken runs, wanting to start and wondering why he hadn't turned up. No one liked loading chickens at night. But it also gave him a moment to think. Stuffing his hat into his pocket, he stepped back and looked at Amos. In the faint light from the street lamps, the broad face looked pinched, his mouth a mere slit. He too had heard the rumours. But this?

Amos put his hand on the man's shoulder.

'Look. I know it must be a bit of a shock. But I need the room.' He paused, 'Please. No questions. It's for me. And Kate.'

Eliezar breathed deeply. Amos. He recalled the two of them as boys, running messages for the *Haganah* defence units in '47, haring up and down the road to Hadar Hacarmel while kicking a ball along the way, to bluff the Red Berets. He also remembered teasing Amos at the camp in Sinai when he had suddenly fallen for the new admin corporal, Miriam. Eleven years since the Sinai War. Eleven years gone by in a flash.

'*Nu*. What can I say? It's your life, Amos.' He paused. 'Listen. Take the room next to Moshe. The key is hanging up in my work clothes cupboard. Number six.' He put his hand on Amos's chest. '*Tishmor, habibi*, take care.' And he stood for a moment, pensive, watching the bulky form disappear into the night.

21

Mrs Schwartz had never seen her daughter like this -- face pale and eyes red -- and showed it when Miriam rang the bell.

'Come,' said her mother after they had greeted, 'I've made myself some chicken soup for supper. You will join me, then we can talk.'

Afterwards, through alternate bursts of anger and tears, Miriam told her about Amos then as she became more composed, the mother began to talk.

'Look. It's all very well having principles, being active in the kibbutz and all that,' she said, 'but in the end though, Miriam, even with all their talk of equality, men want a feminine wife.'

Miriam had always admired her mother, the way she had got over Dad's sudden death, kept up her social work in the *Kupat Kholim* health centre, and still took pride in herself.

'But that's not the way Amos and I want to live, Mum,' she said, eventually. 'Our marriage has always been a partnership of equals. Of respect.' She'd reminded her mother of how pleased Amos been when she qualified as a teacher. Encouraged her to be head of the education committee.

'I don't disagree with you, Miriam. But perhaps after ten years, Amos may be a bit fed up with your being out late most evenings. You on this committee or that, solving this parent's woes and that kid's behavioural problems.'

'But he's busy in the evenings too, Mum.'

'Yes. Yes. But men are different, Miriam. I mean, just look at

your hair. When was the last time you used a real hairdresser?'
Then abruptly closed her mouth. 'Look, Miriam,' she continued,
after a few seconds, 'men still want the room cosy. The nest.' She
smiled. 'Though your Amos would be the last to admit it!'

Sitting at the kitchen table, a coffee-pot between them, they'd
continued talking late into the Friday night, Miriam again breaking
into tears, until so weary, she could hardly string two words
together.

'Come. Let's sleep on it, Miriam.' She got up and put her arm
around her daughter's shoulders. 'Listen, if you want him back,
you have to fight for it.' Then after short pause added, 'and
together with your friends, make a battle plan to get rid of that girl
too!'

She walked with her into the spare bedroom.

'Come. It's *Shabbat* tomorrow. We'll have all day.'

Mrs Schwartz had every Shabbat to herself. Doctor Schwartz
had died from a heart attack three years ago. Still, she had no
regrets. Considered herself lucky. Herman had had the foresight
to leave Heidelberg in the thirties, as soon as the university had
begun to dismiss 'non-Aryan' staff. Persuaded her to emigrate to
Palestine. Most of their Jewish friends and colleagues who'd
remained behind, had ended up in the gas chambers.

Leaving Miriam sitting on the bed, eyes red and hair tangled,
getting undressed, gently Mrs Schwartz closed the door behind
her. Despite his radical opinions and brusqueness, she had always
liked Amos. Yes, he could be impetuous and bull headed — and
attractive men often have a roving eye. But this? It was so unlike
him to cause Miriam such pain.

On Sunday, Miriam caught the early afternoon bus back from Tel
Aviv. She wanted to arrive back early afternoon when the kibbutz

was at its quietest; the men still out in the fields and the children's nurses and cooks taking their afternoon shower and nap. It would also give her time to shower and change before the children came home.

She had had her hair trimmed and shaped, while spending the morning shopping with her mother in Dizengoff Street, and as soon as she reached the room, Miriam plonked two bulging shopping bags on the bed. Without taking off her jacket and town shoes, one by one, she took out and unwrapped a number of small packages. She walked about the room then out to the shower and back again, holding various items up against this wall and that, or by the doorway, head on one side, looking, thinking, then placed them back on the bed.

She stood for a moment, picked up a brightly painted, canvas wall calendar and pinned it to the side of the doorpost. On the back of the built-in wardrobe door, she fitted a flowered, sock-pocket hanger. In the shower, she hung a green and pink toilet roll holder and matching hand towel. Then, after arranging the room, she came back, sat on the bed lips pursed, and slipped off her shoes, wondering how it would begin.

She had showered and was standing by the wardrobe brushing her hair, when Amos came in.

'*Shalom*,' he said, with just a hint of a smile. 'How was your mother?' It was the question he always asked when she came back, especially since her father died. Usually, after that, they'd hug and kiss in greeting. But not now. Instead, he stood awkwardly on the veranda, as though it wasn't his home at all.

'Fine. She's fine,' said Miriam, then added quickly, 'took the chance to buy a few things for the room. She nodded to the calendar, then swung the door open to show the sock pockets and coloured hangers.

'*Nekhmad*,' said Amos, 'pretty,' then turned away. 'I'd better shower before the kids get home.' And went into the toilet, closing the door behind him.

Miriam sunk down on the bed, gripping the hairbrush, her knuckles white. Trying to stifle the tears, she shut her eyes tightly; yellow spots and streaks shooting across the blackness. All the way back on the bus, she had allowed herself the illusion that Amos had thought things over, realised how terrible it would be for the kids, as well as how much she loved him and that deep down, he must love her too.

'Well,' Miriam began again when he came back to the room.

Amos had slumped in the easy chair.

'Amos. You know that if you value your family. Me. The children, there's no way you can see her again.'

For a few seconds, Amos sat staring down at the carpet again. Then he looked up. Their eyes met.

'I've arranged a room and I'm going to fetch Kate from Jerusalem tomorrow,' he said softly.

Miriam stood up, her body trembling, her fists clenched.

'Then you can get out – *now!*'

After he left, Miriam went to the door and slammed it closed. To hell with the neighbours. Then turning round, she slumped full length onto the bed, and sobbed into the pillow.

Number six was cold and bare; a single bed, an old wardrobe, a small table and hard chair, and on the floor a small, threadbare carpet. One of the oldest buildings on the compound, there was a distinctly musty scent to the room.

Though it was hardly the palace he wanted to live in with Kate, it reminded him of the optimism and purposefulness of the first days of the kibbutz lived, though even then there would still have been a few prints on the wall and a bunch of flowers or dried thorns in an old jar.

A tap on the door made him jump.

'Oh. It's you, Amos!' It was the neighbour, Moshe. 'Visitors coming?' he asked.

Amos shook his head.

'No. It's for me.' Adding suddenly, as if in defiance, 'for me and Kate.' Moshe straightened up, his glasses bobbing on his nose.

'*Beseder.* Okay. I…' And abruptly withdrew his head. Amos smiled to himself; between Moshe and his wife Rivkah, the news would travel around the kibbutz at the speed of light. But he couldn't stand here speculating. He must get the key from Brakha to take sheets and towels from the clothes store -- another broadcaster there. Which still left the biggest problem. Taking some of his things from the room, without meeting Miriam.

Crossing the lawn, Amos slipped into the bushes opposite his old room. So soon, and already it had become 'his old room'. The light was off and he wondered whether Miriam gone out, or was still inside lying in the dark? Slowly, he trod onto the veranda and listened. Silence. Opening the outside cupboard, he took out his working clothes and boots. Then took his toiletries and a couple of towels from the shower. The pulse in his forehead throbbed as he gripped the handle and pulled open the door. Silence.

Switching on the light, he stopped. Noa's toys were all over the floor, and the scissors and paper lay on the table where Ran had been cutting out his model aeroplane. Miriam obviously hadn't returned after they'd taken the kids back. He wondered to whom she had gone.

His room, yet not his room. The pictures, the books, the

pitchevkehs they'd bought together. He couldn't take anything now but when he did, they would have to decide who would take what. They'd have to talk; to be civilised about it. Civilised? Suddenly he felt sick, switched off the light, clutched his bundle and hurried out.

After getting the key, Amos went to the clothes store and took out sheets and two blankets, and it had gone ten before he had managed to sort out the room. He'd found a newer rug in the other spare room, as well as a vase and some curtains. He could have taken that room. It was larger, but it looked onto the lawn in front of Miriam's room, again the thought that so soon it had already become just 'Miriam's room'.

Amos lay back on the single bed; it was hard and lumpy; the bare lightbulb glared in his eyes.

Tomorrow, he would have to suffer the sly winks of Meir and Itcho when he ordered a double bed-frame from the workshop. And a new mattress from Tel Aviv.

He switched on the small transistor they used out in the fields and closed his eyes. It was the news, on *Gallei Tzahal*, the forces' programme.

…At the United Nations security council, delegates debated resolution 242, demanding the withdrawal from occupied territories in return for recognition of secure borders…

He lay back on the bed, trying to stop his mind whirling, tired but still too wound up to sleep. Kate must have received the letter by now and would know he was coming tomorrow, Monday.

Amos felt himself dropping off when the door suddenly creaked. He opened his eyes and raised himself on one elbow as, without knocking, Nitza had come in.

He swung his legs onto the floor and sat up. He ran his fingers through his hair and switched off the radio.

'Shalom, Amos,' she said softly. 'I've been talking to Miriam,' and sat on the one chair. 'So. *Mapsoot akhshav?* she asked, her face drawn and tight. 'Now you're happy?'

'Look, Nitza.' He struggled to focus. 'I'm not in the mood for lectures.'

Nitza folded her hands in her lap. Despite the hard expression, she looked calm, her brown hair neatly tied back with a mauve ribbon, her fluffy white sweater fitting close on her still trim figure.

'You're not going to get any, Amos.' And in the small room, alone with him, those deep, long ago feelings began to swell; her voice grew softer and gentle. 'I just want to understand. That's all.'

Amos hunched forward, his elbows on his thighs. He was dog-tired.

'Bit late in the evening for long explanations, Nitza.' He looked up. 'Miriam and I. It was just ticking along. Would have happened sooner or later. And Kate? Well. It was Kate. And now. Now I'm glad it happened.'

Nitza got up and came over to sit on the bed beside him and with her, a faint aroma of perfume.

'Amos. I never suspected. You two seemed so suited.' She put a hand on his thigh. 'Perhaps if – if I'd known…' Amos turned to look into her face. In his weariness, for a few seconds, her breasts proud in the tight, white sweater, he had to fight an urge to reach out to touch her.

When Miriam on occasion teased him, he would laugh and brush it off. After all, it was Nitza who had broken it off when she went off to do her teacher training. And when he had come back from Kenya, she was already sharing a room with Yossi. Sure, Yossi was a nice bloke, but no match for the likes of Nitza. And all he had felt for her since was a deep friendship, but now, in the late hour and his weariness, he felt a sudden sadness.

Before he could shake it off, Nitza leaned forward and hugged him, kissing him full the lips. At first Amos didn't resist, but quickly his head cleared and gently he pulled away, his body tingling.

'Look, Nitza. We've always been close, respected one another.' He shrugged. 'Things are complicated enough, don't you think?' He saw that her eyes were moist too, and strangely, he felt guilty -- though it was a feeling he was getting used to.

Slowly, with her hand to her eyes, she rose and quickly went out, leaving the door open, and him trembling.

Half running, half- walking, down the path, Nitza tried to stifle her tears. But as the cool night hit her, so did the anger. If Amos wasn't Miriam's, then he was hers. And certainly not that bloody slip of a girl's. And she would make sure of that!

22

Sister Francesca was surprised to see Kate, when she booked in at the hostel on Friday evening.

'I thought you were well and truly into the kibbutz by now.'

Kate shrugged.

'I am. But I need a break, I suppose.'

The sister smiled and went back to her office. Personally, she knew little of men, but had long learned to recognise the effect they had.

Sunlight streaming through the window woke her early. Kate cleaned her teeth and dressed, then hurried down to the reception lobby. The post always arrived by eight thirty and was laid on a small tray on the dark mahogany table. There were three letters but none were for her. And Jill hadn't come yesterday, either.

At that moment, Sister Francesca came out of her office. Kate nodded to the table.

'Are these all the letters, sister?'

The nun looked surprised.

'Yes. I always leave them there.'

'Oh, of course. Sorry.'

It could only mean Amos wasn't coming today. Slowly, Kate turned and climbed the stone stairs, trying to stifle her tears. Suddenly, the whitewashed walls seemed even colder, the morning sunlight through the windows harsh. She just couldn't bear another day of lonely uncertainty. Oh God, somehow she had to get through the day. Or at least until lunchtime, the earliest either Amos or Jill could arrive. She had expressed doubts at Shafik's offer when she visited Yusuf yesterday. Now she was glad she hadn't dismissed it completely.

Shafik could hardly hide his surprise when Kate entered the doorway.

'Jill didn't show up,' said Kate, trying to appear nonchalant. 'She must have chosen the later bus from the kibbutz.'

'Well. Nice of you to come, Kate. And early, too. Good.' He had filled the car with petrol, hoping it would be a good omen. It didn't need a full tank but that had helped to swing it with his cousin.

'I hope I'm not imposing, Shafik. I mean the car, the petrol.'

Shafik stepped towards her, a broad smile across his face.

'No. No. I promised. And here I am. We can go.' And he really was pleased -- would show her who was the more reliable and caring...

They walked through the narrow archway of the Lions Gate and crossed the road. Half a dozen taxis of varying ages waited on a patch of rough ground bounded by dusty cypress trees; Mercedes and Peugeots looking for fares to Jericho. Or better still, to the Allenby Bridge for those lucky enough to obtain Israeli military permission to cross into Jordan.

The drivers, stocky, balding men with bushy moustaches, leaned against the bonnets, watching sideways as Shafik unlocked his cousin's small white Fiat and opened the door for Kate to get in. Like Yusuf, they too had lost all their custom from Jordan. And to add to their hard times, they were not allowed into Israel proper to pick up fares.

Soon, they were driving south, through white painted houses of Bettania, the biblical Bethany.

'The old road to Hebron was cut off by the Israelis in 1948,' Shafik explained. 'So this detour had to be built. Much longer. But more spectacular.'

And it was. Suddenly, as though it was a scene change in a film, on either side gleamed bare, parched hills, white and beige in the bright sunlight. Neither tree nor bush and hardly a blade of grass -- and all within the space of a few miles and ten minutes travelling time: the Judean Desert. She had never seen anything so desolate.

Bethlehem was crowded. Low, white-limestone houses and dusty roads. Trucks and buses were parked on Manger Square opposite the Church of the Nativity, as well as clogging the narrow streets around. And among the Christian, foreign tourists, coachloads of Israelis, lining up for their very first opportunity to see the Church of the Nativity at Christmas.

Filing down the winding steps with the crowd, the two entered the vaulted crypt. At one end, a crib of painted and gilded figures was illuminated in the niche where the manger was said to have been. Everywhere, thin candles burned on blackened spikes, gold coloured stars and tinsel hung from the arches above, and artificial flowers were stuck into crevices and vases. The kitsch, icing-sugar sweetness of it all, was too reminiscent of the Catholic shops in Dublin; the hundreds of plaster figurines of the Virgin, or the manger; bottles of Holy Water. After a few minutes, she wrinkled her nose and turned to Shafik.

'Okay. I've seen it,' she said. 'Thanks for bringing me, Shafik. But let's go.'

Out in the streets, where shops and stalls were selling model cribs and mother-of-pearl crucifixes and medallions, she felt no easier. Every window and stall was crammed with tasteless ornaments: camels and donkeys carved from olive wood, and the 'authenticated' bottles of holy water. It brought out the worst of the anti-cleric in her, bringing back painful reminders of the nuns at her convent school, the vicious punishments, the rote catechisms, the warped view of sex. And now her fury at the Pope and his repeated anti birth-control dogma.

'Well, I thought that you would want to see it,' said Shafik, as they reached the car.

Kate raised her hand. 'Please, Shafik. Don't apologise. I'm glad I came to see the church. But…' She paused, searching to express her feelings. 'Just that it was such a sham. All that tinsel. No real reverence. Ugh!'

'Well,' he said, 'we have time. Perhaps you will like Hebron better.'

Kate really had wanted to see Christmas in Bethlehem, but now she wanted to get back.

'Oh. I, er, don't want to be late. You know, Jill…'

'Well, it's not that far.' He smiled. 'And I'm sure you will find it more interesting.'

They drove south along the spine of the Judean mountains.

On either side, small boys chased sheep and goats from one dry, grassy patch to the next between limestone terraces planted with almond and olive trees. In small stony fields, mules or oxen pulled wooden ploughs fitted with an iron 'nail' ploughshare, little changed since the days of old father Abraham.

'This was once part of the ancient route from Damascus to The Nile Valley,' explained Shafik.

Hebron too was full of tourists too, but mainly concentrated around the huge, brown limestone building of the mosque: the Tomb of Abraham -- probably once a Byzantine Church. Being a larger town, it seemed less crowded than Bethlehem, and inside the mosque Kate was struck with the simplicity. No tinsel. No kitsch. Rather gloomy, but no more than many churches in England.

'Abraham,' said Shafik, 'was the father of the Arabs as well as the Jews. "*Ibrahim el Awal*", we call him: Abraham, the First One.'

Yes, Kate was thinking, this was where it all began, the father of the brothers Isaac and Ishmael. The blood feud that had persisted through the centuries -- and was still burning.

Hebrew notices had been added to those in Arabic, and as they came down the stone staircase outside the doorway, Kate suddenly recalled something Amos had told her.

'Is it true that Jews were once not allowed up further than the fourth step?' she asked casually. Shafik jerked his head round.

'Well. Yes.' His face clouded. 'But Hebron has always been a centre of religious fanaticism. Christians wouldn't have got much further up either.' Suddenly, he leaned towards her. 'So where did you hear that?'

'Oh,' Kate tried to dismiss it. 'Someone in the kibbutz, I think.'

'From that man I saw, I suppose.' His eyes narrowed almost to slits. 'But you needn't believe everything he says.'

Kate hung back, her mouth open. Why so angry? And now it certainly wasn't about that fourth step? And why had he supposed it was Amos? God, she had been naïve. He really was jealous!

'Shafik,' she said firmly, as they walked on. 'We need to go back.'

They drove back north, up the road to Jerusalem. Shafik was taciturn, certain she was so anxious to get back because of that man, that Israeli. Probably married and just playing with her. People in those kibbutz places were free and easy; he'd read about them. So if she was late, well he could damn well wait. And if he got annoyed, well Kate would see that he, Shafik, was the more considerate.

Amos stood in the entrance lobby of the hostel, hesitant and awkward. It was a woman's hostel; he couldn't just walk up to her room. He had risen early to catch the six o'clock, direct bus to Tel Aviv, and had been impatient to arrive, to speak to Kate and tell her about the room, to reassure her -- and be reassured.

'Can I help you?' It was Sister Francesca.

Amos started.

'Oh. I believe Kate, Kate McGuiness is staying here?'

'Kathlene. Yes. But she went out this morning.'

Amos tensed. His letter must have arrived this morning and for a moment he was annoyed, but didn't want to show it. Perhaps she had gone to the old silversmith. At the Sister's suggestion, he wrote a note and left it in the tray on the dark, shiny table. Ten minutes later he was hurrying through the Damascus Gate.

Yusuf was sitting at the table. The young boy was with him, laboriously writing homework in an exercise book. It was an old Jordanian exercise book; printed on the back were aircraft bombing a map of Israel.

'Ah. Good morning.' The old man rose and came towards Amos as he hung back in the doorway. 'Please. You look for Miss Kate?' Amos nodded, but before the man could answer, the boy jumped up, grinning.

'Miss Kate. She go Bethlehem. Shafik take uncle's car,' he said proudly, as though Amos would appreciate his friend being taken to see the sights. The blood rose to his head. Two minutes in Jerusalem and already Kate was with that man. To hell with everything. He would get out and go back to the kibbutz, and she could damn well come and look for him.

The silversmith frowned at his nephew, but the boy had meant well.

'They will be back by noon,' he smiled. 'She wanted so much to see Bethlehem at Christmas.'

Amos tried to calm himself and smiled politely. He had nothing against either of them. Nor the man Shafik, he tried to rationalise. But why couldn't she have waited? Jill must have had caught the post van and he was sure Kate had received his letter. And he had deliberately taken the early bus. He glanced at his watch; half past eleven. Why wasn't she here? But he couldn't just stand around and wait.

'I'll come back in an hour,' he said to the old man, smiled and went out.

Like the Friar's letter to Juliet, events had scrambled Amos's carefully laid plans. Coming back from visiting the Beduin on *shabbat* with Roger, and playing silly buggers, Jill had badly sprained her ankle and had to cancel her trip to Jerusalem. Desperately she had asked Roger to take it instead but he couldn't be released from the cowsheds that day. She had hobbled across to Amos's room the next morning to tell him, but he had already left.

Amos strode out of St. Stephen's gate and crossed the Jericho road, glancing at the shining onion domes of the Russian church. Ahead was the garden where he had lain with Kate. To his left, in the distance, beyond the white houses of Sheikh Jarra, was Ammunition Hill; the small hollow in the rocks where they had raised up a small cairn of stones and laid the flowers for Ya'ir. He wondered whether it was still there, but couldn't bring himself to go back.

Amos sat on a rock and closed his eyes. Ya'ir. The curly brown hair, scruffy beard and round glasses. Always unconventional. Joined the Parachutists but insisted on being a medic. Cut down in the dark whilst dressing someone's wounds. What a loss. What a waste. Amos wished so much he was still here, picturing the enigmatic smile when asked his opinion. Would he have approved? Ya'ir had loved kids but never married, had a few relationships that had petered out; couldn't seem to settle.

Amos wondered about that as he walked back into the city and up the Street of the Chain, gazing aimlessly into shop doorways, oblivious of the bustle, the Arabic music and the smells. Eventually he sat and had coffee in the *Suk*, but as the time dragged, he grew more and more annoyed at having to hang around. *Le'azazel.* Kate could wait too!

Shafik had hardly spoken all the drive back. In the tense silence, Kate stared through the car window. The white, barren mountains of Judea seemed even bleaker than before as her anxiety grew. If Amos *was* coming, he would have been there by noon at the latest.

Just before Jerusalem, they were further delayed, at a security road bloc. Observing that it was an Arab car, they had to get out while it was thoroughly searched -- just like Belfast, she was thinking, as the soldiers ferreted in his boot. She sensed Shafik's stifled anger as he stood silent and watched, which made her even more guilty about the trip.

They drove on, the road curving sharply as the old city walls appeared, with the modern incongruity of the Intercontinental Hotel perched up on the hills above. Shafik glanced at his watch. It was gone one o'clock but he had no regrets. That Israeli man didn't deserve a woman like Kate. If he had come, he could damn well wait.

When they pulled up under the dusty cypress trees, Kate turned to Shafik.

'Look, Shafik. I'm really sorry. We both seemed to have got the wrong idea and maybe that was my fault.' Kate managed a smile, adding, 'I hope we can still be friends.'

'It's okay,' said Shafik. 'It is forgotten.'

Amos tried hard to hide his anger when he came to the shop again and found that only Yusuf was there. The old silversmith rose to greet him.

'Ah. Yes. They must be here soon. Before Christmas, there is so much traffic in Bethlehem.' The smile was genuine, but the lined face looked concerned. Amos, knowing nothing of the betrothal issue, thought it was for him. The last thing he wanted was sympathy. He turned to go out.

'Please,' said Yusuf. 'You my guest. Some tea. Or coffee?'

Amos waited; a refusal would offend. And he was fed up with tramping the streets.

'That's very kind.' He swung back and smiled. 'Thank you. Coffee, please.' And came to sit by the table, and his annoyance grew with each minute passing.

About ten minutes later Araf ran in, his face beaming.

'They're back,' he cried out. 'Miss Kate back. I see car!'

A moment later, Kate came through the doorway. And stopped. Her face paled. Shafik, following a pace behind, bumped into her back, sending her tottering into the room.

'Oh God. Sorry I'm late, Amos,' she gasped. 'Didn't know if you were coming, sure. And...'

'Didn't you get my letter?'

'What letter? No. When?'

'We were delayed by army road-blocks,' said, Shafik half smiling and hoping it would help Kate.

Amos, still furious, took it the wrong way.

'The Jordanians had road blocks too, didn't they?'

'Sure,' Shafik snapped. 'So What? They were occupiers as well.'

Both fuelled by their aroused emotions, the argument intensified.

'This city is ours, the Palestinians!' snapped Shafik.

'No. It belongs to both of us,' retorted Amos. 'And it will only be resolved by talking. Negotiating.'

'There will be no negotiation whilst we are occupied.'

'But you refused to talk before, either. That's your trouble. And anyway, if Nasser hadn't blocked Tiran, we wouldn't be here.'

'Ha. You Israelis manoeuvred us into that war, so that you could grab more land.'

Amos knew he was losing his temper, yet couldn't stop himself. Suddenly he saw Motti's face, sneering: *Just show me one Arab who's prepared to talk peace. Force is the only thing they understand!*

'And if you hadn't started this damn war,' he shouted, his voice echoing in the domed room, 'I wouldn't have lost my best friend!'

Kate and Yusuf stiffened from the confrontation. Shafik straightened back and raised his hand.

'We lost friends too. And,' he said, slowly and deliberately, 'we lost more. We lost our freedom!'

'Listen Shafik,' Amos snapped, 'you have a proverb: "With the eating, comes greater appetite." So I tell you one thing. We have our extremists too. And either you talk to Israelis like me. Soon,' he glanced at Yusuf then back to the man, 'or our own fanatics will take even more.'

'You will do that anyway. And you will never leave until we force you out.'

Amos spread his hands.

'Have it your way. Another war will solve nothing. And your own people will lose the most again.'

The argument between Motti and Yaacov in the dining hall flashed in Kate's mind – the fierce tones, flaring eyes, the enmity, the passion, and she now, like then a bystander. Her mind flashed back to Belfast and her body trembled; the Prods and Catholics at each other's throats, the hate and bitterness, the relentless settling of old scores. God, hadn't she gone to London -- and then out here to escape from all that? Yet here she was caught up in it all again, and she fuelling the flames.

Shafik swung round to Kate.

'He talks politics like a master, Kate, but can't you see when you're being used? This pig-headed, married man is using you.'

'None of your damn business,' shouted Amos, clenching his fist, and his body trembled. For a moment Kate feared there would be a fight.

Amos stopped and took a deep breath. What the hell was he doing here, arguing politics when his own life was in turmoil? He swung round.

'Look. I don't need this, Kate.' He ignored Shafik and nodding to Yusuf and the boy, muttered, '*Maah salameh*,' and strode out.

Kate sprang away from the wall and into the doorway.

'Oh. I'm sorry. Er… Goodbye.' She flicked one hand then hurried out into the street.

Amos was striding towards Mujhadin Street, seeing nothing, aiming nowhere. Kate ran after him.

'Amos. Wait. Please,' she called, heedless of the heads turning towards her. Amos didn't look back, but slowed his step. He was still boiling, furious at himself for having lost his temper. By Omariyya school, she caught up with him.

'Amos. Stop! Please.' She ran round and stood in front of him, breathing heavily and he stopped too. 'Listen, Amos. No Jill. No letter,' she panted. 'I didn't know when you were coming. Or even *if* you were coming.' She stopped, regaining her breath. 'Please. Amos. Don't be angry with me.'

Amos felt his head spinning.

'Wouldn't you be angry?' he snapped. 'Two minutes we're apart and already you're dancing off with someone else. And why him? And getting myself into a stupid argument. Did a lot for Arab-Israeli relations that did! Made me look a complete idiot as well!'

Kate felt her neck grow hot. Her Irish temper rose. Why the hell was she apologising. She had waited. Waited and he didn't come; didn't even know whether he was coming. She had more right to be annoyed than he.

'Look, Amos. I'm angry too. But it's all so stupid, so it is. Come,' she hissed, aware of shopkeepers and passers-by staring at them, 'I'm not standing here like this.' She grabbed his hand, she led him through an archway into the Ecce Homo Basilica.

In the cool, semi-darkness, they flopped down on a stone bench between two huge pillars. By the candlelit altar, priests prayed silently and a group of tourists padded across the flagstones between the columns. Amos sat hunched forward, and stared into the dark interior. Kate leaned into his shoulder, waiting for the anger to subside.

'Oh, Kate,' said Amos after a minute or so. 'I was so waiting to see you. To tell you I've done it. And when you weren't there…'

'It was just a terrible mix-up, Amos. I do love you. So I do.'

She raised his hand to her lips. 'More than anything, you know that.' She gripped the hand tightly. 'Look. You didn't come. Jill didn't contact me. No letter. I had to do something, Amos.'

He put his other hand over hers.

'I'm sorry, Kate. You're right. I wasn't thinking straight. But when you weren't at the hostel. *Elohim!*

Kate raised her head and they kissed.

'I'm here,' she murmured. 'I'll always be here, Amos.'

They sat in silence. At the far end, the priests finished the service, and as they filed out through a side door, Amos became conscious of the smell of dust and incense. Strange. Foreign. He turned and kissed her.

'Come. I've come to take you home, Kate.'

23

It was pitch dark and the main gates were closed for the night, but luckily the kibbutz hadn't bothered to padlock them since the war ended. Amos clanged them shut again and through force of habit, shot home the bolt and hooked on the padlock.

Amos wanted to avoid the busy, supper-time dining hall, so he took Kate straight down to the room he had prepared.

Kate sat on the bed. Throughout the whole bus-ride back, they'd both been on a high, kissing on the back seat like a couple of teenagers, talking softly, feeling each other's bodies and giggling about sleeping in the single bed. She would bring her prints and knick-knacks from the hut after supper. Go to town with Amos and buy a bedspread and rug; there was a special budget for new couples, he'd told her.

'I'll just pop down to say goodnight to the kids.' Amos kissed her. 'Back soon. Then we'll go up for a late supper.'

Outside, a cool wind was blowing across the desert. The room was cold too. Kate lay back on the bed and couldn't deny the renewed anxiety at being back in the kibbutz, but weary from the day and the journey, she closed her eyes for a moment. And dropped off.

'Where did you go, daddy?' asked Noa. The children were back and sat at the supper table. Amos kissed her head.

'Jerusalem,' he said. 'Had to see someone, *khamoodi*.'

She clutched the picture book he had bought her.

'Can you read it to me, Nitza?' she called. Nitza glanced up at Amos, then immediately lowered her eyes and looked back to the girl.

'When you're in pyjamas,' she smiled.

Miriam was putting the supper containers outside the kindergarten as Amos passed by on his way back from Ran's school.

'Amos stopped, rubbing his thumbs on his fingers. Miriam straightened up, waiting.

'Have you told — er — do the kids know?' he asked.

'No,' she spat. 'You did it, *khamor gerem*. You tell them!'

The dining hall was almost empty, only the last two tables occupied. They deliberately come up late, so there wasn't much choice. Kate made do with a hard-boiled egg and salad, whilst Amos went into the kitchen to get some hot tea from the urn. Yossi and Hanoch, the duty cleaners, were working their way round the hall, wiping the tables and putting up the chairs for floor-cleaning the following morning.

'How's the sugar-beet dicing going?' called Amos.

'About two thirds done,' said Yossi, wringing out a cloth over a bucket on the trolley.

'I'll see you in the garage at six,' said Amos.

Just before they finished, Miriam came through the swing doors, carrying the containers to the kitchen. It seemed to take an age as she walked through, during which neither of them spoke. She didn't sit down to eat but went straight out. Yossi purposefully carried on clearing and wiping the tables, while Kate looked down at the table, her stomach turning; the euphoria of the ride back was rapidly evaporating.

Amos went to see Uri about keeping the TD6 for a few more

days and Kate went over to her old hut.

'So,' Jill hugged her tightly. 'He's done the dastardly deed.' She leaned away and the two women looked into each other's faces. 'I'll hate losing you from the room, I really will.' She smiled. 'But I wish you all the very best, Kate.'

Kate sat on her old bed whilst Jill related the saga of missing the bus, and apologised profusely.

'If I'd known what was in that letter, I'd have crawled all the way to deliver it, honest,' she said. Kate hugged her. History, she smiled. Amos would come over later and take her bed to the room to make a temporary double bed.

'Strange.' She looked at Jill. 'I feel sort of in limbo, in a kind of trance.'

'So you will, Kate, for a while. Nothing wrong in that.'

'I'll miss being with you, Jill.' Kate fingered her blanket, 'and I apologise for leaning on you these past couple of months. Honest I do.'

Jill came over and sat beside her. 'No sweat, mate. I'm glad to see you so happy. Like I said, jealous in a way. But I'll still be here for a month or so.'

Kate sat up. 'You're leaving! So soon?'

'End of January.' Jill shrugged. 'Going to do a post-grad at Warwick. Industrial relations,' adding — 'if the interview goes okay.' She grinned, 'my kibbutz experience must have intrigued them!'

'Just that, Jill?'

Jill didn't reply at once. She loved Kate and didn't want to hurt her, but then they had always been open.

'Well, I need to leave you and Amos to settle down.' Then she took one of Kate's hands. 'And to be truthful, I suppose I don't want to get involved in any of the upsets that may result.'

Kate thought for a moment. Perhaps Jill had seen further than her. She sat back.

'Well I'm really sorry you're going, Jill. And what about Roger?'

Jill flicked her hand.

'Going back to Oz.' She laughed. 'Anyway, much too macho for anything serious.'

Later, with Kate's sea-grass mattress and blankets slung across his shoulder, Amos carried her metal bed to the room. Kate walked alongside, her belongings in a holdall and rucksack and another blanket around her neck.

'Like the Exodus from Egypt,' laughed Amos.

'More like bloody Irish tinkers,' puffed Kate.

As they passed the dining room, Amos fell silent. Uri had only agreed to let him keep the TD6 tractor for two more days.

'Look, Amos, it's the only light crawler we have, and Joe also needs the orange groves.'

'Yes, but last year we decided that the sugar beet was more pressing.'

'That was last year, yes. But the orange trees have grown denser since then.' Uri had strange air about him, distant. They had always been close and he wondered about that.

In their room, Amos plugged in the kettle; Eli had given him a spare one. Drinking hot, sweet coffee, they talked about the next few days. Kate would take another day off to organise her things. Amos had to work but would pick her up for breakfast and lunch.

'And what about your stuff?' said Kate. Amos looked into his coffee.

'Have to sort that out. Give it a few days. I'll find an

opportunity.' He paused. 'Perhaps when I'm with the children.'

Kate sat for a moment, pensive. Yes, she had reconciled herself to his seeing the children after work in his old room, going to parents' evenings, kids' parties and the rest, he and Miriam together, a world from which she would be excluded. Yes. She'd have to handle that, as well as her sense of guilt over Ran and Noa.

'A grush for your thoughts?' Amos got up and stood behind her, wrapping his arms around her chest.

'Worth more than that,' she murmured, raising his hand and kissing it. 'Come. We've both had a long day.'

'Your side or mine,' muttered Amos as they slipped into the cold sheets. They'd put the two single beds together and the centre bars dug into their sides.

'Mine,' giggled Kate, moving to the side nearest the wall. 'Then it will be warm for me.'

Amos woke with the alarm clock. He rolled over and kissed her neck. Kate woke and put her arms around him and before they knew it, they were making love, quickly and furiously with a passion and intensity born of the restful night.

'Won't be in much of a state for work,' panted Amos as he lay back.

'Gives you energy, they say,' muttered Kate.

'Who says?'

Amos tore himself away, put on his working clothes and went out to wash. When he came in to say goodbye, Kate was asleep again. He stood for a moment, staring down at the bed. In the half-light, her hair was fanned out on the pillow, one hand by her mouth. He smiled, and closing the door gently, his body still tingling, he strode away down to the garage.

Kate was up and dressed when he came to call her for breakfast. The dining hall was crowded, everyone in at the same time. In the summer, many field workers preferred to eat out, but now most wanted a hot breakfast, away from the elements.

Kate felt awkward at first as they walked down the aisle between the tables, greeting the volunteers she knew, but no longer sitting with them. They joined Eli and another cowman, the faint odour of sour milk and manure emanating from their clothes despite having changed boots.

'So,' grinned Eli, 'you're joining us tomorrow, Kate.' Amos had arranged with Aviva for Kate to work in the dairy. Later, the work committee would find a more permanent place. Kate nodded and smiled as she took a plate of porridge from the server.

'Poor Roger. He'll have to moderate his swearing,' said Amos. 'Someone will understand what he's saying.'

Kate was only half listening as the two men spoke. Out of the corner of her eye, she noticed people looking towards their table and passing the odd remark. She caught Orna's eye and the woman turned away. No friends there. Would there be many more like her? It had been Amos's idea to brazen it out and she had agreed. Sooner or later they, and especially she, would have to face public scrutiny. But she was glad that Miriam worked with the children and only came up to the dining hall late in the evening.

Back in the room, Kate began to sort out her clothes in the wardrobe. Hung up some of Amos's shirts. She felt at a loss for what to do and wished that she had started work that day. She went out to the veranda. In these old houses, it was common to two rooms and was open at the front. Her clothes cupboard was dusty and the shelves stained. Taking a bowl from the shower, she started to wash them down.

'Not worth it, Kate.' Kate spun round. It was Batya. Ever since making her miss the bus to Jerusalem that time, through the apologies they'd become quite friendly. Batya was a New Yorker, short and dumpy, with straight black hair and very dark brown eyes. She was in charge of the babies' house. 'Bit of a poet,' Amos had said once. 'She and Ya'ir would always be going on about this one or that.'

'Oh! Shalom, Batya,' said Kate. 'Didn't know you lived around here.'

'I don't. I've come to call Rivkah.' She stepped onto the veranda and came close, whispering conspiratorially, 'never gets to the baby on time for her feed. Anyway,' she continued louder, nodding at the shelves, 'leave that. I've got some shelf paper at home.'

After calling Rivkah, Batya led Kate to her room and delved into a cupboard in the shower.

'Here,' she said. 'It's not a full roll. But it should be enough.'

'Thanks. Thanks a lot, Batya,' said Kate and was about to go, when the woman touched her elbow.

'Hey. You're good at working with kids, Kate.'

Kate smiled. 'Maybe. But I can't go back to the Gan.'

Sure,' said Batya, 'but what about the babies?' Kate shrugged. Batya spread her hands. 'Look. I've got to get back to work. Think about it?'

Amos called her for lunch and again, Kate noticed the different reactions. Most seemed neutral, just curious, while others made a point of being friendly. Some -- mainly women, reflected antagonism. And she couldn't help wondering just how many.

'Look. Everyone has their own problems,' said Amos as he

walked with her back to the room. 'Believe me Kate, it will soon be okay.'

After work, Amos picked up Noa before she got to the room; Miriam's room, he had to keep telling himself. He sat with her on the edge of the sandbox in the kindergarten.

'Look, Noa. I have to tell you something.' The girl looked at his mouth, eyes wide and her fingers playing with the zip of his jacket. 'Now. See. Daddy and mummy are going to live in different rooms. We want it that way.' He paused. Waited. No reaction. 'But we both love you as much as before. More, even and -'

Noa suddenly raised one finger.

'You mean, there's not enough room in the bed for both of you, daddy?' Amos sat with his mouth open. God. The way kids' minds worked. He leaned forward and kissed her.

'Well, yes. Something like that, Noa.' Then he stood up and hoisted her onto his shoulders.

Miriam was drinking coffee as they came onto the veranda.

'Hey. Up!' Lifting her first high in the air, he set the girl down, her shoes stamping a tattoo on the tiles.

'Shalom, mummy.' The girl ran in, holding out a drawing. 'Nitza showed us how to write numbers,' she cried. 'Look.' Miriam took the sheet and cuddled her.

'Lovely,' Miriam smiled. 'Come, we can play with your number cards.'

Amos half smiled. Kids. So much for the anticipated trauma.

He hung about on the veranda, his stomach turning. He had no right to go in and sit down now. Yet he wanted to wait for Ran. He sat on a stool by the working-clothes cupboard, gazing out over the lawn, hoping that Kate didn't feel too left out during these hours. Over the last few days, he had begun to realise just how much more difficult this transition was going to be for her, than for him.

'Amos,' she'd said, hugging him. 'As long as you realise that. As long as we both know. We'll manage.' And he loved her for it.

Miriam's voice suddenly came through the doorway.

'Make yourself a cup of coffee.' She didn't look up. 'And you can sit inside. We're not dogs.' Amos hadn't had the time to drink before he had showered and came over. He took a cup and was pouring the hot water when Ran strolled in.

'Hi, dad. Any luck with the basketball tickets?'

Amos jumped. He had completely forgotten. And Ran couldn't be bluffed. 'No. Sorry, Ran. Been a bit busy.' He went into the room with the boy. 'I'll try this week, okay.'

They played chess. With the board between them, Amos sat right at the edge of the bed, embarrassed now to be on the same bed they had shared for so long. Miriam watched out of the corner of her eye, wanting to hate, yet somehow pitying him.

Ran was at the stage where Amos had to concentrate. One stupid move, and his son would close in on him. As Joe always joked: 'for the first few years, I let my son beat me. After that, I didn't need to try!' Knowing he had to speak to Ran, Amos couldn't keep his mind on the game. Ran had him in checkmate in nine moves.

Miriam took Noa back and Amos walked the boy to the school.

'Ran,' he said as they approached, 'I have to talk to you. Come.'

Ran looked puzzled but said nothing and they went over to the children's farm and stood by the donkey's pen. It was already dark, but a faint light reached them from the fence lamps beyond.

'Look, Ran,' Amos launched straight into it. 'Mum and I have decided to separate.' The boy stiffened and clenched his hands.

'What do you mean, Dad?' Amos felt the blood roaring in his ears.

'Well. We've decided to live apart. And I've moved to the room next to Moshe and Rivkah. Sometimes people are happier that way, Ran.'

The donkey came over and nuzzled against Amos's hip. Ran reached out and stroked its wet nose.

'Was that why Mum was crying in Nurit's room last night, Dad?'

Amos jumped, wondering what the boy already knew.

'Who said?'

'Semadar told me this morning. We're in the same room and she asked me what it was about. I said I didn't know.' Suddenly the boy looked up. 'Will you both be living alone, then, Dad?'

Amos tensed. He'd wanted to break this later; one thing at a time. But he couldn't lie.

'I don't know about Mum,' he said. 'But Kate, you know Kate, she will live with me. But it will your room too, Ran.'

For a moment, Ran said nothing. He took his hand from the donkey and gripped the fence rail, staring at the fence lights.

'No,' he snapped, kicking the fence post and sending the donkey scampering away, 'I won't come to your room! Mum's room is my room and you should stay there!' His voice began to rise. 'You made Mum cry and I hate you,' he shouted. 'I'll never to come to your room, Dad. Never! I hate you!'

Spinning round, Ran hurtled away across the rough ground towards the school, leaving his father standing by the fence, shaking. Slowly, Amos walked to the path and headed for the room, his eyes beginning to water and his stomach clenched. He couldn't go back to the room like this. He dodged into the trees, and clutched at a branch until they dried up. He wondered whether he should tell Kate. No secrets, she'd insisted. But he couldn't burden her with this. Not right now. He waited for a few minutes till his breathing returned to normal — almost, then continued on to the room.

Amos took Kate up for supper, but as they came out into the lobby afterwards to look at the work rota, Menakhem burst through the main door, his face flushed.

'Amos,' he puffed. 'Been looking for you. Can't find Ran anywhere.'

'What do you mean?'

'Miriam said you and he went off for a chat and that was the last she'd seen of him, so we thought he was with you.'

'Well, yes, we were talking then he went off, and I'd supposed back to the school.'

Everyone in the lobby turned to look. Amos felt his face redden and turned to Kate.

'Perhaps go back to the room in case Ran comes there, Kate. I'll be down in a minute.

'You sure?'

'Yes, won't be long.'

Kate hurried out her head whirling. Amos hadn't told her what had happened and she was puzzled. Ran was such a mature, steady kid. So unlike him. They must have had an argument. On the way down to the room she guessed what had brought it on -- and was furious that Amos had kept it from her.

When she'd gone, Amos looked at Menakhem.

'Have you checked with the other kids?'

'Of course. They're all back in the school. None of them have seen him either. And now it's pitch dark.'

For a moment the lobby was silent, everyone thinking and wondering what to do. Suddenly, Miriam burst through the doors.

'Have you found him?' she shouted. Everyone in the lobby turned to stare.

'Not yet,' said Menakhem. He looked around at the small crowd assembling. 'Listen,' he said, looking at Amos and Miriam, 'let us go to my room and think what to do next.'

His wife Hannah was there, and the four of them stood in their room, silent for a moment. Miriam glared at Amos.

'You were the last one he was with,' she snapped. 'It must be because you told him. Had you told him?'

'About you and Miriam?' asked Menakhem.

Amos shrugged.

'Yes. I told him that Miriam and I were separating. He took it badly and ran off, and I thought he had gone to the school — or to Miriam.'

'Well, it's obvious he was so upset that he wanted to be alone,' said Menakhem. 'The point is, where?'

Miriam stamped her foot.

'He could be anywhere, in the cowshed, out in the fields. Anywhere. And in the dark!' She glared at Amos, her head boiling, but didn't want to make a scene in front of the others. His face showed he already felt guilty enough.

'Yes,' said Menakhem, 'upset and anywhere. And it's already late. Listen. We have to organise search parties to find him. Now!' He stood up. 'I'll go and see Uri and Yaacov. And find enough torches.'

'I'll come too,' said Amos. 'Meet you at Uri's in ten minutes.'

Miriam started forward too but Hannah raised her hand.

'Miriam. Best stay here with me,' she said. 'Let them organise the search first. Come, I'll make us coffee meanwhile.'

Miriam was about to protest; Ran was in the dark, jackals, snakes -- anything. Her head felt fit to bursting and her body trembled. And when the men hurried out, she sank onto the chair, her heart thumping against her ribs.

Amos ran down to the room. Kate was sitting on the bed. She jumped up.

'Have you found him?'

'No. We're organising search parties, Kate. Best you stay here in case he comes back. He can't be far.' He went to the work cupboard and took out the large torch they used for night-time irrigation. 'I'll be back as soon as we've found him.' He hugged her and ran out.

Kate stood in the middle of the room for a moment. No one had thought of involving her. She went out to the toilet, and sat and cried.

By now, most of the kibbutz had heard what had happened. Clusters of people stood on the paths, wondering what and why, and offering to take part. Many joined Uri and Menakhem by the dining hall, where they sorted out small groups, making sure each had a torch, then quickly dispersed in different directions; children's farm, cowsheds, garage, around the fence, out to the road, the wadi, and soon from everywhere came shouts of 'Ran! Ran!'

Amos and Menakhem went out to the main road together, turning in all directions, shouting his name. No response. Amos looked into the darkness, his head bursting, trying to see into the distance, and saw a few faint fires glimmering in the darkness.

'The Bedouin,' said Amos. 'We ought to go over and let them know. Keep a lookout. They know the area better than any of us.'

'Yes, good idea.' Menakhem raised his hand. 'You know, I think Ran might even have gone there. Their kids and ours have met a few times, playing football on our pitch and that. Come, let's see.'

They hurried down the dirt track, but as they neared the encampment, three figures suddenly loomed out of the gloom and hurried towards them; a man and two boys.

'*Ahalan,*' said the Bedu. 'We come to kibbutz,' he said breathless. 'He meet my son by sheep-pen. Know him from football.'

Ran came up close to Amos. Head down, hands hanging by his side.

'Sorry, Dad. Hope you weren't worried. Sorry.'

Amos crouched down and hugged him close.

'It's okay. Sure, a bit, yes. Well, more than a bit. So was Mum of course. Come.' He stood up and took his hand. 'Your clever teacher thought you might have come this way.'

Menakhem ruffled Ran's hair then turned and shook the Bedu's hand.

'*Shukaran, shukaran,*' he said. 'Thank you.' They all shook hands again and with Amos holding Ran's hand all the way, walked back and across the road to the kibbutz, and to Menakhems's room.

After he hugged him goodnight -- 'I'll make sure we get tickets for the Macabi match,' Amos left Ran with Menakhem and Miriam and hurried down to the room. Kate would be waiting.

Kate had gone out to the path, but when she saw Amos and Ran with Miriam and Menakhem going to the school, she'd hurried back to the room, shut the door and gone to curl up on the bed. And again, felt an outsider.

24

The night's events gradually melted into the past. Their double bed had arrived and, with Kate's flair, gradually the room became more homely. She became used to Amos disappearing after work to see the children. Ran didn't come round but little Noa did and she enjoyed playing with the child. In the dining hall, although she sensed some hostility, mainly from Nitza's and Orna's tables, most were welcoming and some who spoke English made a point of chatting to her when they passed.

Amos had arranged for Kate to work in the cowsheds and Eli had gone out of his way to make her welcome: a small sized pair of rubber boots awaiting her and one of their work-clothes shelves already cleared out for her use.

'The delicate souls in the dining hall can't stand the smell of real farming,' Eli grinned. They always changed their working boots for sandals. 'Sometimes, we have to change trousers as well when we go up to eat.'

She was given the young calves to look after, giggling at first as their rough tongues sucked at her fingers.

'If you could also come down and feed them once or twice a week in the evenings,' Eli said hesitantly after a few days, 'we'd really be grateful. It's only an hour.' Kate readily agreed. She wanted to contribute, to be a full partner in everything. Eli had his own agenda. He had seen it in other kibbutzim. When marriages split up, one party usually left. He was fond of Miriam too, but Amos; that would be a terrible loss.

After a few days, Eli took Kate into their modern milking parlour and after several tries and much giggling, she'd managed to slip the suction cups onto the teats. Although she enjoyed working there, Kate soon found that livestock would not have been her first choice as a work place. With all its problems, she had enjoyed the children and the kindergarten and after a while, resented the relentless, repetitive routine of the cowshed. But at least it served to remove her from meeting too many people until things had calmed down.

Amos was biting into his second piece of toast after work that day, when the door slowly opened.

'*Shalom Abba!*' It was Noa, swaddled in a thick green cardigan and red pom-pom hat. In her hand she held a piece of coloured card. 'I made this for you,' she said. 'For your room.' She trotted over to where he sat on the bed. '*Neshikah*. Abba. Kiss. Kiss.' Amos hugged her then gently took off her cardigan.

'You found your way on your own?' She nodded. 'Big girl. Daddy's big girl.' And he hugged her again' The girl tucked her chin into her shoulder. 'Mummy pointed me the way.'

Kate tensed for a moment, then came across and crouched down beside her. 'Toast?'

The girl nodded, holding onto Amos's knee.

Kate tapped the jam jar and raised her eyebrows, '*Ribah*?'

Noa smiled. '*Harbeh!*'

Amos had brought some of the toys and books from Miriam's room. He sat her on the bed and whilst she nibbled at the toast, read her a story. Kate sat back by the table watching, pleased that Noa came to the room by herself, as though having accepted her.

The New Year arrived and with it not being much celebrated in Israel, would have passed Kate by completely, had Jill not popped in after supper one evening. She happened to be alone, writing by the small table.

'Happy New Year,' Jill grinned as she burst in.

'Heck. Forgot all about it,' said Kate, waving her over to the bed. Jill sat down and twiddled the radio knob. Suddenly, the King's College carol service came through, relayed on Radio Amman from Jordan.

'There y'are, mate,' Jill grinned again. 'Happy New Year!'

Kate was surprised how quickly it had had come and despite the Christmas visit to Bethlehem, how little she had anticipated it.

Jill had come to invite her and Amos over to the volunteers' New Year's Eve party.

'New Year party?' muttered Amos, when he came in. 'Not for me, Kate,'

'Then come for me,' she said, kissing him.

Will, an American boy, was strumming guitar and croaking out a Bob Dylan lyric when Kate led Amos into Roger's hut. About twenty volunteers were crowded into the small room, the air thick with smoke -- and more than just tobacco.

'Hey,' shouted Roger. 'A real native!' Then carried on drinking from a bottle of Goldstar beer. The kibbutz had provided a crate for the party, as well as biscuits and a large chocolate cake.

Kate and Jill were immediately plunged into deep conversation, but Amos sat on the end of one of the beds and pressed himself back against the wall. He hoped Kate wouldn't stay long.

A couple of boys had been to town and bought a few bottles of brandy and Arak. Having lived 'dry' for a few months, a few were beginning to fall under the influence. The singing grew louder and became more and more raucous and disjointed; two couples were already into heavy snogging on the other beds.

Suddenly Roger and Hans, a Dutch boy, stood up and tottered through the door, arms around each other's shoulders. Standing on the veranda they waved their bottles, shouting into the darkness: 'Happy New Year, everyone!' And, when only silence answered them, grew more agitated: 'Happy New Year you miserable bastards. Come and celebrate. Happy New Year!' Jill went out and tried to drag them in. Roger pushed her away.

'What a miserable load they all are. Never been pissed once, I bet. Any of them.'

Kate looked at Amos, her face taut. He had already stood up.

'I'm off, Kate. See you in the room.' But as he pushed his way out, Roger turned to him.

'Go on. Not good enough for the bloody aristocracy are we?' He tottered against Amos, leaning against him and slurring his words. 'Just good enough to shovel the shit in the cowsheds, eh?' Amos heaved himself away and suddenly without support, Roger fell forward into the bushes, the bottle flying away into the darkness. 'Go on. Hit me, would you… you wait!' he slurred.

Without looking at Kate, Amos strode away, cursing under his breath.

'I needed that like a hole in the head, Kate,' he muttered, when she came back to the room. 'Tomorrow, it will be all round the damn kibbutz.'

'Well I'm annoyed too. It wasn't supposed to be like that.'

'Listen Kate, you're a kibbutznik now. No longer a volunteer.' He pulled off his shorts. 'I'm going to bed.'

For the very first time he couldn't calm down. He had allowed himself to be pushed into going against his better judgement. And was his anger just from that he been coaxed into not just the party, but into everything? And it took a long time to fall asleep.

When Kate woke the next morning, the first day of the New Year, Amos had already gone out to work. Eli had the warm buckets of milk ready for her when she came down.

'The first two pens are new-borns,' he nodded to the shed. 'Leave them till last.' Her head still heavy, Kate fed the small calves then brought a few forkfuls of soft hay to the larger ones.

'Here,' Eli called. 'Take this bucket. For those two, there.' Kate looked at the thick, frothing, creamy milk.

'Why the difference?'

'Called Colostrum,' said Eli. 'Extra rich stuff from a cow that has just given birth.'

She took it and went across and coaxed one tiny newborn towards her. With faltering steps, it tottered across the metal slats, sniffing at the bucket. Gently, she dipped a half-clenched hand into the milk, fingertips protruding the held them to its pink muzzle. The calf sucked on her teat-like fingers then as she drew them down into the foaming liquid, it began sucking up the milk. Soon, it was drinking easily, her tail whipped from side to side and ears twitched.

Kate glanced down. The calf looked so thin and weak, its coat still damp and matted, the shrivelled umbilical cord hanging from its belly. Spontaneously, she began to cry, the tears falling freely into the bucket as it sucked. Somehow, she managed to hold it steady until the tiny beast had finished, then set it down. She took out a handkerchief and hurriedly blew her nose and wiped her eyes.

Eli, happened to be watching from the office doorway. He quickly dodged inside. Kate passed dried her eyes and passed along to the second calf. By the time it had finished, she had managed to compose herself.

In that brief span of time, Kate realised what last night had been all about. Amos was right, she couldn't have it both ways, hanker after being just a volunteer with no real commitments, while at the same time wanting to live with Amos. She had to make the break; become part of the community.

By the time they both came in from work, it was as though the night before had never happened. Giggling, they showered together in the cramped space, each trying to get as much of the hot water as possible, Kate squealing as they rubbed each other dry with the towels.

'Sshh!' hissed Kate. 'God knows what Rivkah will think next door.'

'Just jealous,' said Amos, thinking that he could never have dreamed of doing this with Miriam. He pulled her against him and rested his chin on her shoulder.

'Sorry about last night, Kate. I really am.' He kissed her neck. 'I do love you. I hate arguing with you or your friends!' Kate leaned back and looked into his face.

'We must never fall asleep like that again, ever, Amos. Make up first. Okay?' Amos kissed her again and grinned.

'*Maskeem*!' Agreed.

Winter through January was cold, but with bright sunshine and clear blue skies. Joe was pleased that he could continue to pick avocados daily and take advantage of the export season to Europe. Amos finished preparing the sugar beet field and after a light watering, the new alfalfa crop was beginning to sprout nicely.

He drove out and looked across the field. The new growth made a bright green lawn, which stretched right up to the roadside. But beyond the irrigated area, the new barley shoots were turning pale. For the cereal crops, the promise heralded by the early rains had begun to evaporate. The fear of drought had returned and Motti and the *felakhim* grew morose and short tempered. Despite his personal dislike for the man, Amos always acknowledged the hard work and long hours they put in. But without heavy rains soon, all their efforts would come to nothing.

One in three will be a drought, the Bedouin said, and they'd been here for hundreds of years. But it could be one year out of three, or two together out of five; anything. The only hope was for the two good years to more than cover the loss of the third.

Across the main road, a Bedu drove a camel hitched up to a single furrow, wooden plough. They would sow late, keeping their seed-corn until they were sure that sufficient rain had fallen. But the short growing period gave low yields, and led to severe soil erosion when the rains did come. Amos looked up at the clear sky. Last year had been a drought. A second one this year and after the disruption of the war, would be a real disaster.

Kate came up to the dining hall for lunch, pulled off her yellow headscarf and shook out her hair. The scarf smelled of cows, not nasty but a smell of cowhide for all that, and she stuffed it in her pocket. At work, she didn't notice it at all, but whenever she came away from the cowsheds, her nostrils picked up the faint odour. And it wouldn't go away until she had showered.

At that moment, Batya came out of the lobby, carrying food containers. She saw Kate and stopped.

'Hi. How are the cows?'

'Fine.' Kate smiled. 'Haven't killed many yet.'

Batya arched her eyebrows.

'And you?'

'Me?' Kate shrugged. 'Keeps me out of mischief.'

'Well?' Batya said softly, almost conspiratorially as she came closer. 'Thought about it?'

'Thought about what?'

'The babies' house. Don't you remember?'

Kate felt a flutter in her stomach.

'Sure. But no one's asked me.'

'Well, I'm asking you.' Batya leaned closer. 'I've mooted it at the work committee. We need someone, now that Offra has started maternity leave.'

Kate's palms itched. This wouldn't be just any job; it was a real responsibility, like the *Gan*.

'Really. I'd like that, Batya. Sure. Thanks. Thanks a lot.'

Batya started to walk on, then turned her head and smiled.

'Great. I'll let you know. Some time next week.'

Kate went in to eat with butterflies in her stomach. A proper place of work. An acceptance. She couldn't wait to tell Amos.

Batya carried on down to the babies' house. Apart for being fond of Kate, like Eli, Batya too had her agenda. If Kate was unhappy at work, she wouldn't stay; then neither would Amos.

When Amos drove down to the garage to pick up a grease gun for Yossi, Rami and Shumikeh were loading long aluminium irrigation pipes on to a trailer.

'Where are you taking those?' he called, sliding out of the seat.

'We may have irrigate the wheat,' said Rami. 'All the fields we can reach from the vineyards stopcocks.'

'And with whose water?' Amos asked.

'Dunno.' Rami scratched his head. 'Motti just told us to get the pipes ready.'

All their water came through the national pipeline from up north, and each branch had a strict quota. Amos jumped back into the driving seat, accelerated up the track and round to the office, and braked in cloud of dust.

Uri was at his desk. In front of him, a long, buff-coloured, official form.

'Since when is Motti irrigating the cereal crops?' Amos barked as he burst in. Uri threw down his pen and sat back.

'See this?' he nodded to the paper.

'I know,' said Amos. 'It's for drought compensation. So what?'

Uri shrugged.

'Well. From now on, we'll just get compensation for part of the total area. And only on a complete crop failure. So we have to save as much as we can.'

'But whose water quota will the *falkha* take? And they're our pipes, ready for the alfalfa and sugar beet. Shmuel won't buy any new ones.' Amos strode over to the desk. 'And, anyway,' he tapped his finger on the desk, 'shouldn't this all come to the farm committee first?'

Uri didn't reply for a few seconds.

'Look,' he said. 'Shmuel reckons it'll be more profitable this way and we need the cash flow.' Still uneasy, he continued. 'Also, Motti says he can't sow any spring wheat unless we can save what we can.'

'You mean he's said he won't. Like two years ago, when he threatened to chuck in managing the *falkha*!' Amos slapped the desktop. 'It's blackmail. And I demand it comes to committee.'

Uri glanced up at him, his face strained.

'Listen, Amos. Financially, it's evenly balanced. Always is. Last time, you won.' Again came that uneasy expression. 'This time Motti may have more support. Or rather, you won't have as much.'

Amos's neck grew hot. He leaned down.

'What do you mean?'

'What I said, Amos.' Uri looked straight into his eyes. 'Look. *Shev:* sit down a moment.' Amos shook his head.

'Got to get back to Yossi with the grease gun. One of the disc bearings is binding.'

Uri played with the pen between his fingers.

'Look. You don't seem to realise, Amos. With some people, you are not the most popular bloke at the moment.' He glanced through the window then back to Amos. 'True, mainly husbands of wives with a grudge against Kate.' He paused. 'Me? Well, we know each other of old, and it's your life, my friend. But everyone's fond of Miriam and some see it differently; think she's had a rough deal.'

Amos stepped back, his fists clenching and unclenching, the blood rushing to his head.

'And that's what decides with the farm, Uri?'

Uri hunched forward.

'Look, I'm just the one who's telling you, Amos. Like I said. We know each other from way back. But Miriam and Nitza, Shosh, Motke, Elana, others, not to mention Motti and Orna with their own agenda.'

'Listen,' Amos snapped. 'What the hell has my personal life got to do with the water allocations? If the drought continues, everyone will want more water. And what about Joe's orchards? And the maize area for the silage? It's got to be a rational, economic decision.' He slapped his hand on the desktop again. 'I still demand a full discussion in the farm committee.'

Uri stood up and came round the desk.

'Okay. Have it your way. I'll bring it up this Wednesday. But with Shmuel backing the *falkha* and Shosh's husband Yuval, on the committee too…'

Amos stood for a moment, then said slowly, 'what a petty way to run a farm, eh?'

'I know,' Uri winced. 'But people are people, Amos.' He spread his hands. 'Not a lot anyone can do about that.'

Amos drove out to the fields, fast, his head spun and hands gripped the steering wheel until his knuckles hurt. So much for everything being fine, everything just as usual. How come he didn't notice? His head burned for the rest of the afternoon.

Kate had just finished showering as he clomped onto the veranda.

'Hi,' she called, poking her head out of the door. 'Got some good news today.' Amos sat on the stool and kicked off his boots.

'Uhuh?'

'Batya's getting me a job in the babies' house. Great, eh?'

Amos stood up and kissed her, hoping she knew what she would get herself into. To deal with parents was never easy and with babies' mums, even more delicate and tense. There was bound to be the odd bitchy one -- and after what Uri had said, probably more than one.

He plugged in the kettle, and stared at the wall. When Kate came out, she looked at him.

'What's up?'

Amos knew he couldn't hide things from Kate. Women. Just like with Miriam.

'Looks as though we're going onto a drought regime,' he said. 'Have to decide allocations of emergency irrigation. Everyone will be fighting over water allocations.' He took off his socks. 'Had it last year too. Have to get my boxing gloves on.' Kate poured the coffee. 'Still,' he added quickly, 'let's forget it. Celebrate your new job.'

'Haven't got it yet.' She flicked his nose.

'Huh. If Batya's arranging it, it's pretty definite. We call her the Brooklyn bulldozer.' Amos spread a slice of toast and grinned, 'don't tell her though!'

They sat close, nibbling and drinking, feeling intimate and together. But the impending farm-committee meeting played on his mind and Amos knew couldn't hide his concern.

25

They sat with Joe and Aviva at supper. Kate had noticed that Amos chose where they sat each evening the dining hall, avoiding near where Miriam or others were -- and surprisingly, where Nitza sat too.

'If we can't keep up irrigation on the young alfalfa,' Amos remarked to Joe, 'it will be another season before we can take the first cut.'

'Well, the mature vineyard won't suffer much,' said Joe, biting off a piece of cucumber. He never bothered to cut up a salad -- too much like damned hard work, 'but I'll have to give the two-year-old vines some water to keep them going.'

While the two men agonised over water quotas, Aviva told Kate a little of the babies' house. Hours and parents – especially the troublesome ones. Kate had long sussed out that despite the liberal attitudes and ideals of the kibbutz, men talked work while the women generally talked children.

'Biggest problem is Orna,' said Aviva, 'though Batya will give you the full picture.' Adding softly, almost conspiratorially, 'mind you, with a workaholic husband like Motti, any wife would have problems,' and Kate remembered the way Orna had reacted to her in the kitchen. That was the problem with the kibbutz: always bumping into the same people but in different situations.

After supper, Aviva invited Kate to their room while Amos went to the farm committee meeting. The committee was already gathered, with Uri at his desk. Although only the six elected members could vote, it was always an open meeting, and with the impending drought on everyone's minds, Joe had decided to go to as an observer, as well Barukh, his deputy. Rami and Shumikeh were also there to support Motti.

Uri opened the meeting with a few smaller items: a new hatchery unit for the poultry house, which was agreed in record time, only Shmuel dissenting. As treasurer, he usually dissented on investments outside the yearly plan.

'Right,' said Uri, eventually. 'I've explained the reduced drought compensation package at the previous meeting. The barley is less of a problem at the moment but Shmuel reckons it will pay us to water as much of the winter wheat as we can. So Motti will outline what needs to be done.'

Motti sat up; long, sharp-featured face, smooth brown hair and a bushy moustache. His brown eyes darted from one person to another as he spoke in short, clipped phrases, the speech of a doer rather than a talker.

'So,' he concluded, 'the areas that have already sprouted are wilting. Even if the rains come soon, they will never recover unless we keep them going with at least one watering. Immediately.' He glanced around, avoiding Amos's eyes, then sat back and lit a cigarette.

Amos waited. No one else spoke. He knew that Joe was concerned too but he and Barukh didn't fancy taking on Shmuel and Motti. It would be up to him.

'Okay,' Amos began. 'So we have to try to save the winter wheat. Last year, the Water Company let us go over our quota because of the war. But they won't this year, not without a whacking great penalty.' He paused and looked around the circle. 'So whose water are the *falkha* going to use?' Silence again.

Shmuel opened his diary and slowly flicked over the pages.

Amos knew the signs. The treasurer had banked on it being nodded through. Uri tried to open up the discussion again. Silence. Then Ephraim suggested formulating a revised irrigation programme for the rest of the year. Amos backed it up. Two others spoke but came down neither one way, or the other. Amos could see Motti's face clouding over.

'There's no time to make out programmes,' Motti snapped, waving his arm. 'The wheat is wilting and we have to start now.'

'So will my alfalfa and Joe's vines, and the young silage maize,' said Amos. 'And what about the weed-sprouting irrigation planned for the sugar beet?' He turned to Uri. 'Look. It has to be a balanced, economic decision. Perhaps it would be better to wait and see if the rains do come, then re-sow with spring wheat.'

'And all our work go to waste,' shouted Motti, his face beginning to turn red.

'So will that of others if the *falkha* take their water.' Amos strove to keep his voice down but inside he was boiling.

Motti leaned forward and pointed at Amos.

'You don't care a damn about the wheat. If you just looked at the fields instead of screwing around in Jerusalem with a volunteer, you wouldn't make such stupid suggestions!' In the shocked silence, Rami and Shumikeh looked around, smirking.

Amos's neck grew hot. He almost rose to the bait. Instead, somehow managing to keep his cool, he glared back at Motti.

'That's just about your level,' he retorted, his whole body trembling. 'Just what I could expect!'

Uri stood up and thumped his desk.

'Cut it out both of you. We have to reach a firm decision tonight.' He glanced around. 'There are two proposals: one, to irrigate the nearby wheat areas from tomorrow and two, to make a plan and decide within a week from today.'

'It can't wait,' snapped Motti.

'The committee will decide,' Amos growled. 'Not you alone.'

Motti swivelled round, stood up and strode to the door, his two mates following.

'Well, you can all manage the bloody *falkha* by yourselves now. I've had enough!'

Shmuel closed his diary with a snap.

'Great.' He glared at Amos. 'Satisfied now?'

Amos glared back.

'If you hadn't tried to make arrangements behind everyone's backs, it wouldn't have gone like this.'

Rami and Shumikeh weren't committee members and without Motti voting against, Ephraim's proposal was agreed. Everyone rose to go out, but Amos knew it wouldn't end there. If the rains didn't come, the whole problem would surface again within a week or two.

After the meeting, he strolled across the lawn with Uri.

'Many others got a grudge?' Amos asked.

'Not like Motti,' said Uri. 'But enough.'

'Enough to what?'

'Enough to be a thorn in your backside for a while, Amos.' As they neared the houses, they stopped for a moment. 'I hear Kate is going to work with the babies?' said Uri.

'Uhuh. She's looking forward to it.'

Uri slapped Amos's shoulder.

'Good. *Layla Tov*,' adding as he walked away, 'best of luck.'

Amos watched him go then looked up at the dark sky. Yes, they would need all the luck they could find.

On Friday, Amos went up to the clothes store after work to fetch their clean laundry. With his mind preoccupied, he turned to the shelves along the left hand wall then abruptly stopped. That was his old shelf: his and Miriam's. Old habits. But just as he turned to his new shelf, Miriam happened to come in.

'Oh.' She stopped in the doorway for a second; the clothes store was empty apart from the two of them. 'It's you.' She looked tired and drawn. Amos felt his cheeks burning.

'Just getting my washing,' he murmured and as he hurriedly pulled his bundle from the shelf, Miriam brushed past, then stopped and turned to him. Laying a hand on his bare arm, she began:

'Look. Amos. You are quite sure?' she said softly. 'I mean, perhaps we were a bit, well, impulsive, you know. But for us, for the kids, we could…'

Amos stared down at his laundry.

'Look. I've decided, Miriam,' he mumbled.

Miriam snatched her hand away.

'Well, despite what you've done, Amos, at least I wanted to try. But if that's what you want,' she backed to the door, her eyes like slits. 'Just don't think you and that damned girl can just stay here playing happy families!' And she spun round and ran out.

Amos leaned against the wooden shelves, clutching the clean smelling bundle against his chest, his face flushed and his head whirling. Breathing deeply, he waited for his heart to stop thumping then went out, closing the door behind him.

Kate was in the babies' house. It was her second day working with Batya and she had begun to feel more confident. Working in the *Gan* had been a responsibility, but handling the tiny infants without fear of hurting them or holding them the wrong way, was much more forbidding.

'Just do it naturally,' Batya smiled. 'You seemed in such agony as you tied that nappy.'

'I was,' Kate muttered. 'They look so delicate.'

'Oh. Babies are quite tough really. And they can sense your hands being confident or not.'

Kate had always wondered about collective education, the children sleeping away from home and seeming to owe more to their *metapelet* than their parents. But after her weeks in the kindergarten, she had been pleasantly surprised how everything seemed to dovetail so neatly. And how assured and confident the children were as well, as being so attached to their parents. But babies?

'What about bonding,' she had pressed Batya that morning. 'Sure. The older kids, I can understand. But surely babies need to be close to their mothers when they're so young.'

Batya stirred two cups of coffee. It was a quiet moment, five of the babies asleep and the other two, having been fed, were out with their mothers. She twitched her large, round glasses.

'Look,' she began. 'When they're asleep, it doesn't matter where they are, as long as they are safe and cared for.' Kate could see the nurse had obviously had this discussion more than once. 'And when they're awake,' Batya continued, 'their mothers come to feed them, change them and play with them.'

'But what about when the mothers start full time working after six months. They only see them at odd hours. In town, the mother is with the baby all the day.'

'Some are.' Batya smiled, 'but what about working moms in town who put their babies in a crèche, and the middle-class mothers leaving them with nannies,' adding, 'and in New York, where I come from, most did one or the other.' She put down the cup. 'And what about the Moms stuck at home not coping, driven to distraction. Ever heard of battered babies? Or Moms with postnatal depression? More common than you think, Kate.'

'But most mothers manage?' Kate pressed.

'They do. Or they don't, Kate. And you can see the results on their kids later. Here, at least, we can help, advise, comfort. And Moms can rest and catch up on sleep between feeds. Look,' she said finally, 'no system is perfect. I just think ours -- and we're just a working-class community, remember, is pretty good.'

Kate listened, recalling the way she and Amos used to argue about kibbutz in the fields when she first came, she playing devil's advocate to test his convictions and to find out more. Now she was doing it again, but much closer to the bone. Could she accept the system -- if and when the time came?

What Kate did like about the babies' house was the tranquillity. Sure, there were moments when three or four were screaming their heads off for a bottle, or to be changed. But usually the pace was gentle and calm, the mothers coming in and out, often half asleep, the faint smell of sour milk from the bibs and aprons and no one raising their voice or rushing about as in the *Gan*.

When Orna came to feed that afternoon, Kate was changing her baby's nappy whilst Batya watched. Orna, tall and slim, with long black hair and a smooth dark face, watched too. But as soon as Kate had finished, she stepped forward, lifted the baby and without a word, turned and went into the next room to feed. Batya followed her into the room and Kate heard them talking, too rapid for her to even gain the gist, but she understood the tone, and Orna's repeating the word: *Mitnadevet*: Volunteer.

Crestfallen, Kate went into the small room and began to fold up the clean laundry, trying to stem tears that were forming in her eyes.

'Take no notice,' said Batya when she came back.

'What do you mean?' grunted Kate. 'How can I work here if the parents don't want me to. Don't accept me?'

'The parents are quite happy to have you here, Kate. They all know how well you worked in the Gan.'

'Orna is a parent too.'

'Orna will find fault with anyone.' Batya sighed. 'Anyone except herself. If it wasn't with you, it would be with someone else; believe me. She just doesn't like the system. Or says she doesn't.'

A baby stirred in the adjacent room, then stopped. Batya walked across and stood by the doorway, listening.

'You know, we are the easiest thing for a woman to blame when they don't want to stay on the kibbutz.'

'So why does she stay?'

'She's married to Motti. And Motti is married to the combine harvester!' Then, as though it were Miriam speaking, she added, 'it's always the inadequate ones who find fault with the system: the children's nurses, the babies' house.' She sighed again. 'Anyone except themselves.'

Kate had to wait until all the mothers had come before she could leave. And like Batya had said, most went out of their way to be friendly despite the language barrier. But she still felt a bit awkward. They were all mothers, married with families. She was still 'the other woman', the awkward one.

Amos once told her about the early kibbutzim in the twenties and thirties, where people had repeatedly switched in and out of relationships. Nowadays, the kibbutz was a settled community of families — here, about fifty of them, whereas she, and the one or two other unmarried girls, stuck out like a sore thumb.

By the time she got home, Amos had already washed and changed and gone to be with the kids in Miriam's room. Kate was weary and without showering, made coffee, and munching a few biscuits, stared aimlessly at her Van Gogh print on the wall opposite. Yes, Motti might be married to the *falkha*. But Amos was married to the kibbutz. And what about her? What if she wanted a different future?

In the first week of February, Jill left. Amos and Kate had invited her over for coffee the evening before and they joked about the New Year's party. Roger had apologised to Amos in the dining hall a few days later. He too was leaving too, 'doing Europe' and then on to London to meet his friends at 'Kangaroo Alley' in Bayswater.

'He'll be back, you know,' said Jill. 'Despite all his moaning.'

'And you?' asked Amos. Jill thought for a moment then shrugged.

'Probably,' she said slowly. 'But only for a visit.' She paused. 'I mean, I think it's a great idea. Principles I really hold with. But I don't think I could find a satisfying place of work here.' In full flow, she carried on, 'don't think many women do.'

For a few seconds, there was complete silence in the room. She and Kate had often talked about women in the kibbutz. Then Jill added, as though apologising, 'still. I'm a city girl at heart.'

They talked late into the night, the three of them, though mainly Kate and Jill, laughing over the past months: Jerusalem, the Beduin; other volunteers.

'Gotta go,' said Jill getting up after the umpteenth cup of coffee. 'Let you workers get to bed.'

'Well, you're always welcome back, Jill,' said Amos, shaking her hand warmly. 'Any time.'

After she'd gone, Kate was felt really sad. She didn't know whether she should have begged her friend to stay -- or to take her with her...

The weeks passed, work and daily life soon took over, and the responsibility of working with the babies became completely absorbing. Kate was fascinated by the almost daily changes as each infant grew and developed. There was a routine and a repetitive, almost obsessive, cleaning up, but it was constantly interrupted by the infants waking at odd times, sudden temperatures, doctors' visits, or a mother falling sick with flu, everything noted and recorded, everything carefully explained to her.

'With babies, it's simple.' Batya smiled. 'You take no chances.'

As well as working hours, the evenings too were full. Often they were invited over to Eli's or Menakhem's room, or chatting with Batya or Ephraim, or just she and Amos sitting and talking over the day, then going to bed early, still enjoying the thrill of being alone together.

Occasionally, when a few of them got together, the talk turned more serious.

'Occupation is occupation,' Joe was sounding off, as they all sat in Ephraim's room one night. 'And it can't be justified for any length of time.'

'But you can't just withdraw,' Ephraim butted in. 'Not whilst Nasser and Hussein and all the others won't make peace.'

'It's more to do with the Palestinians,' said Eli. 'We need to find a way of getting through to them. And to do it now.'

'*Bidiyuk!*' added Amos, exactly.

'Wait a minute,' said Ephraim. 'Arafat's Palestinian charter calls for the destruction of Israel. How can you talk to people like that?' His wife was over in the babies' house giving their son his late feed. 'I'm like one of Eli's prize herd, a damn milch cow', she had joked to Kate the day before.

Kate sat on the bed and leaned back against the wall, listening to the argument, while for her benefit, they conversed in English. But soon the exchanges grew more animated and relapsed into a rapid, colloquial Hebrew. Every few sentences, came the key word; '*shetakhim*': the 'territories'; the West Bank and Gaza, and she recalled her conversations with Shafik. She was more in tune with Amos and Eli's way of thinking, but again came the niggling thought: of having exchanged one set of animosities in Belfast, for another out here.

The following day, Kate realised that that discussion wasn't just theoretical. Amos took out a letter from his shirt pocket when he came home after work.

'From the damned army,' he said, shrugging. 'Reserves duty.'

A shiver ran down Kate's back.

'When?' she asked.

'Next week,' he said.

She sat on the bed and he sat by her, his arm round her.

'Just two or three weeks,' he murmured, hugging her close, trying to make it sound as short as possible, though he knew that fighting units could be called for up to thirty days. 'Sorry, Kate.'

'Can't be helped,' said Kate. 'Come, let's have coffee.'

Kate slept badly that night. Outside, the wind was banging the shutters and hissing through the trees. She would be alone, completely alone, now that Jill had gone. Sure, there was Batya, Eli and a few more she could talk to. But there were also the Ornas and Mottis and Nitzas, and others.

She lay on her back, staring at the dark ceiling with Amos breathing deeply beside her, his warm hand on her hip. It was nearly dawn by the time she fell into a troubled sleep.

26

Amos joined his unit at Julis; joyful reunions, men telling of what they had done since the end of the war; some married, some with new babies. They joked about funny incidents in the past; suddenly falling silent as the name of one who was no longer cropped up. And although no one mentioned it, Amos felt the odd curiosity from one or two who were close to him. Gossip travelled fast between the old comrades.

They took the dirt road from Beit Jubrin up the foothills and into the Judean mountains. On either side of the track bare grey rocks were interspersed with terraces of brown earth, stunted green bushes and the occasional oak tree. Here, two thousand feet up, heavy rain had fallen and the road soon turned to a muddy, rutted track.

A young Arab boy stood amongst his flock of black goats staring at the trucks and command cars as they ground past. And in one of the long silences, Amos felt his eyes misting over. Something was missing, would always be missing. Ya'ir.

He wondered for the first time: if Ya'ir hadn't gone, would he have abandoned his marriage for Miriam so readily? Perhaps the two things were connected and in a way he couldn't yet understand.

They drove into Hebron and Amos remembered when they first occupied the town, almost a year ago. His tanks and half-tracks leading a long convoy of supplies' lorries, the local Arabs staring amazed at the procession of civilian vehicles: blue *'Tnuva'* cold-storage trucks, buses, builders' lorries, delivery vans of all shapes and colours that had been commandeered, all winding past and into the town. Could this be the army that had defeated the ferocious Jordanian Legion?

Now however, the shock had passed and the next day when he found himself at his base with some two dozen men, in the centre of Hebron, sullen faces showed the resentment setting in. And though he was worried stiff about how Kate would manage on her own, being away from the tension in the kibbutz seemed to have lifted a weight.

A week later, it was about three in the afternoon. A cold wind was blowing between the stone houses, the towns-people hurrying along the narrow streets muffled against the cold. Suddenly, from a side street, three shots rang out and two young Arab boys came hurtling around the corner. As the soldiers grabbed them, the boys struggled, eyes wide with fear, thin brown legs kicking out.

'*Esh mah?*' snapped one of the soldiers who had a smattering of Arabic.

'*Yahud. Yahud…*' choked the elder boy, '*Boom, Boom,*' pointing his hands as though firing.

Amos took four of his men and ran up the street. It was almost deserted, apart from two local women huddling in a doorway. But at the far corner stood a group of bearded men in civilian clothes with black skullcaps on their heads with two women in long dresses and headscarves. One man held an Uzi, muzzle pointing at the sky.

'What's going on?' said Amos. 'Who fired?'

'I did,' snapped a tall, thin man. 'They looked threatening.' He spoke in a pronounced American accent. Amos realised that they were religious settlers who had taken over a house in the town a few weeks earlier.

'Look, friend. We're here to keep order,' Amos said. 'The town is pretty peaceful. And we want to keep it that way. Okay?'

'We don't need your protection,' grunted the man. 'This is our city. A holy city, where Jews must be able to walk about freely. Not in fear.'

'Well, you won't do it by letting that off.' Amos nodded to the Uzi. 'And anyway, how come you've got that weapon?'

'We shall protect ourselves,' muttered a woman standing beside the man. Her grey eyes were hard. 'Jewish blood will not be spilt for nothing, like in '29!'

During the Arab anti-British riots of 1929, the local townspeople had massacred the small Jewish population.

Meanwhile, local people had gathered at the other corner and heads peeped from nearby windows, fearful yet bemused at Israelis arguing with each other. Amos thought for a moment. He didn't fancy a confrontation with religious zealots. Nor the locals.

'Ami, Zevulun.' He nodded to two of his men, 'see these people back to their house, okay.' The woman was about to protest, but the man, seeing the gathering crowds, turned her away and the small group walked back up the road.

'Like a thorn in the arse,' Amos moaned to his company commander that evening. 'We came to keep the peace and those idiots from Brooklyn come to stir things up.'

Major Gadi spooned sausages and beans from the heated ration tin.

'Not much we can do.' He shrugged. 'Golda should have heaved them out the day after they dived in. No one in the government had the balls.' He wiped a bushy, ginger moustache. 'Now the army is stuck with it.'

'Bloody settlers. Religious fanatics,' snapped Amos, sipping a can of orange juice. 'You should have seen that woman's eyes!' He slapped the tin on the upturned mortar-bomb case that served as the table. 'And where the hell were they before the war? And during the last twenty years? Now it's all over, they come here from Brooklyn and tell us about "Jewish rights" and "Jewish land".'

Later, as he lay on his camp bed, Amos was still furious as he wrote to Kate. He wrote every day, generally in an optimistic mood wanting to reassure her. This time, he couldn't hide his feelings and didn't want to: 'I was so angry, Kate, I wish you were here so I could tell you how gutted I am. Haven't felt like this since that stupid argument with Motti. Remember? And no one seems to have the will to stop these people. And if they keep coming, keep antagonising the Arabs and sowing enmity again, it will put us right back to where we were before the war.'

As he wrote, Amos felt his anger subsiding, imagining Kate's calm face and her soft hands on his back as they lay together. He ended by telling how much he missed her and that it would soon be over, striving not to betray his anxieties at leaving her alone in the kibbutz.

As he folded the sheet into the grey envelope, Amos remembered writing home to Miriam, just before the war, reassuring her too that he was okay. Asking her to kiss the kids for him when she took them back to the children's house…

He shook away the memories, pushed himself up off the camp-bed and went across to the headquarters' hut to slip the letter in the unit postbox.

The evening Amos left, Eli had called round to Kate.

'Amos says I must keep an eye on you.' He laughed, 'dead jealous your man.' And took her over to his room to pick up Bilha for supper. The dining hall was filling up with parents coming in from taking back the children. Eli guided them over to an end table for six. Nitza and Yossi were already seated there.

'Bad luck Amos being snapped up like that,' said Yossi. 'Still, we'll all have to do it now I suppose.'

'Playing policemen,' muttered Eli. 'Sooner we get out of there the better.'

'But we have to make sure the PLO don't re-organise,' said Yossi, waving a piece of tomato at the end of his fork.

'Occupation is occupation,' said Eli.

'You and Amos, and your 'peacenik' friends,' Yossi smiled. Eli opened his mouth to answer, but Bilha cut in.

'Listen, you two. Enough politics for one meal.' She looked across the table at Kate and smiled.

'So things with the babies are going well, eh. Mine too, I hope!'

'Yes. Sure. Yours is a real bruiser! It's all quite new to me,' said Kate. 'And the work is more demanding than the *Gan*, sure. But less hectic.'

Nitza, who'd hadn't taken part in the conversation until then, suddenly broke in.

'Yes. Though Miriam is still struggling to find a decent relief worker.' Kate felt her face redden and looked down into her cup. Bilha turned and glared at Nitza. 'Anyway,' Nitza, pushed back her chair and stood up. 'I've got to get back to the toddlers.' Yossi stood up too and picking up their plates, they walked away, leaving an awkward silence.

'Take no notice, Kate,' said Bilha. 'That's not your problem. It's the education committee's.'

Back in her room, Kate tried to simmer down. The bitch; that had been deliberate. And she wondered from whom else Amos and Eli had been shielding her. She turned on the radio, army songs interspersed with rapid dialogue that could have been Chinese for all she understood. 'Don't worry,' Amos had consoled her. 'The radio is the last thing you'll get to understand. It's too rapid, too continuous.' She turned it down and took out her Hebrew textbook and notebook.

The kibbutz had arranged for Margalit to give her an hour's lesson three times a week and she hadn't done her homework for tomorrow. With the music in the background, Kate tried to fathom out some verbs using the transliteration and matching it to her written Hebrew script, then relating that to the printed script in the textbook. With a reasonable command of French, she had always considered herself quite good at languages. But this: it was so completely different to anything she had known. Holy God. She'd never learn it.

Almost a year now since she'd arrived. Getting involved with a married *kibbutznik* hadn't been in her plans. Now, she couldn't distinguish what it was in the kibbutz that agreed or didn't agree with her, and what was tied up with her and Amos. She got up and plugged in the kettle to make coffee. God knows how she would last three days on her own, let alone three weeks. But as the kettle boiled, there came a tap on the door.

'*Ken?*' she called, having by now familiarised the Hebrew 'yes'.

'It's me, Batya.' Kate stepped across and opened the door.

'There's a film tonight. Coming up?'

'Oh. Thanks. Sure.' The *kumkum* began to bubble. Kate turned and pulled out the plug. 'Must have my fix first, though.'

Batya grinned.

'Fine. We'll save a seat for you.'

But Kate couldn't bring herself to leave the room. Much as she knew she should get out, to try to join in, when she imagined entering the hall she could see only the hostile faces of those she had hurt; those she had let down.

Instead, she sat down to answer Amos's latest letter, all her doubts having raised their ugly heads in his absence. She had almost finished it when heavy footsteps sounded on the veranda, followed by a knock on the door. Surprised, she jumped up and opened it. Yaacov, the kibbutz secretary stood there with an army officer.

There had been 'an incident' in Hebron, he said, and Amos was in Tel Hashomer military hospital. Neither knew details except that it required x-rays and tests.

Kate gripped the doorpost, her stomach turning. Amos and his friends often joked about 'the security situation'. Suddenly, it was real.

'I have to see him,' she blurted out. 'I want to go. Now!'

'No point so late,' the officer grunted. 'Better go tomorrow.' He reassured her that Amos was in good hands. Wished her well. Said goodnight, and left.

Yaacov reached out his hand.

'Listen. I'll go and arrange to take the jeep tomorrow. We'll go at lunchtime. Come to my room for a bit.'

While Yaacov went to Uri to arrange transport, Kate sat in his room with Regina, his wife. She didn't know her well but was glad of her company.

'Can't be too serious,' Regina consoled, 'or they would have *shlepped* you there straight away.'

'Maybe. Maybe,' said Kate. She tried to smile. 'God. Don't know how I'll sleep tonight.'

Miriam was in Nitza's room for coffee when Yossi burst in with the news about Amos.

'Listen, Miriam,' said Nitza immediately. 'He's the father of your kids. You have a right to go and see him – the kids too.'

Regina had just made coffee for her and Kate, when there was a tap on the door and Miriam walked straight in with Nitza.

'Isn't Yaacov here?' she asked deliberately avoiding looking at Kate.

'He's gone to arrange transport for Kate tomorrow,' said Regina.

'Well Miriam has to go with the kids as well,' snapped Nitza. 'They will have heard something.'

Kate felt her blood rising. The cow! She wouldn't let that go and stood up.

'Listen. Yacov is arranging the jeep for me at the moment' she said.

'But we have go.' Miriam snapped. 'He's the father of our kids!'

Somehow Kate found the strength to keep her cool. She wouldn't let the bitch wind her up.

'I'm afraid, I'm going tomorrow,' she said, looking straight at Nitza, 'and that's that.'

At that moment Yaacov walked in and caught the tail end of the argument.

'Listen. Miriam. It's late. I'll sort you and the kids out tomorrow.'

'If not,' she retorted. 'I'll get my mother to take us in her car.'

Kate couldn't stand there any longer. Looking straight at Miriam, then at Nitza, she clenched her hands and strode past them, and out of the door.

'What the hell can I do,' Yaacov moaned to Regina, after they had all left, 'like a damn Brecht drama; the two pulling at the loved one.'

'Well you'll have to arrange time off for Miriam to take the kids as well.' She shrugged, 'arrange it for later in the week perhaps.'

Back in her room, Kate closed the door and sank onto the bed. 'Not serious,' they said. Then why was he in hospital? And suddenly she felt so alone. What would she do if it was more serious than they made out, here on her own until he came out; and what if it left him with a disability? Oh God!

Kate found herself shivering -- and it wasn't from the cold night. Slowly she undressed and slipped into bed. It had always seemed cold since Amos had left; now it seemed even colder. It took her a long time to fall asleep.

The next day, Yaacov took Kate in the jeep. All the two-hour drive Kate was frantic, not able to say nor anything nor think of anything, apart from what she would do if it *was* more serious.

The hospital was a series of long, low, white buildings with large, red Magen David symbols painted on all the sloping roofs. Amos was sitting up in light blue pyjamas, his left arm in a sling and held secure with a broad bandage round his body.

'We were trying to stop a stop a fight, and I got caught with a stone,' he said as Kate and Yaacov came up to the bed, and smiling added, 'nothing fatal! Just badly bruised.' Kate couldn't appreciate the army gallows-humour and leaned down, and kissed and hugged him, taking care not to touch the sling.

He told them that the physio was working on him then nodded to the adjacent beds.

'Much worse cases than me,' he quipped, 'mainly traffic accidents. Army drivers! Anyway,' he said, smiling, 'they are throwing me out next week,' but as he turned, he winced and Kate could see it was more painful than he wanted to let on.

After about an hour, he said he wanted to lie down. They kissed and she and Yaacov left, Kate's head full of 'what if' scenarios again.

On the drive home, Yaacov cleared his throat. 'Kate,' he began. 'The kibbutz has agreed to the children going to see him tomorrow.'

'And Miriam, I suppose,' she said.

Yacov shrugged. 'Well, yes. The kids can't go alone, really.'

All the way back, Kate wrestled with the news. No. She couldn't object. She was still 'the other woman', and the kibbutz called the shots.

Kate went every two days to see him. The kibbutz gave her the days off, but with Amos off the danger list, she had to make her own way, taking the bus the Tel Aviv and then another one to the hospital.

Every time her path crossed with Miriam or Nitza's friends during the day, she felt that she was being judged -- even that what had happened to Amos was some kind of punishment; the influence of her mother's Catholic upbringing she realised later.

Then, on the Wednesday, just as she had finished showering, there was a loud ra-tat on the door, and Amos walked in.

'Threw me out!' One sleeve of his jacket lay flat, his arm strapped to his side under it. 'Command car,' he grinned, 'private transport,' and sat on the bed. Kate couldn't share the army humour. She sat next to him, gently folding her arms around him.

'Oh, Amos,' she murmured, 'the war is never over, is it?' And carefully, they lay back on the bed, silent, just relieved and enjoying the feeling of their bodies close together again. After a while, he sat up and nodded to his pack.

'Something in there.' He grinned. 'For you.' Kate went over and pulled out an Arabic newspaper bundle. Inside was a necklace of coloured glass beads and a blue glass vase. Kate came over and kissed him then draped the necklace round her neck.

'Glass from Hebron!' said Amos, 'would have been a fantasy a year ago. The ancient glass workshop there had almost closed through lack of business,' he said. 'Now, with the occupation, Israeli tourism had given it a new lease of life.'

Amos got up at noon the next day and gingerly showered, holding his arm out to one side. He was lying on the bed when she came in from work early.

'Playing hooky?' he asked, having learned the expression from Joe.

'Well, you're not the only one to get compassionate leave, y'know.' They kissed. 'Batya told me to the afternoon off,' she said. 'Got Margalit to come in. She was only too willing to get out of the clothes store!'

They lay on the bed together, talking quietly and telling of their happenings over the last weeks. Until Amos glanced at the clock.

'Have to get the kids soon,' he grunted, and kissed her as they sat up. 'Let's have coffee.'

Kate smiled but stiffened. She thought she had got used to that…

'What have you brought me?' asked Noa, when Amos picked her up from the children's house and brought her to the room. Ran knew what had happened but they had decided to tell the little one that it was from a traffic incident.

'Look,' said Amos, crouching and holding out a clenched fist, 'from Hebron. Very special.' Noa prised open his fingers and took out a small, blue-glass tortoise. She held it up to the light, turning it this way and that, squinting at the ultramarine glow.

'Eizeh Yofi! Daddy.' And planted a wet kiss on his cheek.

Amos wanted to see Ran too, so after a while, leaving Noa sewing a tiny handkerchief with Kate, he walked back to Miriam's room.

On the path, he bumped into Uri.

'Any news with the water?' he asked.

'Yes. Good news. Rain fell in the north, so the Ministry of Agriculture gave the Negev an emergency quota through the national pipeline. We got forty thousand cubic metres.'

'And?'

'The committee decided to use twenty for the cereal crops, meanwhile.' Amos nodded and walked on. He remembered hearing sprinklers ticking, as they drove in through the gate. With him away, Motti had got most of his way in the end.

Ran was looking through his stamp album as he came into Miriam's room.

'Here,' said Amos, 'bet you haven't got these.'

He handed him four Jordanian stamps he had managed to wangle from the Arab post office in Hebron. 'Couldn't get them franked, though.' He laughed as Ran hugged his good arm, 'the Arab clerk refused to stamp the Israeli army postmark over King Hussein's face!'

'Hey. That's great, Dad. Bet none of the others have got these!'

After a while Ran closed the album and ran out to join his friends, leaving just the two of them. Amos felt more awkward than usual, his head full of when he used to come home from reserves' duty, and remembering Miriam's relief at his safe return from the war; their waiting for the night. And was glad when the kids went back and he could get to his room.

27

March continued with bright sunshine and sudden fierce thunderstorms, often bringing heavy, almost tropical downpours, which pleased everyone except Joe who feared hail damage to his Valencia oranges. At other times, there were only terrifying displays of lightning, and one evening Amos took Kate outside to watch.

Bright bolts shot down into the desert, illuminating huge towers of white and purple clouds in the inky blackness, followed by a sharp, loud reports of thunder. Kate had never seen or heard anything like it. She leaned back against him, his arms tight around her as they stood there staring into the night, watching and listening.

As they stood there, Amos whispered into her ear.

'I asked Yaacov to bring your candidature to the secretariat and the general meeting soon, Kate. Just a formality, he's sure of it.'

Kate didn't react at once. She took a few deep breaths.

'Amos,' she said softly, 'why did you bring it to the secretariat?'

Amos tensed and turned to face her.

'Well, I mean it was the natural thing, Kate. After all, we've been together over three months -- and with your time as a volunteer, it's nearly a year now.'

There was a flash and another crack of thunder. Kate waited until it died away then said gently.

'But we haven't talked about it, have we, Amos?'

'Sorry, Kate,' he said. 'Just wanted to surprise you. Thought you'd be pleased. I -'

'Well maybe I am and maybe... Oh I don't know, Amos.' She slid her hands up and held his arms. 'But it has to come from me, hasn't it? My initiative,' she said, sad that the beautiful night had been in a way, marred. Amos sensed her sadness and reached and hugged her to him.

They stood like that for a while, the lightning flashing and the thunder crashing about them, hugging close, Amos annoyed with himself that he had jumped the gun; Kate wondering whether the idea of living permanently in the kibbutz was creaking before her eyes.

Across the lawn, Yossi and Nili and Shulamit were in Nitza's room. Nili was a member of the secretariat.

'So, Kate wants to become a member?' Nitza began.

'Uhuh,' said Nili, 'Amos asked Yaacov to bring it up this week.'

'Well I for one won't vote for it,' she said, 'bloody volunteer causing chaos and upsets.' Apart from her jealousy, like others, Nitza saw the Amos and Kate saga as opening a Pandora's box.

'Well apart from me and Shulamit, the committee will be in favour,' said Nili.

'Well it will be an interesting general meeting,' said Shulamit, Orna's close friend, one of a small group of anti-Kate members that had coalesced from sympathising with Miriam, each with their own agenda. Now, the notice of Kate's candidature had prompted them to express their feelings.

When they came back from watching the lightning display,

Amos plugged in the *kumkum* and made cardamom spiced Turkish coffee. Then Kate and he sat back on the bed beside one another, both silent for a while. Amos didn't know what to say or how to begin as he sipped the hot, thick liquid. He was annoyed with himself; the one damn time he had taken a firm decision, and it had blown up in his face.

Footsteps sounded on the path then stepped onto the shared veranda; Moshe had come home. A few words with Rivka and the next door closed. Then silence. The silence of the kibbutz after supper, the children gone back, people in their rooms, the silence of the home he had helped to build out here in the huge, wide stillness of the desert.

'So?' Amos whispered. 'Where does this leave us, Kate?' He rested his hand on Kate's back, his fingers played with her hair and his stomach churned.

Kate laid her head on his shoulder.

'I don't know, Amos. I mean, living together has been so wonderful. Better than I had ever imagined.'

'So what is it, Kate?'

'Just that I'm still not certain about making this my permanent home. Our home.'

Amos kissed the top of her head and gently squeezed her arm.

'But you fit in so well here. People like you, Kate.'

'Some people, Amos. Your friends, sure. Perhaps even most. But every time I see Miriam, feel Nitza, or Orna looking at me and others, it feels as though we have created something unacceptable to the community. And they don't like it Amos.'

'Only a few, Kate. And like I said, it will pass. I know it will.'

'Maybe, Amos. But not so quickly.' She turned to look into his face. 'You don't see it or feel it, Amos. But it's there. And I feel I am causing a split in the community here.'

She took a sip of coffee then gripped his hand.

'Sure, most people are deliberately friendly, but though I don't mention it, each day there are incidents. Like when we sit down to eat Amos, sometimes an awkward silence at a nearby table.' Kate paused and sat forward. 'And all the time, the guilt, Amos. Sure, I suppose there is anywhere when this kind of thing happens. But it's living so close, seeing the people we've hurt every day.'

Kate suddenly swung her legs off the bed and stood up. She walked a few paces then turned and came back towards him and sat down.

'Oh, I don't know. Look. In town, Miriam, her friends, we would never see each other. But the kibbutz is so small, just over a hundred adults -- claustrophobic, in a way. So I wonder: can we live like that permanently? And then there's the problem of what I am going to do with my life, y'know. Like, work.'

Amos sat forward, his brow furrowed.

'But you enjoy working with children, I thought. And you're so good at it.' He sat silent for a moment, then sat up. 'Anyway, kibbutz is more than just work, Kate.'

'Yes. I agree. I mean, if you're ideologically motivated, like Batya, work is just a part of kibbutz life. But if you're not, say like Orna, working in the kitchen and using the children's house as an excuse to be dissatisfied with the kibbutz. Or like Margalit in the clothes store when you don't want to, with few alternatives.' Suddenly, her voice grew strained. 'And then the children's house, the system, and although I can see the advantages and know that the kids are happy, I'm not sure about how I will feel when… if. And most of all, Amos, I'm scared. Scared of ending up like Orna, like Margalit, and others. Stuck here but embittered.' Her eyes began to water. 'How would we be then?'

Amos pulled her close and as if desperate to reassure themselves, they put down the mugs and lay back on the bed in a tight embrace. He turned on his side to face her and kissed her eyes, then her lips, then as though some hidden force was about to tear them apart they clung to each other. And like that, they just lay still for a while, close and silent.

It grew late. From the direction of the entrance gate, a truck whined as it changed down a gear, a cow lowed from the cowshed and a little owl screeched from its stump out by the fence. Amos looked into her face again.

'Then where would we live, Kate?' He paused. 'I could never live in another country. And without sounding naff, this is where I belong.' He breathed out audibly. 'It's not some blind patriotism, Kate. This land is special. I've hiked over nearly every square kilometre. Every hill and valley, every place name, has a meaning for me. It's not perfect, I know. And there may always be enmity around us. But…' He leaned up on his elbow again. 'Look. I've been abroad, Kate. Yes, I could work for a while like I did in Kenya, but I could never live there. Another country would never be home for me.'

Amos reached down and kissed her.

'Then there are the kids. I could never leave them to grow up without me, without a father. Can you see that?'

'Of course, Amos. Sure. But there are many other places in Israel -- another kibbutz, town, even?'

'Yes. I know, Kate. But this was just dry, barren earth when we came out here. Building it up been my life's work, making what it is today from nothing. And you know as well as I do, it's not just another village. We are building a new society here, without classes and distinctions. Where people live by co-operation instead of senseless competition.' He cupped her shoulder in his hand.

'And it could so easily be your home, Kate. Everyone has to build his or her life somewhere, Kate. Why not here?'

Kate didn't respond for a while. They had so much going for them, so much to lose if it shattered. Many women she'd known at college were forever following their husbands to places of work all over the world they even hated. Why couldn't she?

Kate didn't respond at once; strove to collect her thoughts. To explain.

'Look, Amos. That's the very point. Kibbutz is not just some other place. It is so definitive -- and for me so demanding.' She wanted to say that she had her own life, her own ideas of what she wanted to do. Then thought for a moment. Had she?

And strangely, as if telepathic, Amos suddenly said;

'So. What do you want to work at Kate? What would you do, somewhere else?'

'To be fair, I don't know exactly what I want to do, Amos. And perhaps that is the problem. But outside at least, I would have the possibility of trying out different things, workplaces, of discovering what I want to do.'

Kate paused and squeezed his hand, then sat up.

'Look, Amos. I love you. Want to live with you so much. But I can't make a commitment to the kibbutz yet. And above all, I don't want to live here just as "Amos's wife". Can you understand that?'

The room was silent for a moment, a heavy silence. Kate turned to him and tried to smile.

'God I've screwed things up, haven't I?'

Amos leaned forward and kissed her.

'No. No. It had to come out, sooner or later -- and better now than later.'

Amos began to breathe more slowly and more easily. At the beginning of the conversation, he'd feared that Kate's mind was already made up. But the longer they talked, the more he sensed that all was not lost. But it hung in the air, and Amos knew it wouldn't go away. Meanwhile, he would see Yaacov.

On Thursday, two weeks after Purim, the usual notice of that coming Saturday's General Meeting was posted on the dining-hall notice board. Joe was surprised that Kate wasn't on the agenda. He wasn't the only one.

'Thought Kate's candidature was coming to the general meeting,' said Yossi as he barged into his room that afternoon. 'But it's not on the -' He stopped abruptly. Miriam was in the room having coffee with Nitza.

Nitza had been teasing Miriam about Eldad's visit.

'Dead sweet on you, your old schoolfriend. So sad about Ronit. No justice.' Eldad's wife had recently died of cancer, leaving him with two young children.

'He's just an old friend,' said Miriam, a little annoyed but trying not to show it. 'And he's vulnerable at the moment. That's all.'

At that moment, Yossi had blundered in.

'Oh. Don't mind me,' smiled Miriam. 'I'm getting used to it.'

Yossi blushed then deliberately glanced at his watch.

'Anyway,' he said. 'Got to get back to the work roster.'

'Well, well,' said Nitza, after he had gone. 'Second thoughts, maybe?' She poured out more coffee. 'I would have abstained, that's for sure.'

She looked sideways at Miriam, thinking then said hesitantly, 'Tell me it's none of my business if you want, Miriam, but if it all fell through. You know… Would you take him back again?'

Miriam didn't answer at once. She took several sips of coffee, staring into the cup, her brow furrowed.

'No. I don't mind you asking. I've thought about that possibility myself, Nitza. More than once, I can tell you.' She paused. 'My pride makes me want him to go to hell. Then I think of the kids. And that essentially, Amos is not a bastard. Just a damn idiot. An immature, stubborn idiot!'

She held out her cup for more coffee. Nitza poured.

'And then,' Miriam continued, 'I feel that because he is so stubborn, he would stay with her even if he had made a mistake.' She half smiled and brushed back her hair. 'Or perhaps that's my ego talking.'

'Sure,' murmured Nitza. 'Who knows. Then again, she might make the decision.'

Across the lawn and three rows of houses along, Amos and Kate were talking too. More than just talking. Kate had stormed in. That morning, Batya had remarked that her candidature wasn't on the agenda.

'I didn't know what the hell to say,' she said. 'You've done it again, Amos. Without asking me!' Kate stood by the small table leaning on one hand, her lips tight and pale, trying to control her anger.

'Look, Kate. You didn't want it brought to the meeting. You said so. I had to get it crossed off the agenda.'

'Yes. But again you're making decisions for me.'

'No.' Amos punched one hand into the other. 'I messed it up. It was for me to sort it out.'

'I know. I know.' Kate shook her hand. 'But we can talk first, can't we?'

'We did. And you didn't want it, Kate. You can't have it both ways!'

Amos sat down on the bed, his shoulders hunched and the blood roaring in his ears. Kate opened her mouth to respond then closed her mouth. They'd been shouting at each other. My God, fighting like her Mum and Dad when he came home drunk. She had sworn never to be like that. Stepping across the room, she sat beside him and laid her head against his. Stroking his cheek, she breathed out.

'That wasn't like us, Amos,' she said softly.

'No. It's not, Kate.'

She kissed his neck. 'I'm sorry. Shouldn't have blown up like that.'

'It's past, Kate. Let's forget it.' He turned to face her. 'Look, Kate. You know, for both of us, it's been like a pressure cooker ever since we came back here together.' He leaned forward and kissed her. 'We need to get out a bit. Need to be on our own.' Amos paused, his eyes wide in the soft light. 'We never had a real honeymoon, did we, Kate? A holiday.'

Kate's eyes widened. 'No. But…'

'So,' he said, 'how about taking a few days off and going down to Eilat?'

The boots of the night guard crunched on the path outside then faded into the darkness. And in the silence that followed, they quickly undressed and slipped into bed, and as if to drive away the bad feelings, gently made love.

Afterwards, as they lay back, their bodies wrapped in one another, Kate knew that nothing had been resolved. But on this trip, away from the pressures of the kibbutz, perhaps it could be.

28

A faint breeze ruffled the water, scattering the moon's reflection into slivers of silver. It was their second night at Eilat, sleeping on the seashore like a couple of backpackers.

'Amos,' Kate murmured, 'this is such a magical place.'

'It is, Kate. And there are so many more throughout the country. Each holiday, we can go somewhere else.'

'I want to, too, Amos.' Kate paused and raised herself on one elbow, looking down at his broad, angular face glowing faintly in the starlight. 'And I am trying, honest I am, Amos.'

Amos eased her head down gently and kissed her.

'But if…' Kate raised her head again, hesitant, 'if it doesn't work out in the kibbutz… You know. And if we do love one another, we could live together anywhere, sure. Couldn't we, Amos?'

'Maybe. But where?'

Kate didn't reply. She laid her head on his chest again, rising and falling with his regular breathing. In the distance, a truck whined in from the Arava rift-valley. Across the head of the gulf, came music from one of the new hotels.

Amos stroked her hair, staring up into the sky. Kate tensed as he continued.

'Apart from anything else, I couldn't bear leaving my kids. They don't deserve that, growing up without a father?' He turned his head to look at her. 'Why not stay, Kate? Is it so terrible?'

'No. It's not terrible at all. Just that. Oh, Amos. I don't know.' Suddenly, she sat bolt upright and flung out her arms. 'Be positive, Kate,' she shouted out across the sea. 'Positive!'

Amos reached up and put his arm around her shoulder, kissing her neck.

'You're crazy,' he laughed. 'But not so loud! The Jordanian border guards over there might take it the wrong way.'

Amos lay back. He pulled Kate against him and felt his eyes closing. It had been a long day, walking along the shore, swimming around the corals with a face-mask. He pulled Kate against him and they lay close. And, like that, fell asleep.

The next morning, after a last longing look at the deep blue water of the gulf, they headed for the road out of town to catch a ride north. Amos had used up so much of his yearly holiday allowance going up and down to Jerusalem, that he could only take three days.

They were just passing one of the large hotels to walk out of town and catch a lift, when a loud voice called out from the car park.

'Hey, *ya fighter*! What are you doing here?'

Amos stopped and spun round, then spread his arms.

'Jukha, you old bastard. Me. I'm on holiday.' Amos turned to Kate and introduced her to a slim, bronzed man, with horn-rimmed glasses. 'Yokhanan,' he smiled. 'From my unit.' He punched him playfully in the stomach. 'Intelligence officer —— though you'd never believe it.' The man grinned and shook Kate's hand. Amos noticed that his eyes showed little surprise but much curiosity. News travelled fast on the old comrades' bush telegraph; half the country probably knew by now.

For Kate's benefit, they spoke in English for a while. Yokhanan was studying philosophy at the Tel Aviv University.

'I'm a tourist guide during the holidays,' he said. 'Most Israeli students have to work their way through college.'

A few minutes later, the two were swapping news and scandals about others in the unit and mutual acquaintances, quickly slipping into a Hebrew so rapid and colloquial, that Kate was completely lost. And even though she tried not to show it, once again she had that feeling of being an outsider.

Suddenly Yokhanan stopped and winked at Kate,

'Hey. Hey.' He prodded Amos in the stomach. 'Where are your manners, Amos?' Despite his accent, he spoke a perfect English, 'boring the lady with our *shtuyot.*'

'Sorry, Kate.' Amos squeezed Kate's hand. 'Just catching up on the news.'

'Gossip, he means,' said Yokhanan, speaking directly to her. 'So, are you staying in Eilat for long?'

'No. We're on our way out,' said Kate, adding without thinking, 'unfortunately.'

'Well, stay another day. I can find a find somewhere for you both around the hotel.'

Kate glanced at Amos.

'Nice idea,' said Amos. 'But I'm owing days as it is.'

'Oh Amos, please?' asked Kate, beginning to feel a little annoyed. Couldn't he forget the kibbutz for just a few more days?

'Can't now Kate.' He slipped his arm around her. 'But we can come again. No problem.'

Yokhanan broke the awkward silence that followed.

'So, how are you going back?'

'By *tramp*,' said Amos, as the Israelis called hitchhiking.

'*Shtuyot!* Hordes of tourists coming since the war.' He waved towards the car park. 'Look. There's a coach load of Americans leaving in ten minutes, through Ramon. Only half-full.'

Amos leaned back. 'You sure?'

'*Ein baayot*,' he said. 'For a native! A soldier and his girl! No problem.' He smiled at Kate again. 'They'll spoil you both rotten.' And they did.

The coach accelerated and sped north along the broad, sunbaked valley with its high, bare mountains on either side. Amos was impatient to be in their own room again, but Kate was thoughtful at leaving Yokhanan and what he represented; the wide, open world.

At Timnah, the coach stopped and they joined the guide showing the ancient workings of King Solomon's Copper mines, then around the huge natural pillars of red sandstone, reminding Kate of what Amos had told her about Petra.

The coach sped on north and from time to time, one of the grey-haired Californians would turn and smile in admiration, or come up and hand out filled rolls and bottles of orange juice.

Being of the Holocaust generation, they had watched anxiously during the months leading up to the war, listening to the vicious propaganda from Cairo threatening Israel's destruction. For them, Amos was the modern David slaying Goliath, epitomising the young Israelis who had so brilliantly defeated their combined Arab enemies. Amos disliked being treated as a hero. But a free bus ride up north couldn't be scoffed at.

On and up through the mountains of the Negev, Kate fascinated by the bare, rocky moonscape, then the steep incline up the Ramon Crater wall, followed by the flat, desolate, stone strewn *Hamadas*. But as the miles flew by and they passed Beersheba, Kate felt a growing tightness in her chest.

The coach was going up to Tel Aviv, and passed right by the kibbutz turn-off. After a myriad '*Shaloms*, 'Good Lucks' and 'God bless yous,' they walked away, turning back to wave at the sea of smiling faces and hands pressed against the windows.

'Embarrassing,' muttered Amos. 'Being treated like damn celebrities.'

They arrived back too late for Noa but Amos managed to see Ran in his schoolroom. He was in his pyjamas, 'kibbitzing' at two friends who were playing chess.

'Hi, Dad.' He jumped up to greet him. 'How was it?'

'*Atzoom!*' Amos gave him a hug and ruffled his hair. 'A lot of tourists but still terrific. Fantastic.' He gave Ran a small paper parcel. 'Take a look at that?'

The two boys stopped playing and looked on Ran opened the paper and took out a large, shrivelled seed head.

'It's called a Jericho Rose,' said Amos. 'Picked it near Yotvata. Seen one before?' Ran shook his head, puzzled. 'Amram,' Amos nudged one of the boys. 'Bring a cup of water. You'll see.' When the boy returned, Amos took the plant, dipped in the head for a few seconds then took it out and handed back to his son. As they watched the seed head began to open, each spine slowly straightening out and stretching back, until it was twice the circumference and exposing rows of small seed-pods. Ran held it high.

'Hey. Like magic!' He twisted it around in his fingers. 'Great, Dad.'

Amos took the plant from him.

'It's from the Arava desert. Waits for a flash flood -- could be two, three years, even more, then it opens up and the seeds get washed away and scattered.' Amos smiled at the boys. 'Neat, eh?' He stood up. 'Tomorrow, when it dries, it will ball up again and you can repeat the trick.' He stood up. 'Come. It's late.'

Amos took Ran into his bedroom room to lie down. He kissed his forehead, said goodnight and went out, wondering how long it would take his son to accept Kate; to accept the new situation and come to the room. It pained him, and knew it upset Kate too -- and didn't help her to adjust.

He hurried across to Noa's house and left two pieces of bright green malachite stone from Eilat on the chair by her bed, with a note in large letters: 'From Daddy', and four large kisses. He would try to pop in at lunchtime tomorrow to say hello.

Joe teased Amos about the tourist coach when they ate in the dining hall later.

'Typical of you socialists; relying on the American bourgeoisie for the journey home.' He winked at Kate. 'Just like Trotsky and his first-class train carriage.'

'Meaning?' asked Kate, puzzled, when they all laughed.

'Well, before the revolution,' Joe continued, 'when Trotsky came back to Moscow from meeting comrades in Ukraine, the Communist leadership gathered at the station to meet him. When the train came in and everyone had got off. Nothing! Then from a first class carriage at the far end, Trotsky descends.

'Comrade Lev Davidovitch,' they asked, astonished. 'First class?'

Trotsky thinks for a moment, then straightens back and throws his fist in the air.

'Come the revolution, everyone travels first class!'

And they all laughed again.

Kate laughed too, but it was an 'in' joke, and again she couldn't help feeling the outsider.

Miriam was crossing the lawn from Nitza's room when she noticed light shining through the shutter-slats of Amos's room. For a split second she stiffened, then carried on to the room. Sitting on the bed, she stared aimlessly at the bookcase opposite. Where his books used to be she had placed dried flowers and small ornaments, but still the empty spaces seemed to glare at her.

Nitza had teased her about Eldad again: 'He really is sweet on you. Enjoy it whilst you can. The bastard might come crawling back sooner than you think.' Miriam had noticed the bitterness with which Nitza spoke about Amos. Soft spot? More perhaps? After this, nothing would surprise her.

The room felt cold. She leaned over and turned up the 'Fireside' paraffin heater. It was only ten o'clock and she wanted to read. Yes. A strong cup of coffee. On the veranda, she plugged in the kettle and stood as the water boiled. Eleven years together, damn him. Damn her. How long would it take to get him out of her system? Perhaps never...

Miriam poured the coffee, stirred in a spoonful of sugar and went back to sit on the bed. Holding the hot mug between her hands, she thought about Eldad, an old schoolfriend and now a Sociology lecturer at Tel Aviv University. But he would never come to live down here. He disliked kibbutz life. Anyway, it was too soon after his wife's death. And too soon for her -- yes, her grief too. Would she want to move to town, take the kids out of the kibbutz and away from their friends? She had devoted her life to the kibbutz, but then wasn't her personal life important too?

Miriam brushed back a strand of hair and sipped her coffee, the warming drink slowly diffusing through her body -- and thinking about her future.

29

It was Seder Night, the eve of the Passover celebration and the highlight of the kibbutz year. It was one of the few nights that even the very young children and families all sat together, to eat in the dining room.

Amos left the children in Miriam's room and came in to get dressed in a clean white shirt. Kate finished brushing her hair then stood up and went over to the built-in wardrobe. Gazing aimlessly into the cupboard, she recalled hearing the choir rehearsing as she crossed the lawn the evening before, the music echoing from the windows of the dining hall and away into the darkness of the silent desert. She had glanced up at the crescent moon. *Pesakh.* Passover. Easter. A year here now.

She ran her hand along the clothes' rail and chose the blue dress, reminding her of their very first day together, then tied a white sash around her waist and left her hair loose – and no make-up.

'God, you look marvellous, Kate,' said Amos, pulling her against him. 'I could eat you.'

'Get your fill of *matzo* first,' she giggled, pulling away and fluffing out her hair. 'You'll make me look a sight.'

At eight o'clock, in the cool, still night, they joined the families on the paths all making their way up to the dining room.

The tables were arranged in long rows, covered with white lining-paper and laden with flowers, cakes and fruit and *Matzot*, the crispy, unleavened bread. Around the walls, Shoshannah's decorations depicted the festival themes: the Exodus from Egypt, The Ten Plagues, Spring, Slavery to Freedom, the First Harvest, and one sombre corner commemorating the revolt of the Warsaw Ghetto at Passover 1943.

The men and children were all in white shirts, but the women wore their best dresses, and some had lipstick and make-up, which had become more acceptable over the years. Ran was standing on a chair and he called them over to where he and Noa sat with Miriam. 'Here, Dad. I've saved places.' Kate saw that he had saved two seats -- an acceptance at last?

The evening opened with songs by the choir followed by the traditional '*Mah nishtenah*' questions from one of the youngest children.

'Why is this night different from all other nights,' the girl read from the Hagadah, the decorated booklet relating the Passover story.

'For on this night,' another answered, 'we sit and eat together, parents and children, to tell of the Exodus from Egypt, from Slavery to Freedom.'

Kate glanced around. Yes, all together: she at one end next to Amos, then Noa and Ran, and at the other end, Miriam.

'We've got to just tough it out, Kate,' Amos had tried to reassure her a few days earlier. 'You and I are a family. And my kids are also my family. That's our reality, Kate.' He had hugged her close and stroked her hair. 'And together, we can manage it. I know we can.'

The evening continued with community singing and readings and with the choir on an improvised stage at one end of the dining hall. Kate was glad that Eli and Bilha and their six-year-old were sitting opposite and the conversation flowed easily between them. She had become quite friendly with Bilha, feeling that she had a more open mind than Batya. In time, she wanted to talk more with her about the babies' house.

Further along from them sat Yossi and Nitza and their two children. Nitza was sitting diagonally across from Amos and opposite Miriam. But instead of her just friendly attitude, all through the evening she was ostentatiously laughing at his jokes, looking him straight in the eye. At first, Kate dismissed it as fertile imagination. But it wasn't. She was damn well flirting and it was for her, for Kate's, benefit.

As if to rub in salt, when Amos got up to join the dancing group's presentation on the stage, all the capable dancers had been roped in by Semadar. By chance it was Nitza partnered him, flashing smiles as they danced and Amos, as though oblivious, grinning back and clutching her waist as they swayed together in a gentle, Yemenite dance.

'Those two,' chirped Eli, 'think they're still sixteen and in the youth movement.'

'Still a great dancer, your Amos.' Bilha smiled at Kate as she jabbed her husband in the ribs. 'Eli's just jealous, Kate. Has two left legs and can't put three dance steps together.'

Kate tried to smile, but watching the two dancing, her forehead was burning. And when the dancers finished and weaved their way back, Nitza sat down, face flushed and smiling at Miriam, then at Amos's kids.

At that moment, Amos flopped down beside Kate. 'God. I'm getting too old for all this,' he wheezed as the soup began to be served. 'The younger ones can take over next year.'

It was real chicken soup. Kate knew that the cooks had worked wonders to provide the feast for so many people and she had been hungry on the way up. But now her throat felt blocked and the smell of the food made her nauseous. Eli was cracking a joke but abruptly, stopped, caught Amos's eye and nodded towards Kate. Amos turned to her. She was gazing at the soup plate, aimlessly twisting a spoon in her fingers.

'Thought you were hungry, Kate. Your favourite: chicken soup with noodles?'

Kate shrugged.

'I was. But it's not the damned food,' she muttered. 'It's. It's… I feel sick, Amos. And my head aches.' Amos, still flushed from the dancing and Eli's joking, leaned close.

'Evening sickness?' he whispered jokingly. When occasionally she felt tired on the odd morning, they'd joked about what might happen if…

Kate swung round to face him.

'No it's not,' she hissed. 'And I'm not joking, sure.' She flicked her hand towards Miriam and Nitza. 'It's all -- all this; them. And you don't see it, Amos. You just don't see it!'

Out of the corner of her eye, Kate saw Nitza staring at them. Would it be like this at every festival evening? She glanced at Eli and Bilha. God. If only there were more like them.

Amos placed his hand on her thigh under the table.

'No one is bothered, Kate,' he said softly. 'No one thinks it anything special any longer, Kate. That's how it is, how we are.' But Kate could sense faces turning towards them, eyes looking, ears pricked up.

'No, it isn't,' she cut in, her body quivering, but keeping her voice low and controlled. 'You don't see it Amos. You just don't see it. But it isn't.'

Tears began to well up into her eyes. Kate knew she wouldn't be able to hold them back much longer. Quietly she pushed back her chair and despite her anger, rose calmly, then weaved her way between the rows towards the door, feeling every eye on her, and imagining Nitza grinning across the table to Miriam.

Still fighting to keep control, she gently pushed open the door and went into the lobby, then out through the swing doors, running down the path, eyes streaming and sobs choking her throat, up onto the veranda and into the room, where she threw herself on the bed, sobbing into the pillow.

How on earth had she thought this could work…

Amos had half-risen as Kate went out and remained like that for a few seconds, deliberating; but if he hurried out after her, it would attract even more attention. Slowly he sat down again, his head hot and his stomach turning. Noa was tucking into her leg of chicken but Ran was staring up at him, concerned.

'Anything up with Kate, Dad?'

'It's okay. Just a bad headache.' Amos ruffled his hair. 'Gone to get a pill.' He spoke calmly but loud enough for others to hear. 'She'll be back soon,' he added, half-smiling at Eli and shrugged. Eli was gripping Bilha's hand under the table and further along the row and Joe looked at Aviva, all with the same thoughts. If it carried on like this, Kate would leave. And Amos…?

Amos had already broken *matzo* into his soup, an old Pesakh habit from childhood. He loved to eat it quickly whilst it was still crisp. Now it was soggy and the soup cold. He loved crispy roast potatoes too, but he couldn't stomach them either. Beside him, the empty seat seemed like a hollow space in his body.

He glanced around the crowded tables, everyone enjoying the festival. It felt as if all that was pulling him to one side, whilst the empty space beside him pulled to the other.

30

Kate lay in bed in her nightshirt, reading by the small bedside-lamp, her hair loose and falling over her shoulders. She looked up and tried to smile as he came in.

'I'm really sorry about that, Amos,' she said. 'It was just too much.'

'It's okay. It's okay, Kate. Eli and Bilha wished you well. Told them you had a bad headache.' Amos undressed and sat on the bed. 'Ran was the star in the *Khad Gadya* and Noa flaked out as soon as I took her back.'

He undressed but as he picked up the covers to take out his pyjamas, he noticed Kate's nightdress rucked up around her hips. Immediately, he became aroused.

'I'd like to Amos, but I can't. Not after all that,' said Kate, pulling down the hem. 'Please don't be annoyed.'

Amos slipped in beside her, his head buzzing. It was the first time this had ever happened between them.

'No problem, Kate,' he murmured, 'better we sleep it off.' But the very moment he lay beside her and pulled up the covers, there was a tap at the door.

Amos raised his head, annoyed.

'*Ken! Mi zeh?*'

'It's me, Ephraim.' Amos knew he was on night guard and cursed, supposing that it was an incident with the tractor left out in the field. 'Telephone call,' continued the voice, through the door. 'For Kate. From London. To phone back. Urgent.' Kate slid out and jumped onto the floor. In the pitch darkness, she pushed her face against the mesh screen in the door.

'Who from? What about?'

'Your aunt,' replied the night guard. 'About your father, she said. Said you have the number.'

Amos came over and joined Kate by the door.

'*Beseder*. Thanks Ephraim,' he called through the screen.

The footsteps crunched off the veranda, and Amos pulled Kate's trembling body against him.

'It must be serious, Amos, she said. 'Dad has his bad moments, but this must be life or death, sure. I know my aunt. She would never phone if it wasn't.'

Amos kissed her.

'Come. You're shivering,' he said. 'Let's get dressed. I'll come with you and get the key from Uri, and we'll go over to the office.'

Uri was half-asleep as he handed the telephone key through the half-open door.

'Remember it's expensive to *khutz l'aretz*,' he mumbled then went back to bed and the two of them hurried across the lawn.

In the office hut, Amos caught the gist of the conversation. There had been a drunken brawl at a pub. Kate's father had fallen badly and knocked his head. He was in hospital, and her aunt had phoned because her mother was too distraught to phone herself.

Kate put down the receiver and stared at the phone. In the bare, single lamp of the office, her face was chalk-white.

'My aunt says he's stable but in intensive care.' Kate clutched at his arms. 'Oh God, Amos. Why did this have to happen now?' She fell against him, tears streaming down her cheeks. 'I've got to go, Amos. Got to see him. 'I don't want to -- but I'd never forgive myself if he… if…' She couldn't finish the sentence. 'And for my mother too, I know I have to.'

Amos held her close. And as Kate laid her head against his body, her tears wetting his chest, with the shock and anxiety came a strange lightness.

'I know. I know Kate,' Amos murmured, stroking her hair. Like we say in the army, Kate: "Life is not an insurance policy." Anything can happen, to any of us.' He hugged her more tightly, fearing losing her, and added: 'and does.' Already in his mind, was that perhaps that was what was happening…

Kate travelled to a ticket agent in Tel Aviv the next morning. There were no direct flights. The only way was through London. She would have to buy an onward there, to Belfast.

'A return ticket?' asked the girl behind the desk.

The next day was so rushed that they had little time to talk about the future -- or avoided it. The evening before, she had posted a brief note to Jill. Now, while jeep hummed along the newly surfaced road on the way to Lod airport, both were preoccupied and silent.

When they passed Masmiyya Junction, Amos glanced to his right up the road to Jerusalem, so did Kate. The city that would always have a special meaning for both of them. She reached across and clutched his elbow.

Slowing down to the speed limit through Gedera, Amos thought back to the day before. Noa had come to the room to say goodbye to Kate.

'Will you bring me something from Ireland when you come back, Ket?'

Kate had become quite fond of the little one, sitting on her lap in the small room, often playing with a lock of Kate's long hair. The child's plaintive voice had cut right through her and Kate hugged her, trying to hide her eyes watering.

'I'll bring a *'hafta'ah'*; a surprise,' she'd said, and gently put her down. Then, just as they were about to take her back to the children's house, Ran had sauntered onto the veranda, for the very first time -- as though it were nothing special.

'I come to say goodbye Ket,' he said in faltering English, having obviously rehearsed it. 'I very sorry for your father.' Then he walked with them along the path, before peeling off opposite Miriam's room, called *'Lehitraot'*, see you soon, and with a bashful smile waved. Kate waved back then looked at Amos, eyebrows arched. Amos had shrugged, then just gripped her hand and smiled.

At the airport, Amos parked the jeep and carried Kate's rucksack into the terminal. Holding hands, they clung to each other as the queue crept towards the security check counters. Armed soldiers were everywhere. Only a short time before, three Japanese Red Army maniacs had sprayed the hall with automatic fire, killing some thirty people, including a leading paediatrician.

The uniformed security girl asked Kate to open her pack, and was about to search through, when she noticed Amos.

'You with him?' she asked. Kate started then nodded. The girl smiled.

'*Shalom*, Captain Amos.' Amos looked up.

'*Ahallen*, sergeant Ruthie.' He grinned. 'Sure. She's with me -- I hope!'

Kate looked from one to the other.

'Does everyone know everyone in this country?'

'Almost,' said the girl, zipping up the pack and smiling. '*Derekh*

Tzlekha. Safe journey.'

With an hour to wait, they had coffee in the crowded bar then sat on one of the hard plastic benches, munching chocolate biscuits.

Kate sat silently, just looking into his face as through a mist, desperate to retain the memory -- all their wonderful shared memories. She was afraid that if she opened her mouth, tried to say anything, it would provoke a flood of tears.

The flight was called, and when they stood up to go, Amos reached into his jacket pocket. Her stomach heaved -- the jacket he had worn in Jerusalem. He pulled out a small, red paperback.

'Tchernikhovsky,' he said, his eyes sad. 'One of our greatest poets. A restless soul, torn between two worlds. It was Ya'ir's favourite.'

Kate took the book and flicked through the neatly printed Hebrew pages.

'I know you can't understand it now, Kate,' he continued, 'but it's something from me. Of me. And if you have the opportunity, there must be a few Jews in Belfast who can read Hebrew and will translate a few verses.' He kissed her. 'I wanted to buy you a real present, Kate, but well, there was no time...'

'I'll treasure it, Amos, so I will. And I've something for you too.' She pulled a paper wrap from the shoulder bag Jill had left her. It was the small, clip-framed Van Gogh chair print.

'I've had this with me ever since I left university. It's been in our room... and I want you to keep it.'

The flight was called for the third and last time. They rose and walked slowly towards the departure gate.

'Think of me,' whispered Kate, unable now to hold back her

tears.

'Me too,' said Amos.

'I'll write,' she whispered. 'Will you still love me?'

Amos gripped her hands.

'Oh God, Kate. What a question. I'll always love you. And you?'

Kate leaned forward.

'Need you ask Amos, need you ask?' She closed her eyes and kissed him, a long, passionate kiss, and had to pull herself away.

Amos watched her ride up the escalator, her hair glinting red in the fluorescent light. Kate looked down through the tears, wanting to hold the image of that upturned, bronzed face and unruly fair hair. She blew a kiss. Then he was gone. She was gone.

Amos waited in the airport car park, leaning back against the jeep, his whole body trembling. Perhaps he would glimpse her on the tarmac. Perhaps the plane would be delayed? Cancelled? Perhaps; perhaps. And he waited — waiting until with a whine and a roar, the Dan Air flight sloped up into the cloudless sky and headed out over the sea.

The sun was setting to his right as Amos drove down the last stretch of road south from Faluja. The ruins of the Arab village where the young Colonel Nasser had been surrounded in 1948, had been bulldozed into oblivion, the mud huts returned to the earth whence they came. Just a large mound covered with thistles and grass, like an ancient *Tel*, where layer upon layer of settlement destroyed in one war or another over thousands of years, lay buried. Amos wondered whether his own children would ever know that the village had even existed.

Like Ein Husb, Huleikat, Yibneh and a myriad of other places, the junction now had a Hebrew name: Plugot. And in his melancholy mood, he thought of the children of those villagers, now refugees in the camps of Gaza. They would never be allowed to forget. Yes. Two peoples with the one land, needing a judgement of Solomon, and no one with the wisdom. As Ya'ir would mutter, quoting the sages: '*Shalom. Shalom, ve'ein shalom*': Peace, peace, yet no peace.

Amos parked the jeep behind the dining hall, switched off the engine and sat for a moment. Closing his eyes, he saw Kate's tearstained face on the escalator. He glanced at his watch. Her 'plane would be circling over London by now. She would not be back.

A hot, dry, *hamsin* wind was blowing from the east. He looked around the courtyard and down the track to the cowsheds. His kibbutz, but for how long? On the way back, he had called in to have a chat with Azriel at Rehovot. Amos glanced at his watch again then swung his legs out of the jeep; time to pick up the children.

The engine noise softened; the plane lost height and made its approach run. Kate looked down. Docklands. So, what now? Take up her Masters' option -- though she would have to find a job to finance it? She'd dropped a note to Jill and would ring her once she was settled; arrange to meet. Together they would know.

As the landing wheels thumped on the tarmac, Kate knew that she had had to come home. How long would she stay in Belfast? If Dad didn't improve, much as she wanted to support Mam, her sister would have to play her part too. She had her own life to lead; in a few years she would be thirty.

Closing her eyes, Kate pictured Amos sitting in their small room, alone, her Van Gogh picture on the wall. Suddenly remembered the incident with the Arab boy that had brought them together. God, how she still loved him -- would always love him, a love that had given her something so precious she would never forget. But it was just not to be… And with that, came the final acceptance, that she couldn't, wouldn't go back.

Her eyes grew moist, then watered, tears streaming down her cheeks. Hurriedly she snatched a tissue from her bag, but she let them flow -— they wouldn't be the last. She glanced out of the window again but couldn't see anything as they taxied along the runway.

The plane came to a halt; the cabin lights came on. Kate wiped her eyes and blew her nose. Talking a small brush from her bag, she brushed and brushed her long hair until her scalp tingled — like that day she'd met Amos in Jerusalem…

She rose and took down her holdall. Next stop, Belfast.

———————————

Also by David Merron

Goodbye East End – An Evacuees Story

Collectively Yours – Kibbutz Tales

On The Job – A Building life

Borderline – Border Incident

Life, Death and In-Between – Short Stories

Available worldwide from

Amazon and all good bookstores

———————————

www.mtp.agency

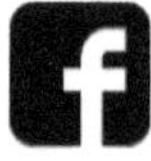

www.facebook.com/mtp.agency

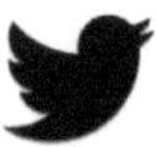

@mtp_agency